Pierre Batcheff and Stardom in 1920s French Cinema

'Focusing on a single major star, Pierre Batcheff, Phil Powrie's new book offers a productive, alternative approach to writing the history of a crucial period of French cinema, that of the late 1920s and the transition to sound.

On the one hand, Batcheff often exemplified the *jeune premier* of commercial fiction films during the period (notably in *Le Joueur d'échecs*): handsome, seductive, well-bred, and charming. On the other, his characters' "normality" just as often was undermined by an element of "foreignness" or uncanny "otherness" and by a behavior shaped by irony and/or self-parody.

Taking Batcheff as an iconic figure, Powrie and Rebillard's book counters the long-held notion that such a persona differs radically from the iconic male figures of the American or German cinemas of the period, and thus challenges the all-too-common denigration or dismissal of French male stars in most histories and critical studies.'

Richard Abel, University of Michigan

Pierre Batcheff and Stardom in 1920s French Cinema

Phil Powrie with Éric Rebillard

EDINBURGH UNIVERSITY PRESS

Edinburgh University Press Ltd
22 George Square, Edinburgh

Typeset in Garamond
by Servis Filmsetting Ltd, Stockport, Cheshire, and
printed and bound in Great Britain by
CPI Antony Rowe Ltd, Chippenham, Wilts

A CIP record for this book is
available from the British Library

ISBN 978 0 7486 2197 2 (hardback)

Contents

List of illustrations

Preface

Pierre Batcheff is in all probability best known to those interested in cinema as the Man of the avant-garde classic, *Un Chien andalou* (1929), by Luis Buñuel and Salvador Dalí. The paradoxical combination of dreamy beauty and surrealist-inspired frenzy in a provocatively nonsensical and often disturbing narrative is likely to be what most remember about him. What is much less well known is first that he played a major part in the making of the film, a fact conveniently forgotten by the film's many commentators, and, second, that he was a major star at the time of the film, while its makers were almost complete unknowns. The tables have been turned since 1929, however, and it is Batcheff who has sunk into obscurity, while the two Spaniards became in their different ways major icons of the twentieth century in film and in painting respectively.

Batcheff was one of a small group of prominent commercial stars in the 1920s. Unlike them, however, he was linked to intellectual circles, particularly the surrealists and groups surrounding poet and scriptwriter Jacques Prévert. His involvement with the avant-garde led to tensions in his film performances as he strove to balance the demands of the commercial cinema and his interest in the avant-garde film. Unlike most of his fellow stars of the 1920s, he had a strong social conscience and engaged in voluntary work, organising film projections in prisons and even in asylums. Like many intellectuals of the period (Antonin Artaud and Roger Gilbert-Lecomte amongst them), he became addicted to drugs. Striving to keep his addiction secret, he finally died of an overdose in mysterious circumstances in April 1932 – an apparent suicide – just as he was about to embark on a new career as director and scriptwriter. *Amour . . . Amour . . .* (September 1932) was directed by Robert Bibal after Batcheff's death, from a script by Jacques Prévert and Batcheff.

By the time of his death, he had made twenty-five films (including dual language versions), of varying quality, many of which he quite openly despised. Amongst them, however, there are a number of films by major silent cinema directors: Raymond Bernard, René Clair, Jean Epstein, Henri Fescourt, Abel Gance, Marcel L'Herbier. Although we shall explore all of his films, we have focused in this study on those that are now more readily available. *Un Chien andalou* (1929), *Le Joueur d'échecs* (1927) and *La Sirène des tropiques* with Josephine Baker (1927) are currently available on DVD. In addition, a number of films have been screened in theatres or on television over the years, sometimes in a restored version: *Feu Mathias Pascal* (1925), *Napoléon vu par Abel Gance* (1927), *Les Deux Timides* (1928), *Monte-Cristo* (1929) and *Baroud* (1932). Seventeen are available for viewing in archives. That still leaves eight films which are not extant, at least to our knowledge (see the Filmography for details); to explore Batcheff's performance in context we have relied on documentary archive material for these (as well as for those that are extant, of course), as detailed below.

Considerable work has been done on French silent cinema in recent years, by Richard Abel in several ground-breaking volumes (Abel 1984, 1988, 1994), by younger researchers in the USA, and by members of the Association Française de Recherche sur le Cinéma; it is particularly useful to single out François Albera's extraordinary study of the Films Albatros, not least because Batcheff made several films with this studio (Albera 1995). This kind of work has generally been broad-sweep history, analysis of conditions of production/reception, analysis of genre and analysis of directors, rather than our focus for this study, the analysis of the stars of the period.

Star Studies is now a key component of current cinema studies. Introduced as an academic discipline by Richard Dyer at the end of the 1970s, it has since developed considerably, not least in French cinema studies when Ginette Vincendeau published a groundbreaking volume on Jean Gabin (Gauteur and Vincendeau 1993), followed by an equally important study of French stars (Vincendeau 2000); this was complemented by Guy Austin's study of French stars after 1945 (Austin 2003).[1] Susan Hayward has worked extensively on Simone Signoret (Hayward 2001, 2002, 2003; Hayward and Leahy 2000), Sarah Leahy has worked on Bardot and Signoret (Leahy 2002, 2003, 2004; Hayward and Leahy 2000), and there has been a recent collection devoted to one of the other iconic female stars, Catherine Deneuve (Downing and Harris 2007). But apart from the books by Vincendeau and Austin, neither of which focuses exclusively on male stars, and occasional journal articles (O'Shaughnessy 1994 on Belmondo; Hayes 2004 on Delon), there is as yet no major work on a male star, still less a star in the silent period.

Our study therefore sits squarely within a major direction taken by French cinema studies in the last decade; but its focus on a silent cinema star, and to some extent its focus on a male star, is novel. Vincendeau's 2000 book only covers one silent star, the comic Max Linder, to whom one of ten chapters is devoted; Austin's book is on post-1945 French stars; the 2003 Popular European Cinema Conference's focus on stars was more generally European, and did not have a single paper on a French silent cinema star. A study of

Batcheff will allow us to understand how stardom worked in the 1920s in France for a genre-crossing star. Unlike Max Linder, for example, who specialised in comedies, Batcheff worked in mainstream cinema, usually as the lover in escapist fantasies or spectacular historical reconstructions. However, he also acted in one of René Clair's comedies, *Les Deux Timides*, and in Buñuel and Dalí's *Un Chien andalou*. Batcheff's ubiquity makes him a more profitable figure to study than some of the other male leads of the period – such as André Roanne (1896–1959) or Albert Préjean (1893–1979) – with whom the film press of the time tended to compare him. He is an exemplary figure of the avant-garde, but, fascinatingly, a major star; indeed, he is one of the key male 'pin-ups' of the 1920s, with many parallels between him and Anglophone matinee idols such as Valentino and Novarro in the USA, and Novello in the UK. We shall refer to some of the work that has been done in this area, particularly with regard to Valentino, with whom Batcheff has frequently been compared (see Hansen 1986 and 1991, and Studlar 1996 for Valentino; Williams 2003 for Novello). Unlike the American stars, however, Batcheff was intimately involved in the intellectual avant-garde of his time, leading to a tension between the star as commodity, his persona moulded by the demands of the market, and the star as auteur pursuing a personal agenda. This study will tease out the tensions he exemplifies between the 'popular' and the 'intellectual' during the 1920s and early 1930s, while engaging in a star analysis whose focus is on star performance.

We begin in Chapter 1 with Batcheff's biography, where we encounter the gap between his activities as a commercial star and his gradual engagement with a variety of intellectuals in the period, most revolving around the surrealist group. This led to a sharper sense in Batcheff of what he really wanted to do: drop acting, particularly in commercial films, and move towards directing. Chapter 2 places this basic tension in the context of the film industry, and in particular the role of the *jeune premier* in French cinema in the 1920s. We chart the rapid rise but equally rapid mutation of the *jeune premier*, and suggest that Batcheff represents a particularly interesting variant of this feature of the French film industry, gesturing towards a transitional masculinity. After these two opening chapters, we treat Batcheff's films mostly in chronological order, most chapters dealing with a group of films. Chapter 3 looks at Batcheff's first three films, which set up a complex persona combining the innocence of the ephebic youth, a longstanding motif in French pictorial culture, with darker streaks of duplicity, the uncanny and hysteria, which we link to the concerns of the surrealists in the 1920s. Chapter 4 groups together Batcheff's historical reconstructions, spread over several years (1925–9). We have changed our adherence to chronology partly because he did not have a lead role in the four films in question, and partly because they illuminate particular aspects of his image which are elaborated in his other films from this period. One aspect is his static performance, which combines with roles where he is either passive to start with, or made passive by the narrative, to elaborate a masochistic form of masculinity. Chapter 5 turns to the other films from this period where he plays the Lover. In these films, a trope that was already in evidence in previous films comes to the fore: Batcheff is 'other' or alien in a number of ways, either by his presumed nationality, or by virtue of narratives where an oppressive family situation causes him to escape. Interestingly, the last film of this group, *Le Perroquet vert*, suggests that Batcheff wished to change his image of the apparently innocent but corrupted and almost catatonic alien.

His next two films, both comic and violent in different ways, mark a significant shift not just in his star persona, but also in French cinema more generally. For that reason, we have devoted a whole chapter to *Les Deux Timides*, one of René Clair's great silent comedies, and two chapters to the film that many will remember Batcheff by, *Un Chien andalou*. These two films reprise and foreground the darker sides of Batcheff's image, characterised by the detached and troubled alien. This is more obviously the case in *Un Chien andalou*; in the two chapters devoted to this film, we review both contemporary and later views of the film, in whose creation Batcheff himself played a significant part, before considering fracture and disarticulation in the film as a function of Batcheff's star body. We pick up themes covered in earlier chapters, such as madness and masochism, and focus in on a key image little analysed previously, that of the death's-head moth, to show how anamorphosis, a preoccupation of Dalí's at the time of the film, can be profitably used to explore Batcheff's function. Batcheff's final films are a disappointment, but in terms of our study are illuminating; they show how difficult it was for him to extricate himself from the stereotypes established in his previous short career. They try to engage with some new elements for his image, but in the end, the abiding sense of Batcheff's final couple of years is, as we call it, melancholic destitution.

Our conclusion returns to surrealism, using the Freudian notion of the uncanny to tie together the various aspects of Batcheff's image that we have identified: apparent innocence underlain by brooding menace and troubled identity; an innocence bordering on a masochistic helplessness, apt to break out suddenly in spurts of activity tinged with violence; or, as we attempt to characterise it, the young lover uneasily and convulsively combined with the rebel-criminal. We finish with André Breton's notion of convulsive beauty as the most apt expression of this extraordinary star, who shot to fame in less than four years, and burnt bright at the end of one period, the silent period, in two heady years 1928 and 1929, before burning out just at the time when the industry was turning to sound.

Sources

Much of our archive work is based on the popular film press of the period, available in particular in the Département des Arts et Spectacles at the Bibliothèque Nationale in Paris. Sources include the following: *Cinéa-Ciné pour tous*, *Cinémagazine*, *Ciné-Miroir*, *Cinémonde*, *Mon ciné*, *Mon film* and *Pour vous*. This material has been augmented by documentation from an extensive private archive held by the only surviving relative of Batcheff: his niece, Madame Claude Roche. The biography of Batcheff relies on the same sources, and on material from the family, mainly Claude Roche and Batcheff's wife, Denise Tual. We have indicated both in the biography outlined in Chapter 1 and in the summary biography in the Appendices the months when particular films were being shot. Sometimes it is apparent from details of location publicity exactly when and for what Batcheff was available. In most cases, however, we have had to piece together a broad time-frame for the shooting of films, and it is clear that Batcheff would not have been shooting throughout the whole of the period concerned.

Acknowledgements

Our study is the culmination of a project begun by the two authors in 1999 and which led to a British Academy-supported paper on Pierre Batcheff at the Buñuel conference held in London in 2000. This led to a publication (Powrie and Rebillard 2004), from which this book has grown, bringing together a longstanding interest in Batcheff on the part of both authors. Éric Rebillard acted as principal researcher of archive material, and conducted indispensable interviews with members of Batcheff's family (Denise Tual and Claude Roche). Phil Powrie is responsible for the architecture of the project and the drafting of the text, which both authors have then extensively revised.

The book contains brief extracts from previously published work by Powrie in the fields of surrealism, and cinema and gender studies:

- 'Masculinity in the Shadow of the Slashed Eye: Surrealist Film Criticism at the Crossroads', *Screen* 39:2 (Summer 1998), pp. 153–63 (critical accounts of *Un Chien andalou* from the 1940s to the 1980s).
- 'The God, the King, the Fool and ∅∅: The Oedipal Trajectory in the Films of Beineix', *Gender in the French Cinema*, edited by A. Hughes and J. Williams (Oxford: Berg, 2001), pp. 195–208 (theoretical considerations on anamorphosis).
- 'Of Suits and Men in the Films of Luc Besson', in *The Films of Luc Besson: Master of Spectacle*, edited by Susan Hayward and Phil Powrie (Manchester: Manchester University Press, 2007), pp. 75–89 (theoretical considerations on the male suit).

Chapter 3 includes a reworked version of an article published by Phil Powrie with Éric Rebillard, 'Marcel L'Herbier au carrefour des avant-gardes: *Feu Mathias Pascal* et le dédoublement', in *Marcel L'Herbier: l'art du cinéma*, edited by Laurent Véray (Paris: Association Française de Recherche sur l'Histoire du Cinéma, 2008, 79–90). An extended version of the section on *La Sirène des tropiques* was given as a paper at two conferences in 2008: the eighth annual Studies in French Cinema conference at the Institut Français, London; and the fifth Women and the Silent Screen conference in Stockholm. Parts of Chapter 2 and the Conclusion were given as a plenary paper at the ninth European Cinema Research Forum in Dublin in 2008.

We would like to thank the following: the British Academy for financial support in archival research, leading to the Buñuel conference paper mentioned above; Claude Roche for her readiness to share her archives on Batcheff with us, and for her agreement that we could use many of the photographs from her collection to illustrate this book; Kevin Brownlow for material on *Destinée*, including the loan of an indispensable 17.5mm copy of the film, the only extant version as far as we know; Marie-Ange L'Herbier for access to her father's archive; Sarah Leahy for her sympathetic reading of the final draft of the book; the Robinson Library, Newcastle University, for their help in obtaining a wide range of archival material; Éric Le Roy from the Centre National de la Cinématographie for material on Donatien; Robert Short for material on *Un Chien andalou*; the viewing services of the British Film Institute (London), the Centre National de la Cinématographie (Paris), the Cinémathèque Française (Paris), the Cinémathèque Royale de Belgique, the Forum des Images (Paris); and Sarah Edwards, our editor at Edinburgh University Press, who never lost faith in our ability to complete the project.

Particular thanks go to Richard Abel whose work on early French cinema is a constant source of inspiration, and to whom all of us who have an interest in early and silent French cinema are deeply indebted.

Phil Powrie and Éric Rebillard
January 2008

Note

1. We are referring here and below to academic work on stars rather than popular star biographies, of which there are many. These are often useful secondary material for basic historical data and for framing the reception of stars, but of little use in terms of the close analysis of star performance within the films themselves.

CHAPTER 1

A short life

'C'est ça, le cinéma.'
(Batcheff) me répondit très sèchement:
'C'est votre cinéma, ce n'est pas le mien.'
             (Buñuel 1982: 109; on *La Sirène des tropiques*)

'Well, I guess that's the movies,' I remarked.
'That's *your* movie,' (Batcheff) replied drily, 'not mine.'
             (Buñuel 1984: 90)

Pierre Batcheff was labelled the best French actor of the period 1925–9 by Georges Sadoul in 1975 (Sadoul 1975: 106). He was one of the foremost *jeunes premiers* of the 1920s, a term normally taken to refer to handsome young actors who played young lover roles. His biography is striking for his rapid rise to stardom and the fact that he was, unlike many of his peers, an unwilling star. He considered the majority of the films he acted in to be no more than hack work, and longed to become a director. This was no doubt partly because his wife-to-be, Denise Piazza (later Tual), introduced him to a number of intellectuals in the mid-1920s; but his desire to be more than just a commercial star increased following *Un Chien andalou*. He met Luis Buñuel on the set of a film he made with Josephine Baker in 1927, and collaborated closely with him for *Un Chien andalou*. Not long afterwards, he met Jacques Prévert and his entourage, with whom he planned screenplays for films that he might direct. In what follows, we will outline the major elements of his life as an unwilling star.

ORIGINS AND CHILDHOOD (1907–22)

Pierre Batcheff's mother, Maria Renter, was from Estonia. A woman of great beauty, she had a very strong personality, and was involved in early protests against the Tsar. She was part of a large family, most of which would sadly disappear during the Stalin era. In 1905, she married a Russian businessman by the name of Mikhaïl Petrovitch Batcheff, much older than her and from Oranienbaum, near Saint Petersburg. The nature of his business is unclear, except that it required frequent travelling. Denise Tual reports in her auto-biography that he was Jewish (Tual 1987: 86).

Pierre Batcheff himself was born Benjamin Batcheff in Harbin, in Manchuria (where his father had gone on business for a couple of years) on either 22 or 23 June 1907.[1] He took the name Pierre from his father only later, when he started in the cinema. Batcheff had an elder sister, Sophie (called Sonia), born on 27 July 1905 in Saint Petersburg.

The family did not stay long in Harbin, moving to Riga and then back to Saint Petersburg. When war broke out in the summer of 1914, the mother and children were on their annual holiday in Switzerland, where they subsequently stayed – on the father's recommendation, as he assumed it was a safer place for them to be – first in Lausanne, and then in Geneva. The father kept travelling between Russia and Switzerland, but around 1917 he went bankrupt in the turmoil surrounding the Russian revolution, and the family found itself in reduced circumstances. They had to move to cheaper accommodation, and Batcheff's mother returned to her occupation as a nurse.

Batcheff himself took on bit parts in Georges Pitoëff's theatre company in Geneva. Later interviews tell us that he acted in *Hamlet* amongst other plays, but, as he ironically put it, 'je jouais les valets de chambre' ('I played valet roles'; Sannier 1930: 665). He went to school in the Collège Calvin in Geneva's old town from 1919 to 1921 (the same school as the film actor Michel Simon), where he did well (sixth out of thirty boys, according to the college archives and interviews with one of his classmates), leaving in mid-June before the 1921 end-of-year exams to go to Paris with his mother and sister.

It is not known why the family moved to Paris. The father did not follow them, and times were hard. They were soon joined by Batcheff's aunt, who had managed to escape from Russia. Batcheff found himself the only male surrounded by three females – his mother, his sister and his aunt – for whom Batcheff was their only support and the centre of all attention.

Batcheff began his acting career in Paris at the age of fifteen, playing Apollo in *La Nuit des muses* by Robert de Jarville, which opened on 22 December 1922 in the Théâtre de la Potinière on the occasion of the 112th anniversary of the birth of the Romantic playwright Alfred de Musset. He also played bit parts for a small local theatre near Pigalle, the Comédie Mondaine. His theatrical work was in all probability undertaken to pay for drama lessons.

From the very start he knew that he wanted to be in the cinema, and in 1922–3 he was moving around the studios, starting at a low level, helping on the sets as a stage-hand or painter, and then as an extra (Bernard-Derosne 1929: 16; Mital 1931: 6). But his looks were so exceptional that very quickly he was noticed by a director who was looking for someone very young for his next film.

Figure 1.1   Batcheff around 1925–6 (Courtesy of the Bibliothèque Nationale, Paris)

THE RISE OF THE STAR (1923–6)

In the summer of 1923, Batcheff was shooting his first film, *Claudine et le poussin*, at the Château de Troissereux near Beauvais, in which he plays Claude de Puygiron, the inexperienced lover of a rather more experienced female artiste. The film, described as a mixture of sadness and gaiety,[2] was premiered on 15 January 1924 at Le Select (8, avenue de Clichy), to considerable interest. More than fifty cinemas rented it for its general release in March (*Cinématographie française* 1924a), and it was later distributed in the USA under the title *Baby Boy*.[3] Later that year, in May–June, he was shooting *Princesse Lulu* – in which he plays Prince Raoul, a young lover and foil to the villain played by the film's director, Donatien – near Geneva, as well as in Montreux and Lausanne (Hennard 1924: 3–4), before returning to France in July for the remainder of the shoot.

Marcel L'Herbier was one of the major figures of French cinema during the 1920s, with a reputation for a highly aestheticised art cinema, thanks to *Eldorado* (1921) and *L'Inhumaine* (1924). It is unclear how Marcel L'Herbier came to hear of Batcheff for the small role he plays in *Feu Mathias Pascal*, made for Films Albatros, a studio run by Russian émigrés. L'Herbier may well have seen Batcheff's first film, *Claudine et le poussin*; in addition, he knew Georges Pitoëff well,[4] and it may be Pitoëff who alerted him to Batcheff's emerging talent. Contemporaries remarked on the close resemblance between L'Herbier and Batcheff, and this may have been an additional and deeper motivating factor, particularly when we consider that L'Herbier and another prominent *jeune premier* in much the same mould as Batcheff, Jaque Catelain, worked closely together during the 1920s.[5] Be that as it may, from that date, L'Herbier appears to have taken Batcheff under his wing to some extent, and helped him obtain a foothold in the cinema world.

Batcheff was a late addition to *Feu Mathias Pascal*. The first shooting script[6] does not have his character, Scipion, the slightly deranged brother of the villain, and the various lists of actors in the film press do not mention him until a very late stage of the production.[7] By that time, he had already been working on another film, *Autour d'un berceau*, signalled in the film press in late December 1924, and completed at about the same time that Batcheff seems to have been working on *Feu Mathias Pascal* with L'Herbier, in February 1925. In *Autour d'un berceau*, he plays Pierre de Sombierre, the suave gambling friend of the hero, who steals money and runs away, thus causing all sorts of problems for the hero. His aristocratic-sounding name recalls that of his first film, and to some extent set his persona as an elegant upper-class lover, often with a tragic flaw.

While Batcheff was working on these two films, another film with Albatros was announced in February, by the well-known filmmaker Jean Epstein: *Le Double Amour*. In this film, Batcheff plays Jacques Maresco, the gambler son of a mother played by Natalie Lissenko. The film was made in a very short space of time, between March and mid-April (Ploquin 1925: 12), and was premiered a month before *Feu Mathias Pascal*, the reason for this being that L'Herbier had additional scenes to shoot as late as May (*Cinéa* 1925a: 16–17). As a result, Batcheff had his first magazine cover, as L'Herbier's Scipion, for *Mon ciné*, on 30 April 1925, but also with mention of Epstein's film. This placed Batcheff firmly in the public gaze, especially given the stature of Epstein and L'Herbier in the film industry.

Destinée, Batcheff's first historical reconstruction, was announced in that same month of April 1925, directed by another major figure, Henry Roussell. Batcheff played yet another aristocratic lover role, that of Roland de Reuflize, an officer in Napoleon's army. Shooting started in mid-May, the main exteriors being located in the South of France (Avignon, Arles, Nice and Marseille) in June and July; further exteriors were shot in various locations in Paris, such as Palais-Royal, the interiors being shot at the Éclair studios, in Épinay, between July and November.

Not surprisingly, given that much of the film was shot in the South of France, it was a French regional newspaper that ran the first major article on Batcheff at the end of June 1925 (see Appendices). It is significant that one of the few personal traits evoked in this article is one which will mark his persona in the years to come: melancholy. This film appears to be the first one to elicit the term *jeune premier* with regard to him, as well as epithets that were to remain with him throughout his career: elegant and charming (*Cinématographie française* 1925e: 26).

In January 1926, Batcheff was making *Le Secret d'une mère* in the studios at Saint-Laurent-du-Var, with exteriors in Rome; he played the role of a son abandoned by his mother, but who eventually forgives her after a painful moral tussle. This was followed by a film by another major filmmaker of the period, Raymond Bernard, whose *Le Joueur d'échecs* was being made in Joinville's Réservoirs studios. Batcheff was once again cast in the role of the aristocratic lover, this time Russian: Prince Serge Oblonoff. This film seems to be the one which made him a star; an interview piece from 1931 says that in this film, Batcheff 'sut donner à son personnage un tel relief, qu'il se détacha de l'ensemble' ('managed to create such a convincing character that he stood out from the rest'; Mital 1931: 6). The sudden celebrity occasioned by roles in films by three major filmmakers – L'Herbier, Epstein and Bernard – led to the beginning of fan mail.[8]

Meanwhile, Gance's epic *Napoléon* continued, shooting having started back in January 1925. Batcheff's role was that of General Hoche; one of his few scenes in this film was the 'Bal des victimes', which we analyse in Chapter 4. The film press tells us that shooting for this scene took place in the Billancourt studios in July 1926 (*Cinématographie française* 1926a: 23), even though Batcheff is not mentioned, and had not been mentioned previously as being engaged for the film (the first mention of him in relation to this film is almost at the end of shooting, in the 2 September issue of *Mon ciné*).

The year 1926 was an important one for Batcheff's private life, as he met Denise Piazza, daughter of Henri Piazza, founding director of the well-known Éditions d'art, that specialised in deluxe editions (she later married Roland Tual, at the time a surrealist sympathiser and later a film producer, publishing her autobiography under that surname). She had first seen Batcheff in passing on a location shoot for *Le Joueur d'échecs* near Barbizon, where she lived, and it was love at first sight. She arranged a meeting subsequently on the set of a film,[9] where Batcheff could not speak with her as arc lights had made his eyes stream with tears. They met three days later, and Tual's description of Batcheff is worth quoting extensively for the insights it gives us into his character:

> (J'étais) stupéfaite et subjuguée à la fois par sa beauté qui venait de l'intérieur, sorte de magnétisme qui comptait plus encore que ses traits (. . .) Obsédé par l'idée de faire un jour de la mise en scène, il n'aimait pas le métier d'acteur, qu'il considérait comme une véritable prostitution. Il ne se reconnaissait pas de talent comme interprète, et se demandait pourquoi il avait tant de succès. Il haïssait l'idée de s'exhiber comme un portemanteau. Il écrivait des scénarios, mais autour de lui, personne à qui lire ses écrits. Acteur, il n'était pas pris au sérieux comme écrivain, et s'en désolait. Son âme slave le poussait au désespoir. À vingt et un ans – il avait débuté à quinze ans – il se trouvait très vieux, il n'avait pas le temps d'attendre, ayant derrière lui une carrière de films alimentaires qu'il détestait, avec des partenaires impossibles, vulgaires. En réalité il cherchait un scénario qui lui offrirait un rôle plus intéressant que ceux de jeune premier fade et prétentieux dans lesquels on l'enfermait. (Tual 1987: 88–9)

> (I was astounded and enthralled by his beauty which came from the inside, a kind of magnetism which was even stronger than his good looks (. . .) Obsessed by the idea that he might one day direct films, he didn't like acting, which he considered to be tantamount to prostitution. He didn't think he had any talent, and couldn't understand why he had so much success. He hated the idea of exhibiting himself like a coat stand. He wrote screenplays, but he had no one around him who would read them. As an actor no one took his writing seriously, which filled him with chagrin. His Slav soul led him to despair. At the age of twenty-one – he had started acting at fifteen – he thought himself old, he didn't have the time to wait, with nothing but bread-and-butter films that he hated to his credit, with impossibly vulgar co-stars. What he was really looking for was a story that would give him a role somewhat more interesting than the insipid and pretentious *jeune premier* roles in which he felt imprisoned.)

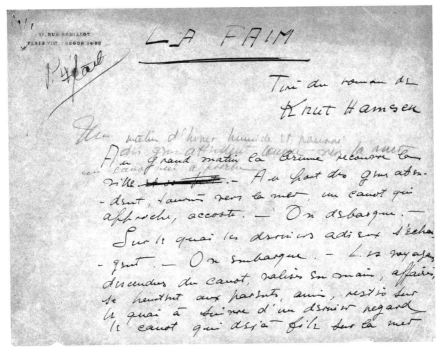

Figure 1.2 The first page of Batcheff's script for *Sult* (Collection Roche-Batcheff)

Tual at the time was already married, to Camoin, an antique dealer, and abruptly decided to leave her husband, gradually moving in with Batcheff.[10] She was to have a key influence in his life as she introduced him to the avant-garde and the surrealists. For example, Batcheff met and became friend with poets Robert Desnos and Paul Éluard, and with composer Igor Markevitch. Tual explains how she talked to him about *Sult* (*Hunger*, 1890), a novel by Knut Hamsun (1859–1952) about alienation and the descent into madness. Batcheff subsequently read the novel and drafted a screenplay.

She and Batcheff were invited to visit Rex Ingram in Nice in 1926; Ingram was looking to launch another Latin lover after Rudolph Valentino and Ramon Novarro, and tried to persuade Batcheff to take on the role of a Berber. Batcheff laughed at the idea and decided against it in 1926, although he was to take it on five years later for his last film, *Baroud*, after his attempt at becoming a director failed.

Éducation de prince, directed by Henri Diamant-Berger, was announced in October, Batcheff's role as Sacha, the European prince who needs 'educating' and who falls for a Parisian dancer, not being announced until December. There is no doubt Batcheff was happy being cast with Edna Purviance,

Chaplin's leading actress, Chaplin being one of his idols. In November, he briefly substituted for Jaque Catelain who had fallen ill while making *Le Diable au cœur* (1928) for Marcel L'Herbier; Catelain appears to have recovered sufficiently quickly, as Batcheff is not credited for this film.

Meanwhile, he acted in a play at the Théâtre Montmartre, *La Comédie du bonheur*,[11] by the well-known Russian playwright Nicolas Evreinoff (1879–1953).[12] The play was staged by one of his co-actors in *Le Joueur d'échecs*, Charles Dullin. Dullin was a theatre director; he had grouped a small number of actors around him, known as 'l'Atelier' (workshop), amongst them Antonin Artaud. The play ran for 250 performances, from November 1926 to May 1927. In the play, Evreinoff used the device of a company of actors sent out into 'real life' to perform the parts chosen by their director; Batcheff played the part of the *jeune premier* of the company. He did not enjoy his part (interview with Denise Tual, 1994), getting mixed reviews. Some commented favourably: 'Il danse farouchement' ('He dances fiercely'; *Presse* 1926). But he was still too used to the silent screen, and many complained that he could not be heard: 'Il parlait bas, si bas, qu'à plusieurs reprises on dut lui crier "Plus haut, plus haut"' ('He was speaking low, so low, that several times people shouted "louder, louder"'; *Paris-midi* 1926).

From the mainstream to the avant-garde (1927–9)

The year 1927 was tiring for Batcheff from the start. Before Christmas 1926, Diamant-Berger's company had gone on location to the old town of Pérouges near Lyon. The company was soon back in Paris, and the film press reported that Diamant-Berger had erected lights in such a way that he could shoot *Éducation de prince* night and day.[13] The film was also the first to be made in Natan's new studios in rue Francœur, inaugurated by a visit from the Minister for War, Paul Painlevé, at the end of January, while the film was being made. No sooner was shooting for this film finished than Batcheff was back in the studios at Épinay for Gaston Ravel's *Le Bonheur du jour*, followed by location shooting in Nice during the course of April. In a story which recalled *Le Secret d'une mère*, Batcheff was the lead as Jean Plessiers de Chavignac, a son from an aristocratic family (as his name once more suggests) who thinks he is illegitimate.

In July, shooting started on two films in which Batcheff was again the male lead, although refreshingly not aristocratic: *La Sirène des tropiques*, as the engineer André Berval, the young lover playing opposite Josephine Baker; and *L'Île d'Amour* (called *Bicchi* until the end of shooting), where he plays a local Corsican boy who falls in love with an American heiress, who eventually makes him presentable in polite society. The latter film once again took him to Nice, and then beyond to Corsica.

Batcheff, in need of money, had decided to act opposite Josephine Baker in her first feature film since her success on stage in La Revue Nègre in 1925. Tual recounts the famous tantrums of the American star: 'Insupportable, elle faisait des caprices, piétinait les colliers de verroterie qui lui servaient de cache-sexe, exigeant une cape de chinchilla sans laquelle elle refusait de tourner. Pierre assistait impassible à ses scènes, pendant qu'un jeune assistant stagiaire se précipitait pour ramasser les fausses perles' ('She was unbearably capricious, stamping on her glass necklace G-string, demanding a chinchilla cape without which she refused to act. Pierre watched impassively as a young assistant rushed to pick up the false pearls'; Tual 1987: 98–9). Baker was no doubt uppermost in Batcheff's mind when he later commented dismissively on screen partners, emphasising the disjunction he felt with at least some of his co-stars: 'Être acteur, c'est exprimer devant l'appareil de prise de vues toute la poésie latente que l'on sent en soi. Mais comment y parvenir si l'actrice, de son côté, a un jeu sans poésie, un jeu banal?' ('Being an actor is expressing for the camera all the latent poetry you feel inside yourself. But how can you do that if the actress on her side acts without poetry, in a banal way?'; Doré 1929a: 183).

It was while making this film that Batcheff met Buñuel, who was an assistant director, and began talking about a collaboration which was eventually to become *Un Chien andalou*, a radical departure from the kind of film they were both engaged in, the kind of film that Batcheff increasingly despised, as reported in the exchange between him and Buñuel in the epigraph at the beginning of this chapter. According to Tual, Batcheff accompanied Buñuel to meetings of the surrealist group (Tual 1987: 99).

In September, Batcheff was back in Natan's studios, where both *La Sirène des tropiques* and *L'Île d'amour* were being made at the same time.[14] Shooting for *L'Île d'amour* finished towards the end of October, *La Sirène des tropiques* in November, although it is likely that Batcheff was no longer involved by this time. The end of the year finished on a high note, with Batcheff featuring alongside Edna Purviance, his co-star in *Éducation de prince*, on the cover of the 23 December issue of *Ciné-Miroir*, although any pleasure he may have felt might well have been mitigated by the fact that Josephine Baker made the cover of both *Cinémagazine* and *Ciné-Miroir* two weeks later.

The year 1928 was significant for the release of Batcheff's first comedy: one of his best films, René Clair's *Les Deux Timides*. The year began under a cloud, however, with the suicide of Batcheff's partner in the as yet unreleased *L'Île d'amour*, Claude France. Aged 33 and unhappy in love, she had gassed herself, according to the suicide note she left behind (Dupont 1928: 59–60). The film was as a result released without a press showing, apparently to capitalise on the publicity surrounding France's death. The same month, Batcheff began shooting *Le Perroquet vert* at Natan's studios, with exteriors the following month in Nice. The story-line involved incest, and Batcheff played another aristocratic role as Félix Soltikoff, the young lover who turns out to be the brother of the female lead. He then went to Berlin for *Vivre*, as the Baron Derozier-Schell, yet another aristocratic lover role, this time as lover of the male lead's wife.

He had been identified as a *jeune premier* in 1925 and had had his first cover in 1927; his first star interview was published in March 1928 (although it had taken place on the set of *Éducation de prince* a year earlier), with two more before the end of the year (see Appendices); and he had had another cover, for *Cinémagazine*, when *Les Deux Timides* was released in December 1928, one of his greatest performances as Jules Frémissin, the awkwardly shy young lawyer of a nineteenth-century farce by Labiche. As a journalist of *Cinémagazine* countered, when a reader suggested that Batcheff had a great future, he was already very much in the public eye: 'Un brillant avenir lui est promis dites-vous? Mais il a déjà atteint une enviable situation puisqu'il ne cesse d'interpréter des rôles de premier plan' ('You say that he has a brilliant future ahead of him? But he already has enviable status as he is constantly in major roles'; *Cinémagazine* 1928a: 155). This was quickly followed up in the same magazine by a long piece on *jeunes premiers*, where Batcheff figured alongside Jaque Catelain, L'Herbier's protégé, as the adolescent type of *jeune premier*, a couple of weeks before the release of *Vivre*: 'Pierre Batcheff, au visage mobile et exalté garde encore la touchante fragilité de l'adolescence' ('Pierre Batcheff, whose animated and elated features are still marked with the touching fragility of adolescence'; Alby 1928: 423). A reply to a reader's comment in July reiterated the fact that he was one of the best *jeunes premiers*, but also pointed out that he had aspirations to be a director (*Cinémagazine* 1928b: 80), just at the time when he was starting on *Les Deux Timides*.

René Clair, who, along with his brother Henri Chomette, was a friend of Denise Tual, had wanted Batcheff as his lead for the film, even if on the face of it, it did not seem like the kind of role for which Batcheff was well known. The producers of the film at Albatros, the Kamenka brothers, insisted that the role should be adapted for Batcheff, by now a major star and, as Tual puts it, a guarantee of success for a film (Tual 1987: 91).

In November he started shooting Henri Fescourt's adaptation of Dumas's *Monte-Cristo*. Although he only appears in the 'second epoch', as Albert de Morcerf, the son of the villain (played by Gaston Modot), we know from reports in the press that Fescourt was shooting the magnificent opera sequence in which Batcheff plays a significant role, at Billancourt with 1500 extras, in the last weeks of that month.

It is clear that 1928 marked the apogee of Batcheff's rapid rise to stardom, with major roles in no less than four films. One interviewer put him alongside a small handful of French stars to rival the Americans, and called him 'l'un des jeunes premiers les plus originaux qu'on puisse voir ces temps-ci sur l'écran' ('one of the most original *jeunes premiers* on our screens at the moment'; Frank 1928: 9). It was hardly surprising, then, that in late 1928 he was chosen to star alongside an international star some ten years older than he was, Pola Negri (1897–1987), even if her career was waning. She had had a brilliant career in German cinema, making key films with Ernst Lubitsch, amongst them *Die Augen der Mumie Ma* (1918), *Carmen* (1918), *Madame DuBarry* (1919), *Sumurun* (1920) and *Die Flamme* (1922). They were so successful as a team that both of them went to the USA, Negri signing up with Paramount, where they made one film together, *Forbidden Paradise* (1924). Negri starred in no less than twenty-one films while she was in the USA between 1923 and 1928, and was famous for her reported romance with Rudolph Valentino.

The film in question was *Le Collier de la reine*, by the same team that had made *Le Bonheur de jour* (Gaston Ravel and Tony Lekain), adapted from the novel by Alexandre Dumas *père*. The film was announced in mid-December 1928, with Batcheff's participation announced a month later.[15] Clearly, much like Ingram in 1926, the directors and producers had felt that of all the French *jeunes premiers*, Batcheff was the most obvious to take up Valentino's mantle. However, both of the leads withdrew from the film before their scenes were shot. Negri terminated her contract by mid-March, probably because of a better offer from the UK for what was eventually released as *The Way of Lost Souls* (Paul Czinner, 1929; see *Ciné-Miroir* 1929: 167). Batcheff paid a hefty penalty to pull out a few weeks later, because he wanted to progress his work on *Un Chien andalou*,[16] which was premiered in June. Batcheff and Negri's roles were taken by two then inexperienced actors, Jean Weber and Marcelle Jefferson-Cohn (later known as Marcelle Chantal).

Once he had cancelled his contract for *Le Collier de la reine*, Batcheff threw himself into his collaboration with Buñuel and Dalí. They were keen to have Batcheff, partly because they wanted their lead actor's 'complète participation' ('complete participation'; Tual 1987: 100); Buñuel had asked Batcheff to be his assistant, according to Tual, which was bound to appeal to Batcheff's increasing feeling that the profession of actor appealed to him far less as the years were going past. But they also wanted him because his presence would ensure financial backing.

Participation meant in the first instance working on the screenplay together, according to Tual, who describes how the three men generally worked during the night. She recounts how on one occasion Buñuel and Batcheff, who had clearly worked throughout the night, woke her up at sunrise to ask her opinion on something they could not agree on, and that on another occasion they entered her room as she was fast asleep to read part of the

Figure 1.3 Denise Tual, Pierre Batcheff and the 35mm projector in their flat (Collection Roche-Batcheff)

screenplay to her excitedly (Tual 1987: 101–2). She appears to have been the first spectator of the film itself, as she and Batcheff had a 35mm projector in their flat, on which she saw the image of the slit eye for the first time, followed shortly afterwards by a private screening of the film to Jean Cocteau and members of Cocteau's entourage. Cocteau was a friend of the Piazza family; amongst his entourage that day were Cocteau's secretary, Maurice Sachs, Sachs's lover Robert Delle Donne, and Marie-Louise Bousquet, whose salon was a rallying point for the smart set and the intellectual elite (Tual 1987: 102–3).[17]

The public screening of *Un Chien andalou*, on 6 June 1929, has been described many times, so we will not dwell on it here. It was shown at the

Studio des Ursulines, an independent cinema opened in January 1926 by the actors Armand Tallier and Laurence Myrga, and devoted to avant-garde films. To Buñuel's amazement, it was well received by the audience which included a high proportion of artists and intellectuals. Tual lists the following: from the surrealist group there were André Breton, Louis Aragon, Robert Desnos, Paul Éluard, Max Ernst and Georges Hugnet. Amongst others, from a number of different 'tendencies', there were Jean-George Auriol, Brancusi, Jacques-Bernard Brunius, René Clair and his brother Henri Chomette, Marcel Herrand, Jean-Paul Le Chanois, Fernand Léger, Igor Markevitch, Darius Milhaud, Charles and Marie-Laure de Noailles (in whose property in the South of France the accompanying film by Man Ray, *Les Mystères du Château de Dé*, had been shot), Pablo Picasso, Georges-Henri Rivière and Jean Wiener (Tual 1987: 103–4).

Two of the names amongst *Un Chien andalou*'s audience listed above are of some importance. Batcheff had become friendly with Auriol, who was the director of a new film journal, started in December 1928: *La Revue du cinéma*. Auriol had asked Batcheff to obtain Buñuel's permission to publish the screenplay of *Un Chien andalou*, which Batcheff duly did. This aroused the wrath of the surrealists, who had intended to publish the screenplay in a special number on surrealism of the Brussels-based journal *Variétés*, an episode recounted at some length in Buñuel's autobiography. Brunius, who was a critic working for *La Revue du cinéma*, was key in introducing Batcheff to the Prévert brothers in the winter of 1929.

On the same day as the premiere, Batcheff was on the cover of the 6 June edition of *Mon ciné*, although the image of him was in the as yet unreleased *Monte-Cristo*. *Un Chien andalou* subsequently ran for some eight months at Studio 28 from November 1929, so that audiences in that month would have been able to see Batcheff in no fewer than four films: the avant-garde *Un Chien andalou*; a comedy, *Les Deux Timides*, on general release since March; a historical reconstruction, *Monte-Cristo*, on general release in October; and a historical epic, *Le Joueur d'échecs*, released in 1927 but still showing.

At about this time (May–June 1929), Batcheff managed to persuade Louis Nalpas to buy the rights to H. G. Wells's *The Invisible Man*, for which he himself had begun a script.[18] Batcheff spent much time working on the screenplay, trying to tackle the technical challenges of such a scenario, but he was never to direct the film. Nalpas later sold the rights to Universal, and it was released in 1932 with James Whale as director.

In September, Batcheff began shooting *Illusions* (in the Limousin and in Paris locations, including the Bois de Boulogne and Place de l'Opéra), where he played an unusual role for him; although for part of the film he plays the normal typecast young lover, the end reveals an old man who has stayed

Figure 1.4   Far from the studios (Photo: Élie Lotar, Collection Roche-Batcheff)

faithful to the woman with whom he has an affair at the start of the film. The shooting was finished before Christmas, and the film, released early in 1930, did not do well.

Meanwhile, in October, he had adorned the cover of *Pour vous*, with the caption 'Pierre Batcheff, qui s'est révélé comme un des meilleurs jeunes premiers de l'écran' ('Pierre Batcheff, who is one of the best *jeunes premiers* of the screen'),[19] echoed in a piece a few months later: 'Il s'est révélé dans *Un Chien andalou* (. . .) Il me paraît être l'un de nos meilleurs jeunes premiers et son talent sensible, très émotif, le place en tête des acteurs de notre cinéma' ('He made his mark in *Un Chien andalou* (. . .) I think he is one of our best *jeunes premiers* and his sensitive, emotional talent makes him one of our top cinema actors'; Tribourg 1930: 9).

Batcheff and his wife moved from the cramped flat where *Un Chien andalou* had had its first screening, swapping it for his mother and sister's somewhat larger apartment at 3, square de Robiac in the seventh *arrondissement*. It is clear that Batcheff was extraordinarily busy in 1929, and this, coupled with his disaffection for the commercial films in which he had to play typecast roles, may well account for increasing complaints by fans that he was not answering mail.

Far from the studios and from his star persona, Batcheff enjoyed playing tennis or boating. 'Il aimait la nature, il adorait les enfants, il adorait les bêtes, il ne se plaisait que dans les milieux paysans ou à la campagne' ('He loved nature, he loved kids, he loved animals, and only felt comfortable among peasants or in the countryside'; interview with Denise Tual 1996). And he declared in a 1928 interview: 'J'aime le peuple parce que j'aime ce qui vient du cœur bien plus que ce qui vient du cerveau' ('I love the popular because I love what is coming from the heart more than what is coming from the brain'; *Ciné-Miroir* 1928: 215).

Batcheff had a strong social conscience, and at that time, together with Denise, he started to engage in voluntary work, organising concerts, conferences and film projections in prisons (La Petite-Roquette and La Santé). He spent considerable time and energy trying to convince prison management that films were good for the inmates, as is proved by a number of draft letters in his notebooks: 'Notre but n'est pas de distraire, mais (. . .) d'élever le niveau moral et intellectuel des détenus' ('Our goal is not to entertain, but to lift the moral and intellectual level of the prisoners'; Collection Roche-Batcheff). The films shown were usually educational or documentaries – the first screening at La Petite-Roquette, for example, on 29 June 1929, was a documentary of Prince Achille Murat's travels to Indochina (van Etten 1929: 11) – but Batcheff was even considering the possibility of making his own films for the same purpose, and started drafting screenplays. The journalist Max Frantel, one of Batcheff's friends, describes one of those sessions in a 1932 article, published after Batcheff's death:

> Il avait pour les malheureux et pour les déshérités de la vie une pitié qui allait jusqu'à la tendresse (. . .) Il m'a été donné de le voir, pendant cette heure de musique à Fresnes et à la Petite-Roquette. Il était là, recueilli et en proie à une émotion qu'il maîtrisait à peine. Le rachat moral de ces malheureux lui paraissait un absolu devoir pour tous. (Frantel 1932)

> (He had for the poor and the disinherited a pity that extended to tenderness (. . .) I was able to observe him during one of those hour-long music sessions, at Fresnes and La Petite-Roquette. He was there, meditative and overwhelmed by an emotion he could scarcely control. The redemption of those poor people seemed to him everyone's duty.)

He soon got involved with Dr Toulouse, the renowned psychiatrist,[20] and took his activities to asylums where, as Tual recounts, 'les réactions étaient imprévisibles, déroutantes, souvent émouvantes' ('reactions were unpredictable, disconcerting, often moving'; Tual 1987: 131). Toulouse was trying to improve the conditions of the mentally ill. In his newly created psychiatric service, a cinema session was organised once a week. Batcheff's role was to intercede with the film companies to obtain prints (Toulouse 1931: 116; cited in Le Sonn 2004). Such activities were very much at odds with his *jeune premier* image, and would have been completely unknown to his fans at the time, except for a brief allusion in a star portrait (see Bernard-Derosne 1929).

THE LACOUDEMS (1930–2)

Shooting for Batcheff's next film and his first talkie, *Le Roi de Paris*, began in February 1930, mostly in Berlin. Batcheff and Tual took advantage of their stay in Berlin to attend the premiere of *Der blaue Engel* on 1 April, somewhat prophetically given the criticisms of Batcheff's next film, *Les Amours de minuit*, for its recycling of some of the motifs from the German film. No sooner had shooting in Berlin finished than they returned to Paris to marry on 8 May. *Le Roi de Paris*, in which Batcheff played a young lover role as foil to the villain, was released in August, and was poorly received both by critics and by the public; it was booed, and led to a sustained series of negative reader comments in the film press. The same month, Batcheff signed up for a new film, *L'Ensorcellement de Séville* (1931), directed by Benito Perojo with Gina Manès, who had worked with Batcheff in Gance's *Napoléon*. The production ran into financial difficulties, however, and by the time the shooting could resume in November, Batcheff had dropped out of the film. By then, he was already working on *Les Amours de minuit*, the first talkie to be made at the Billancourt studios (and, during the night, at the Gare Saint-Lazare); his role returned him to earlier characters where he had a problematic relationship with money, either as a gambler or, as here, because he steals money.

At the end of 1929, Batcheff had confided to Brunius that he was looking for a collaborator to further his ambitions: 'Il cherchait un collaborateur avec lequel il puisse "dialoguer", "avoir une réplique sur des sujets qu'il avait en tête"' ('He was looking for a partner with whom he could have a "dialogue", with whom he could "debate some ideas he had in his mind"'; Tual 1987: 105). As a result of this, Brunius had introduced Jacques Prévert to him. Prévert was at that time an unpublished author who associated with the surrealists. He and Batcheff hit it off straight away and became close friends, to the extent that Prévert and his wife Simone moved into the Batcheffs' flat.[21] The group of friends also included Jacques's brother, Pierre Prévert, and Brunius, as well as Jean-George Auriol, Jean-Paul Le Chanois, Louis Chavance, Lou Bonin, and by extension Denise Tual and Batcheff's sister Sonia.

Bonin had invented the term the group used to describe themselves, the 'lacoudems', referring to the slight fluttering of the elbows ('coude') against a fellow group member's elbows as a sign of recognition and solidarity. The group spent much time in cafés, often making fun of customers or passers-by, and generally being disruptive. Batcheff and Tual managed to get work for members of the group as extras (for example, Jacques Prévert and Lou Bonin were extras for *Les Amours de minuit*).

In the winter of 1930, they all went off to Chamonix, at the Col de la Voza, where Batcheff out-skied the rest of them, rushing back the next day for a shoot (probably for *Les Amours de minuit*) that turned out to be cancelled. Then they all went off together to the Cotentin in Normandy, attending the fish-market on the quays of Cherbourg.

Batcheff, Brunius and the two Prévert brothers worked on a screenplay from an idea by Jacques Prévert, called *Émile-Émile, ou le trèfle à quatre feuilles*, a comedy full of black humour about a sculptor who is making an elephant out of bread; he runs out of money, has to beg and is eventually killed by lightning, his ashes being sucked up by a vacuum cleaner (Brunius 1987: 92; see also Courrière 2000: 169). Convinced that he was about to make the long-awaited breakthrough into direction with this rather surreal screenplay, Batcheff allowed the impending *Émile-Émile* to be announced in the film press throughout October and November 1930. So, for example, he was on the cover of *Le Courrier cinématographique* on 11 October, with the following caption: 'Pierre Batcheff qui va tourner le principal rôle du film *Amours de Minuit* de Genina, pour la société Braunberger-Richebé, et qui par la suite, doit réaliser lui-même un film comique tiré d'un scénario des frères Prévert intitulé *Émile-Émile*' ('Pierre Batcheff who will star in *Amours de Minuit* by Genina, for the Braunberger-Richebé company, and who will then himself direct a comedy from a screenplay by the Prévert brothers entitled *Émile-Émile*'). In a short piece for another journal a couple of weeks later, he explained what he was trying to do with this comedy:

> Je pense que le public aime, et j'aime moi-même, tout ce qui est débordant de vie, de mouvement; la brutalité avec laquelle les Américains nous présentent la psychologie des personnages de leurs films comiques, personnages qui résument les péripéties de leur existence en quelques gags. En Europe on a complètement négligé ce genre de cinéma où brillent pourtant les acteurs les plus aimés du public: Keaton, Laurel et Hardy, Charly [sic] Chase, etc . . . Avec un premier film dont le prix de revient sera peu élevé, nous allons essayer d'aborder ce genre, en nous servant de dialogues populaires comme d'une satire de la vie de la rue. C'est ce qui, nous l'espérons, rendra ce film familier au public français. Il y reconnaîtra aussi, d'ailleurs tournés au ridicule, certains de ses travers, certains de ses préjugés. (Batcheff 1930)

> (I think the public likes, just as I do, everything that is bursting with life and movement; the brutality with which the Americans give us the psychology of the characters in their comedies, characters who sum up a life in a few gags. In Europe we have completely neglected this type of cinema, despite the fact that it has the best-loved and brilliant actors: Keaton, Laurel and Hardy,

Figure 1.5   Denise Tual, Jacques Prévert and Pierre Batcheff at the Col de la Voza
(Collection Roche-Batcheff)

Charly Chase, etc . . . With a first low-budget film we will try this genre out,
using popular dialogue in a satire of street life. We hope that this will make the
film more approachable for French audiences, who will also see their foibles
and prejudices made fun of.)

The script for *Émile-Émile* was now fully finished. Igor Markevitch, a friend
of Batcheff, was approached to compose the musical score (interview with
Tual 1996; see also Pierre Prévert 1965: 54). It was submitted to the producer,

Figure 1.6 Batcheff on the quays in Cherbourg (Collection Roche-Batcheff)

Émile Natan, and other producers as well. They all rejected the screenplay. The reason given by Tual is that Natan felt that the title of the film was in some way a disobliging reference to him. His rejection probably had more to do with the hostile reaction to Buñuel's *L'Âge d'or* in November 1930; the scandal created by the film had led to the ostracism by polite society of its wealthy aristocratic backers, the de Noailles. It is reasonable to assume that Natan, given the subversive nature of Batcheff's screenplay alluded to in the extract above, probably did not feel that it was appropriate to make the film, despite Batcheff's high star profile. Batcheff, given his hopes that he might make interesting films as a director rather than star in uninteresting films, was understandably devastated. The fact that his last two films, *Illusions* and *Le Roi de Paris*, were poorly received – two films in a row with bad press – would clearly not have helped.

Batcheff had better reviews for *Les Amours de minuit*, released in January 1931. The film was successful enough that it was decided to shoot a German language version later that year, *Mitternachtsliebe* (released in Berlin in September 1931). The Batcheffs went to Berlin for that, Tual now trained as a sound editor.[22] Meanwhile, Batcheff was also working in the Joinville studios on a film originally called *Le Général* but eventually released as *Le Rebelle*, his role being the rebel in question, Boris Sabline, another Russian role, this time a scientist who revolts against military discipline.

His next film after *Mitternachtsliebe* was announced in June in the film press as *Vingt-quatre heures de la vie d'une femme*, directed by the Moravian Robert Land (who had been directing films in Germany since the early 1920s), adapted from a play by Stefan Zweig and co-starring Marcelle Chantal. There are no reports of Batcheff completing this film,[23] the German version of which was released under the title *24 Stunden aus dem Leben einer Frau* in October 1931, with Walter Rilla and Henny Porten in the starring roles. It is likely that Batcheff dropped out of the film because he had lost control when Marcelle Chantal had bumped into him and he had slapped her, in a display of erratic behaviour no doubt brought on partly by his depressive state following the rejection of *Émile-Émile*.[24]

Batcheff, almost perversely given that he knew that Ingram wanted to make him the new Latin lover of the silver screen, contacted Rex Ingram and took him up on his much earlier offer of a film based in Morocco. *Baroud*, Ingram's first talkie and his last film, started shooting in August 1931 in parallel French and English language versions, finishing in December. Batcheff played Si Hamed, the son of a tribal chief and friend of the lead male role, played in the English language version by Ingram himself. The time spent in Morocco appears to have done Batcheff good, according to Tual; he returned relaxed and tanned, as we can see in a shot of him on the beach (Figure 1.7).

AN EARLY DEATH (1932)

Life in Paris was increasingly hectic. Tual recounts how their combined passion for the cinema had led them to support films that they felt had been insufficiently distributed, by organising private shows and lobbying distributors. Their busy lives as cinema professionals, combined with their frantic social life – going to night clubs, dancing until early in the morning – left little time for sleep, and Batcheff's health began to suffer. He was becoming more and more irritable, and subject to sudden changes of mood: '(Il) était désinvolte, capricieux, instable, fantasque (. . .) totalement imprévisible, déroutant' ('(he) was careless, capricious, unstable, fantastical (. . .) totally unpredictable, disconcerting'; Tual 1987: 94). He would get nervous when the phone was not ringing. 'Non, je ne suis pas oublié de tous,' he writes repeatedly in his notebooks ('No, I am not forgotten by everyone'; Collection Roche-Batcheff). His relationship with Denise Tual was becoming strained; they both had strong personalities and violent tempers, and were subject to fits of jealousy. Batcheff's depressive state did not help.

The first months of 1932 saw Batcheff devoting all his time and energy to a new screenplay, *Pour ses beaux yeux*, based on a story by Jacques Prévert. It told the story of Paul, the shy employee of a jeweller, who loves Jacqueline,

Figure 1.7 Batcheff on the beach during the shooting of *Baroud* (Collection Roche-Batcheff)

who in her turn loves Max, a thief and con-man. Max robs the jeweller but is caught, while Paul and Jacqueline get together. Ironically, this screenplay, unlike *Émile-Émile*, was accepted; but by the time the shooting started in June, Batcheff was already dead.

On the evening of 11 April 1932, he confessed to his wife that he had been taking drugs since his beginnings in the theatre with Georges Pitoëff in Geneva. Tual felt betrayed and reacted badly to this deception, not realising that he had kept his addiction a secret to spare her his ordeal. Jacques Prévert dropped by, as was his custom, and they all went to a Montmartre[25] night club later that night. After a while Batcheff returned home, telling them he was tired. When Prévert and Tual, concerned about him, went back to the flat on the morning of 12 April, they found him close to death. Prévert phoned the doctor, who rushed to the apartment, but Batcheff was already dead.[26] He had left a suicide note. Ironically, he died, according to newspaper reports, just hours before he was due to sign the contract for the film he had scripted himself.

The suddenness of his death was a shock for his friends and family. Le Chanois, for example, describes how they were left in a stupor by his unexpected and tragic suicide (Le Chanois 1979: xxi), sentiments echoed by Tual: 'Il me laissait, ainsi que son entourage, dans le désarroi le plus total (. . .) Depuis la disparition de Pierre, une partie de moi était morte' ('He left me, and his close friends, in the greatest distress (. . .) With Pierre's death, a part of myself had also died'; Tual 1987: 134). Those involved were still in shock a long time after the event. Pierre Prévert wrote in 1965: 'Il est toujours présent et vivant en moi. J'entends souvent son rire généreux' ('He is still there and alive in my mind, I often hear his generous laughter'; Pierre Prévert 1965: 54). And Marcel L'Herbier recounts in his 1979 autobiography how the memory of Pierre Batcheff was still haunting him (L'Herbier 1979: 210).

Batcheff's death has always been surrounded by mystery. One of the main reasons is the reluctance of Denise Tual and other protagonists to discuss it (Tual's account of his death was only published in her autobiography in 1987, fifty-five years after the event). Then there is the stigma and silence related to drug usage, often only referred to obliquely in the press: 'Les sentiers dangereux des paradis artificiels' ('The dangerous paths of artificial paradises'; *L'Œuvre*, 17 April 1932). Batcheff's death was covered in great detail in the newspapers between 15 and 17 April 1932, and the results of the first medical findings were publicly disclosed (heart attack resulting from a toxic substance). The press coverage then suddenly stopped, and the results of the second autopsy were never revealed.[27]

We will not dwell on misleading and inaccurate statements by Dalí, according to whom Batcheff 'in unstable equilibrium on the borderline between the conscious and the unconscious, (. . .) kept himself drugged with ether in order to remain present to the world, and swung between life and death until at last committing suicide on the final day of the shooting schedule (of *Un Chien andalou*), like a holocaust offered to Moloch for my greater glory' (Dalí [1976] 1973: 77). Others later raised questions about his death. L'Herbier thought it might not be suicide (L'Herbier 1979: 210), and Le Chanois suggested that he might have committed suicide 'pour des raisons sentimentales' ('for sentimental reasons'; Le Chanois 1996: 55). There is no doubt in our minds, however, that Batcheff killed himself, and that it is likely that he chose as the means the very drug he was addicted to (we can only speculate here whether it was cocaine or another substance).

Another reason why Batcheff's suicide remains shrouded in mystery is a series of bizarre touches. Two weeks before his death, he took Jacques Prévert to the Cimetière du Père-Lachaise in Paris, where they visited the crematorium, Duhamel reporting that 'ils s'étaient bien marrés' ('they had a good laugh'; Duhamel 1972: 303). Batcheff died at 2am on the morning of 12 April 1932. At 10am that same day he had an appointment planned with Léon Poirier to sign the contract for the direction of the film he had been working on for the previous three months.[28] It is strange, to say the least, that he committed suicide the very same day when he was about to fulfil one of his main ambitions, that of becoming a director.

Pour ses beaux yeux, the film that Batcheff might have directed, began shooting in June, under the charge of the very minor director Robert Bibal, and starring Henri Marchand, who had been Émile in René Clair's *À nous la liberté* (1931). It was released under the title *Amour . . . Amour . . .* on 26 September 1932, some six months after Batcheff's death, to mixed reviews. Two days later, the English version of *Baroud* had its premiere in London, and the French version was released in November.

Amongst the welter of news items and tributes released in the film press and the general press, we would like to single out the following extract from an interview (originally published eighteen months earlier), in which Batcheff discusses what he was trying to achieve in his screenplays. We find a peculiar combination of realism and comedy, a perception of the need for everydayness, but also a stepping back, a self-deprecating distance, an irony:

> Je voudrais que mes personnages disent des phrases comme on en dit dans la vie. N'avez-vous pas remarqué que, dans la vie, certaines gens sont comiques à chaque instant sans le savoir. Ils disent sérieusement des mots burlesques – burlesques pour les autres. Je voudrais mettre dans des films non seulement de l'ironie, mais de la farce, de cette grosse farce qui fait notre joie dans les comédies de Mack Sennett, avec des échelles qui tombent sur la tête du héros, des plats pleins de sauce qui se renversent, toute cette lutte sournoise que les objets et les animaux mènent parfois contre les maladresses des hommes. Oui, répéta-t-il avec force, tous les acteurs devraient, au lieu de se regarder dans les glaces et de se prendre au sérieux, apprendre à tomber par terre sans se faire mal, à recevoir des tartes à la crème, des gifles, des coups de pied. (Guérin 1932: 291; previously in Doré 1930: 647)

> (I would like my characters to speak like people do in real life. Have you noticed how, in real life, people are comical all the time without realising it? They say funny things seriously, funny at least for other people. I would like

my films to contain not just irony, but farce, the slapstick that we love in Mack Sennett comedies, with ladders falling on to the hero, platefuls of gravy being overturned, that insidious struggle that objects and animals engage in faced with human incompetence. Yes, he repeated forcefully, all actors, instead of looking at themselves in the mirror and taking themselves seriously, should learn how to fall without hurting themselves, how to take custard pies, slaps and kicks.)

What combines the two poles of realism and comedy is a clear valorisation of the popular. Arguably, this is precisely what the 1930s screenplays of Jacques Prévert, one of France's greatest popular poets and screenwriters, were to achieve. It is tempting to see Batcheff's legacy in some of these films of the classical French cinema, as it has often been called, scripted by Prévert: *Le Crime de Monsieur Lange* (Jean Renoir, 1936), *Drôle de drame* (Marcel Carné, 1937), *Le Quai des brumes* (Marcel Carné, 1938), *Le Jour se lève* (Marcel Carné, 1939) and, finally, perhaps the greatest French film, *Les Enfants du paradis*[29] (Marcel Carné, 1945). The peculiar combination of melancholy and popular realism, or poetic realism as it later came to be called, is already there in Batcheff's performance, and in his aims as a screenwriter and director.

Notes

1. The marriage certificate indicates the first, the death certificate the second. The discrepancy is probably due to a mistake when converting the original birth date recorded according to the Russian Orthodox calendar.
2. 'C'est une comédie très sentimentale qui, si elle frise plutôt la mélancolie, atteint aussi à la gaîté la plus franche' ('It's a very sentimental comedy, which, although slightly melancholic, is also full of cheer'; *Cinémagazine* 1923: 374).
3. *Mon ciné* 1925b: 5.
4. Talking of how he came to make *Feu Mathias Pascal*, he explains how Pirandello's *Six Characters in Search of an Author*, which he saw in Paris, was staged by his friend Pitoëff, who had also staged a play by L'Herbier in Geneva (L'Herbier 1979: 114).
5. For example, Jacqueline Lenoir wrote at the time of *Monte-Cristo* that 'je fais un rapprochement mental entre Marcel L'Herbier et Batcheff qui offrent une frappante ressemblance physique' ('I make a mental connection between Marcel L'Herbier et Batcheff, who closely resemble each other'; Lenoir 1928c: 17).
6. Private collection of Marie-Ange L'Herbier.
7. The beginning of production was announced in October 1924 (*Cinématographie française* 1924b: 29), but there is no mention of either the character or Batcheff in what is called a 'complete list' in December (*Cinématographie française* 1924c: 11), or in a 'complementary list' in early February 1925 (*Mon ciné* 1925a: 14). The first mention of Batcheff is on 21 February, in an article signalling the end of production for a week later on 28 February (*Cinématographie française* 1925a: 21).

8. The address given for him at that time is that of L'Herbier's company, Cinégraphic, in a short note in the 1 April issue of *Cinéa-Ciné pour tous*.

9. There is some doubt in our minds about the accuracy of her account, as she says she met him on the set of a comedy he was making with Colette Darfeuil (Tual 1987: 86); Batcheff never made a film with this actress.

10. It was only in 1930 that she obtained a divorce and was able to marry Batcheff.

11. Created in Russia in 1921 as *Samoe glavnoe*, adapted into French by Nozière as *La Comédie du bonheur* (meaning 'The Illusion of Happiness'), and known in English under the name *The Main Thing* or *The Chief Thing*. The play was later made into a film with the same title by Marcel L'Herbier (1940), adapted by Jean Cocteau and starring Michel Simon.

12. In the cinema, Evreinoff co-directed *Fécondité* with Henri Étiévant (1929), based on a Zola novel and starring Albert Préjean.

13. Reported in the 8 January issue of *Cinématographie française*.

14. Reported in the 3 September issue of *Cinématographie française*.

15. Reported in the 15 January 1929 issue of *Cinéa-Ciné pour tous*, and again in the 24 January issue of *Pour vous*.

16. Reported in the 1 April issue of *Cinéa-Ciné pour tous*; see Tual 1987: 100–1 for confirmation of his penalty for pulling out.

17. Denise Tual affirms that Cocteau had already completed his film *Le Sang d'un poète* (1929), and that he therefore could not have been influenced by *Un Chien andalou*, as was subsequently claimed.

18. See *Pour vous*, 22 (6 June 1929) and *Cinéa-Ciné pour tous*, 136 (1 July 1929).

19. *Pour vous*, 48 (17 October 1929), p. 16.

20. Dr Édouard Toulouse (1865–1947), psychiatrist and journalist. He was one of the most famous French psychiatrists between the wars. He considered mental illness to be a disease, and attempted to treat the mentally ill, if possible, by searching for the cause of their problems. He advocated open and free treatment for them, creating an open psychiatric service in Paris to that effect (at the Hôpital Henri Rousselle, part of the Hôpital Sainte-Anne complex). He was also Antonin Artaud's doctor and close friend around 1920–3, encouraging his first literary efforts.

21. The brief account that follows is based on Tual 1987: 106–34, with some additional elements from Courrière 2000 (who himself relies very much on Tual's 1987 account, augmented by interviews with her) and from Prévert and Prévert 1965.

22. She had worked on *L'Amour chante* (Robert Florey, 1930) and *La Chienne* (Jean Renoir, 1931).

23. A short film, *Une Nuit à Monte-Carlo* (1932), is listed in the French film archives of the Centre National de la Cinématographie, and appears to be what is left of *Vingt-quatre heures de la vie d'une femme*. It is not known if it was released at the time.

24. We believe that Tual confuses this film with the earlier *Le Collier de la reine*, which Batcheff dropped so as to work on *Un Chien andalou*. It is hardly conceivable that

he would have signed up for a film with Chantal two years after slapping her on set (Tual 1987: 131–2; this account is not in Tual 1980).

25. Tual says Montparnasse, but all contemporary newspaper accounts indicate Montmartre.

26. Pierre Batcheff was cremated at the Cimetière du Père-Lachaise. In 1972, he was transferred to the Cimetière du Montparnasse, together with his mother and sister, after the latter's death in 1971.

27. In all probability due to steps taken by Denise or Batcheff's family.

28. See *Ami du peuple*, *Paris-Midi*, 15 April 1932, or *L'Intransigeant*, *Paris-Soir*, 16 April 1932, among others.

29. It is worth noting that *Les Enfants du paradis* includes a scene that was originally in the *Émile-Émile* screenplay: 'la pantomime où Baptiste veut se pendre avec une corde à sauter d'enfant' ('the pantomime where Baptiste wants to hang himself with a kid's skipping rope'; Pierre Prévert 1965: 54).

CHAPTER 2

Stardom in the 1920s

The star system in France emerged around 1910 as theatre and music-hall stars crossed over into film (Vincendeau 2000: 5), but only really took off in the 1920s with the establishment of a wide-ranging film press, and the sharp rise in cinema attendance in the mid-1920s (see Abel 1984: 49). The press that interests us here is less the dailies which began to run film reviews in the early 1920s (such as *Le Figaro*, *L'Humanité*, *L'Intransigeant*, *Le Journal*, *Le Matin*, *L'Œuvre*, *Paris-Soir*, *Le Petit Journal* and *Le Quotidien*), or the up-market literary journals (such as *L'Esprit nouveau*, *Mercure de France* and *Les Nouvelles littéraires*), than the trade and popular film press on which we have relied significantly for this book. Some had been established early on as trade journals, such as *Ciné-journal* (1908), *Courrier cinématographique* (1911) and *Hebdo-Film* (1916), *Filma* (1908), *La Cinématographie française* (1918) and *Cinéopse* (1919), with *Filma* (1908) and *Le Film* (1914) aimed at cinephiles. There was an explosion of journals around 1920, however. There were cinephile journals, such as *Ciné pour tous* (1919) and *Cinéa* (1921), these merging into *Cinéa-Ciné pour tous* in 1923, and *Cinémagazine* (1921); but there were new types of journal aimed at a wider public, such as *Mon ciné* (1922) *Ciné-Miroir* (1922) and *Mon film* (1924), followed later in the decade by *Pour vous* (1928) and *Cinémonde* (1928).[1] It is in this popular film press that we can observe an emerging star culture, albeit one which found it hard to disentangle itself from a world-wide star culture, given the portability of silent film.

French actors had to contend, then as they do now, with American or American-based stars in particular. It is telling, for example, that in the first year of Louis Delluc's weekly magazine *Le Journal du Ciné-club*, 1920, the majority of its covers and of its star profiles focused on non-French stars. In its first two months, for example, readers would have learnt from a full-page report how the American star Fanny Ward was thinking of settling in France after making films with Jacques de Baroncelli and Henry Bernstein (no. 1, p. 2); they would have read a three-page article on the US star Pearl White (no. 2, pp. 6–8); seen Theda Bara on the cover of no. 4, and former Ziegfeld girl Mae Murray on the cover of no. 7. In these first months, there were only two French actors who made the cover of the magazine. One was female, Emmy

Lynn, whose career had started in 1913, and who had starred in Abel Gance's *Mater dolorosa* (1917; see Abel 1984: 87–9). The other was male, 43-year-old Marcel Levesque, whose career started at the same time as Lynn's. He would have been familiar to audiences from the series of Louis Feuillade and (briefly in 1919) those of Jean Durand. The *jeune premier*, or Romantic male lead, emerged very quickly, however. Charles de Rochefort, for example, is on the August 1920 cover of *Ciné-club* (no. 33), captioned as the *jeune premier* starring in Henri Pouctal's super-production *Gigolette* (1921);[2] and Eric Barclay (Swedish-born, but who made his career in France in the early 1920s, principally in films by Jacques de Baroncelli) is similarly identified on the cover of the June 1921 issue of *Cinéa*, starring in Baroncelli's *Le Rêve* (1921).

Jean-Louis Croze complained that the French did not understand how to foreground their stars compared with the Americans, as can be seen from the title of his article: 'Nous avons nos vedettes . . . mais nous ne savons pas les imposer' ('We have our stars . . . but we don't know how to impose them'; Croze 1925a: 77). None the less, by the end of the decade there was a flourishing star culture comprising both French and non-French names. So, for example, *Cinéa-Ciné pour tous*, like many other journals, ran advertisements for photo-portraits of stars. In a 1929 list, we find Maurice Chevalier, Jean Angelo, Jaque Catelain, André Roanne, Jean Murat, Pierre Batcheff, Georges Charlia, Ivan Petrovitch and Adolphe Menjou;[3] Chevalier and Petrovich were by then associated with the American cinema, and Menjou was American, while the rest are French-based stars. The list also exemplifies the rise of the *jeune premier* as a key feature of the industry; a survey by *Mon ciné* suggested that young women readers in particular wanted to see more *jeunes premiers*, rather than men in their forties (Desclaux 1927: 19). Batcheff was an important figure in this group of stars; indeed, we shall be arguing that he is key in the transition from the ephebic and melancholy *jeune premier* to the healthily athletic *jeune premier*. He foreshadows the popular heroes of the 1930s, while still looking backwards to both the Romantic hero of the nineteenth century, as well as the exotic New World star most keenly represented by Rudolph Valentino.

BATCHEFF, THE *JEUNE PREMIER*, AND THE PAST

As we pointed out in Chapter 1, Batcheff was at the height of his stardom in 1928. *Pour vous* ran a competition late in the year, just after the premiere of *Les Deux Timides*, to decide who the top six *jeunes premiers* were. Batcheff was the only clear French star in a list made up of American and British actors: Walter Byron, Alexandre D'Arcy, Reginald Denny and Douglas Fairbanks, along with

Figure 2.1 'Pierre Batcheff, who is one of the screen's best *jeunes premiers*' (*Pour vous*, October 1929)

Eric Barclay whose career began in the UK in the early 1920s and who made films in both France and Germany in the mid-1920s (*Pour vous* 1928b: 12–13). Two of these, along with Batcheff, can be found in a *Cinémagazine* article that year devoted to 'ideal masculinity'. The article lists principally American and

British stars as examples of a confident and what might be called 'athletic' masculinity: for the Americans, John Barrymore, Richard Dix, Douglas Fairbanks, John Gilbert and George O'Brien; for the British, Ronald Colman and Reginald Denny; and the Frenchman Charles Vanel, whose film career had started before the First World War. All of these actors had been born before the end of the nineteenth century. But the article also devotes a section to young 'adolescent' stars, listing Novarro, Batcheff, the American Charles 'Buddy' Rogers[4] and the dancer Ernst van Duren:[5]

> Et voici les éphèbes au corps mince, au visage encore puéril, aux yeux pleins de flamme généreuse. Ramon Novarro est sur la lisière.[6] On l'aurait cru plutôt un homme si, dans *Ben Hur* [1925], il n'avait semblé si jeune. La caresse de son regard est celle d'un adolescent, ainsi que son corps svelte et robuste; mais le cou musclé, l'expression précise des traits, annoncent l'approche de la maturité. Pierre Batcheff, au visage mobile et exalté garde encore la touchante fragilité de l'adolescence ainsi que Jaque Catelain, ce jeune dieu de lumière. Charles Rogers ne peut maîtriser ses beaux yeux vagabonds. On y lit, malgré lui, l'étonnement naïf et la sincérité de l'enfance. Plus assuré est Van Duren, que les Allemands comparent au célèbre Apollon du Belvédère. (Alby 1928: 423)

> (Here are the young ephebes with their slender bodies and childlike faces, their eyes full of the fire of generosity. Ramon Novarro is on the edge. He is more like a man, if it had not been for *Ben Hur*, where he seems so young. His silky eyes are those of an adolescent, as is his slender and sturdy body; but the muscled neck, the precise features, are harbingers of maturity. Pierre Batcheff, whose animated and elated features are still marked with the touching fragility of adolescence, as well as Jaque Catelain, that young god of light. Charles Rogers cannot prevent his handsome eyes from roving. He may try to hide it, but you can see the naive astonishment and the sincerity of youth in them. More self-assured is van Duren, whom the Germans compare to the famous Apollo Belvedere.)

The key point to retain from this description is the youthfulness and feminine grace of the *jeune premier*. This is part of a well-established tradition in French iconography of the nineteenth century, as has been shown by Abigail Solomon-Godeau, who explores the figure of the androgynous ephebe in history painting after the Revolution, pointing out how these figures 'connote effeminacy, passivity, debility, helplessness and impotence' (Solomon-Godeau 1997: 150).

It is worth remembering that the *jeune premier* figure also had his antecedents in the novels of the nineteenth century, as is suggested by a writer reviewing the figure of the *jeune premier* in 1943. She points out how the *jeune premier* 'est la consécration vivante du Prince Charmant, dont rêvent les jeunes filles. Jusqu'ici, il n'y avait que les romans pour leur donner une idée assez positive de cet être inaccessible et désiré (. . .) Étonnons-nous que le jeune premier de cinéma connut la grande faveur!' ('He is the living incarnation of the Prince Charming dreamed of by young girls. Up until now only novels could give them a positive idea of this inaccessible and longed-for creature (. . .) It isn't surprising that the *jeune premier* of the cinema became so popular!'; Mohy 1943: 6).[7] Batcheff conformed to this image of the Romantic hero. A description of him on the set of *Monte-Cristo* in 1928 plays on key Romantic figures, such as Don Juan, Alfred de Musset and Lord Byron, as well as a key figure for the surrealists from later in the century, child-poet Arthur Rimbaud:

> Des lèvres de Don Juan jeune, un rire qui s'éteint vite, une voix capricieuse, par à-coups . . . Musset à dix-huit ans. Et le regard volontaire et vague à la fois que devait avoir Byron (. . .) Mince comme une lame, nerveux et rapide, (. . .) on pense au mauvais garçon des légendes. Il n'est pas encore décoiffé, en guenille, tout en yeux comme Rimbaud, mais les romantiques auraient reconnu en lui un frère. (Frank 1928: 8–9)

> (The lips of a young Don Juan, short laughs, a capricious voice, that comes in fits and starts . . . Musset at eighteen. And the wilful but also faraway gaze that Byron must have had (. . .) Slim as a razor, nervous and quick, (. . .) he makes you think of the bad boy of legends. His hair isn't ruffled yet, his clothes are not rags, he doesn't have those wide eyes like Rimbaud, but the Romantics would have seen him as a brother.)

Even as late as 1931, we find the following description of him on the set of *Les Amours de minuit*, in terms that recall the melancholic and brooding hero of the Romantic period: 'Il est immobile dans quelque coin du décor, tassé sur une chaise, l'air absent, l'œil perdu entre les projecteurs éteints, on dirait un rêveur . . ., un poète . . ., un être chimérique, presque irréel, qui semble poursuivre éternellement un rêve ou un regret. Quand on lui parle, il semble revenir de loin, de très loin' ('He sits immobile in lost corner, slumped in a chair, his eyes vacant, staring between the darkened projectors, a dreamer . . ., a poet . . ., a phantom, almost unreal, who seems to pursue eternally a dream or a regret. When you speak to him, he seems to return from somewhere far away'; *Spectateur* 1931).

Given that the *jeune premier* was, at least in the French case, so anchored in the iconography and the literature of the nineteenth century, we should not be surprised that the figure might well have been seen more as a throwback to the past than to the future. The future seemed to belong, judging by the mass hysteria they elicited, to more exotic, foreign New World stars such as Novarro and Valentino. The French *jeune premier* signalled not just the past, however, but a potentially more stable past, where social and physical grace had not yet been tainted by the Great War. It is understandable that the French should have desired a return to the Belle Époque, seen as a mythical period of stability (see Becker and Berstein 1990: 155, 391; Vavasseur-Desperriers 1993: 53); and equally understandable that the image of the impotent youth should reflect not just a reaction against the virility of the soldier damaged in the male-dominated and very public theatre of war, but also a wish to return to a more private scene, that of domestic and maternal bliss, as Janine Bouissounouse argued in an article in *Cinémonde* in 1933. Her intentionally ironic sketch, with its almost blasphemous and no doubt unintentional references to the Pietà, could not better describe Batcheff's role in *Claudine et le poussin* at the age of sixteen in 1924: 'Après la guerre, pour se délasser sans doute des soldats (. . .) les femmes aimèrent Chérubin, un éphèbe pâle et fragile qu'on eût voulu bercer en chantant la romance, couvrir de fleurs et dorloter' ('After the war, no doubt to find relief from the soldiers (. . .) women loved Cherub, a pale and fragile ephebe that you would have liked to cradle in your arms while singing a romance, cover with flowers and pamper'; cited in Cadars 1982: 21).[8] Her argument does not just apply to film stars, but to some of the surrealist group (and by extension, one might argue, to many French intellectuals of the 1920s). Denise Tual explains in an interview in 1985 that Batcheff, 'sans être homosexuel (. . .) était un "homme féminin", un phénomène très particulier relatif à cette époque (. . .) Prenez Aragon, Dalí, Éluard: tous étaient des hommes extrêmement féminins qui avaient pris l'habitude de se regarder dans une glace. Leurs attitudes, leurs comportements, sans avoir d'analogie avec l'homosexualité, plaisaient beaucoup à certaines femmes' ('without being homosexual, (Batcheff) was a "feminine man", something specific to the times (. . .) Take Aragon, Dalí, Éluard: all of them were extremely feminine men who had the habit of looking at themselves in the mirror. Their attitudes, their behaviour, without being specifically homosexual, was attractive to some women'; Gilles 2000: 191). The following description of Batcheff in *Le Bonheur du jour* is typical of this view; he is 'trop "joli", à cause de cette beauté presque efféminée' ('too "pretty", because of his almost effeminate beauty'; Roque 1928).

BATCHEFF AND TRANSITIONAL MASCULINITY

The post-war period led to a reaction against virile men, and a refuge in images of beautiful and aetheticised childlike impotence; but it was clear that this kind of image could not last long. It was too static, too perfect, and increasingly out of step with shifting attitudes to masculinity. Mohy encapsulates these points well in her 1943 review, articulating the negative views Batcheff himself had of the roles he played:

Le jeune premier fut ce personnage trop bien habillé, admirablement cosmé-
tiqué et doté d'un physique avantageux, auquel était dévolu la tâche de donner
à sa partenaire des baisers sur la bouche. On ne lui en demandait pas beaucoup plus. Son rôle se réduisait à celui d'élégant mannequin, accessoire indispensable du film à succès (. . .) Prisonnier du frac éternel ou du smoking
cintré, le jeune premier s'étiolait. (Mohy 1943: 6)

(The *jeune premier* was the character who was always too well dressed, too well
made up, with a too perfect body, whose job it was to kiss his partner on the
mouth. He didn't have to do much else. His role was to be an elegant dummy,
the indispensable accessory for a successful film (. . .) Imprisoned in his
eternal morning coat or his dinner jacket, the *jeune premier* was wasting away.)

But in reality, the *jeune premier* was considerably more various than this
thumbnail sketch allows. As early as 1926, a sketch of André Roanne began
bluntly by saying that 'pour être un bon jeune premier, il faut être sportif,
élégant et plein d'entrain' ('to be a good *jeune premier*, you have to be sporty,
elegant and full of energy'; *Ciné-miroir* 1926: 178), hardly the epithets – apart
from elegance – that we might associate with Batcheff, or the even more
effeminate Catelain. Indeed, Roanne came to prominence in the same film as
Simonne Mareuil (who was to star with Batcheff in *Un Chien andalou*), *Chouchou
poids plume* (Gaston Ravel, 1925), where he plays a boxer. There was clearly a
shift towards the more active star; a feature in *Mon ciné* in 1928 on sport and
cinema began 'le sport est le roi du jour' ('sport is king'; *Mon ciné* 1928: 9), and
later that year there was an article entitled 'Le Public aime les héros sportifs'
('The Public Likes Sporty Heroes'; Desclaux 1928: 12).

Mohy's sketch of the figure of the *jeune premier*, in which she argues that
there is an evolution during the 1920s, in reality suggests that these were coex-
isting variants rather than developmental stages in the figure. This is because
they were all active as stars during the mid-1920s. She begins with the effeminate Catelain, but immediately points to the less conventionally beautiful Ivan
Mosjoukine and Jean Murat. She considers that a more virile version of the
jeune premier was represented by Valentino and Batcheff, or more proletarian
types such as Albert Préjean and Jean Angelo. These last four correspond to
what she calls 'l'homme séduisant certes, mais fort, protecteur, aussi éloigné
que possible du type créé par un Jaque Catelain par exemple' ('the seducer, yes,
but strong, protective, as far away as possible from the type created by a Jaque
Catelain, for example'; Mohy 1943: 7).

The disjunction between Mohy's 1943 view (that Batcheff is quite unlike
Catelain) and Alby's 1928 view (that Batcheff is much the same as Catelain)
can be at least partly explained by Batcheff's career after 1928. Up to and
including 1928, Batcheff was probably seen rather more in the mould of the
effeminate Catelain, as can be surmised from the fact that L'Herbier used him

briefly as a replacement for Catelain in *Le Diable au cœur*, as we saw in Chapter 1. Perceptions of Batcheff changed after *Les Deux Timides* (premiered five months after Alby's article in 1928) and *Un Chien andalou* in 1929, films he made precisely so as to escape from the typecast *jeune premier* roles he had previously had.

Seen from the vantage point of the mid-1940s, Batcheff might well have seemed – and this is a view we also hold – a transitional form of masculinity. Batcheff in 1929–30 signalled a crossing over from the effeminate Catelain type, with whom he had been associated until 1928, to what became the more dominant *jeune premier* by the turn of the 1930s, the athletic type. It is undoubtedly no coincidence that the *jeunes premiers* listed by Mohy who had a significant career beyond the silent period were those who were the more virile and athletic type. Murat, Petrovitch, Roanne and even more so Préjean carried on into sound cinema, as did Batcheff briefly,[9] while Catelain, the effeminate *jeune premier* par excellence, did not. Catelain himself was very aware of the shift we have identified, as we can see from the following extract from an article in 1930: 'Ceux qui plaisent actuellement sont les garçons francs, nets, sains, avec un bon sourire clair, le cœur sur la main (. . .) On apprécie moins aussi le personnage mélancolique ou romantique (. . .) L'acteur qui vous fait partager ses tristesses, ou des pensées trop hermétiques, ennuie indiscutablement' ('Those in favour at the moment are honest clean-living lads with a smile on their face, their heart on their sleeve (. . .) People don't like the melancholic or the Romantic (. . .) The actor who shares his sorrows or his deepest darkest thoughts with you, is unquestionably boring'; *Cinémonde*, 6 November 1930, quoted in Cadars 1982: 15). It is in this respect significant that the photos of Batcheff used in the 1920s tended to stress the melancholic type, while Sannier's star portrait of 1930 has three pictures of him, the most visible one, cutting across the headline, being of Batcheff playing tennis (Sannier 1930: 665). Another star portrait of him the same year articulates the same shift away from the Romantic hero to the more sporty type, reporting that, having just married, Batcheff and his wife spend their time playing table tennis, the writer commenting on how odd this might seem to those familiar with Batcheff's image: 'Allez donc vous fier, après cela, aux regards mélancoliques et à la fatale pâleur que ce jeune premier offre, sur l'écran, à ses admiratrices? Je commence à soupçonner secrètement que, sous l'apparence romantique de Batcheff, se dissimule un personnage facétieux' ('I'm not sure we can trust the melancholy looks and the sickly pallor of this *jeune premier* so attractive to his female admirers. I am beginning to think secretly that under Batcheff's romantic appearance, a more mischievous character is hidden'; Doré 1930: 647).

Batcheff's choice of films at this juncture in his career is clearly important. In late 1928, his role as Félix Soltikoff in *Le Perroquet vert*, while being linked, as we shall see in later chapters, to aspects of his mid-1920s star persona, also suggests a shift to a more athletic image – as a review points out, emphasising 'un nouveau Batcheff, non plus un jeune premier joli, mais un homme, un partisan plein de vigueur' ('a new Batcheff, no longer the pretty *jeune premier*, but a man, a partisan full of vigour'; *Cinémagazine* 1928a: 163).

Batcheff can be considered a transitional *jeune premier* type for another reason. Unlike Catelain, who suffered from the shift away from silent elegance to the sonorous athleticism of sound cinema, Batcheff had an exotic dimension. This linked him firmly with Valentino, not least when Batcheff accepted Ingram's Berber role in *Baroud*. Batcheff's role as Si Hamed was a clear reference to Valentino's *The Sheik* (1921) and *The Son of the Sheik* (1926), and Novarro's *The Arab* (1924). In this optic, Batcheff was not at all, or at any rate no longer, like the pale and fragile nineteenth-century European melancholic; he was much more like the New World *jeune premier* so attractive to audiences on both sides of the Atlantic. Batcheff, in other words, had consciously manipulated his image. The *Baroud* role can therefore be seen much less as a resigned acceptance of the inevitability of typecasting, and more as a clever shift to the dynamic and exotic *jeune premier* associated with the New World; it is a conscious reconfiguration, as *Les Deux Timides* and *Un Chien andalou* had been, but for different reasons, of the *jeune premier* role he had played in the mid-1920s.

Indeed, Batcheff more generally did everything he could to undermine the image of the *jeune premier*. The Sannier interview is extraordinary in this respect, given that he had made his mark as a *jeune premier*. In this interview, he undermines that role, not just by rejecting it, but by emphasising its stupidity, in terms that recall those of Mohy above:

> Je ne suis pas un 'jeune premier'. Les gens qui m'ont confié de tels rôles se sont trompés. D'ailleurs cette appellation est empruntée à un langage périmé qui, avec sa 'mère noble', son 'ingénue' et son 'vilain', a empêché les scénaristes de nous montrer, jusqu'à présent, autre chose que deux jeunes gens qui s'avouent leur amour dans la première partie du film, qui le voient contrarié par de 'méchantes gens' dans la seconde, mais dont un gros plan réunira les lèvres dans la troisième. Je rêve de films qui sortiraient de ces stupides conventions (auxquelles sacrifient les auteurs stériles en donnant comme excuse que c'est 'pour plaire au public'). C'est faux, et la meilleure des preuves en est la réaction à laquelle nous assistons actuellement. Voilà pourquoi je crois le moment venu de réaliser un film qui serait, à l'esprit français, ce que les films de Laurel et Hardy sont à l'humour américain. (Sannier 1930: 665)

> (I am not a *'jeune premier'*. Those who have given me these roles were wrong. Besides, the word comes from an old-fashioned language, which, with its 'noble mother', its 'ingénue', its 'villain', has prevented scriptwriters from

showing us anything other, until now, than two young people who declare their love in the first part of the film, who have obstacles put in their path by 'bad people' in the second, but whose lips meet in a close-up in the third. I dream of films which would drop these stupid conventions (which sterile writers follow claiming that it is to 'please the public'). This is misguided as we can see from the reaction to these conventions at the moment. It's why I think the time has come to make a film which would be for the French what Laurel and Hardy are for the Americans.)

Batcheff's dealings with fan culture also show us how he was the unwilling star we identified in Chapter 1, and which this interview underlines.

BATCHEFF AND FAN CULTURE: THE UNWILLING STAR

Fan culture determined that everything should reinforce the image of the *jeune premier*. While there was not the kind of merchandising with which we are now familiar, with stars promoting specific designer clothes or other consumer items, none the less there was a general use of the star as a beacon of elegance, the word that constantly crops up where Batcheff (and some others) are concerned. So, for example, *Pour vous* ran an article in 1930 on costume in the cinema, in which publicity photos of Batcheff were used, with the caption 'Pierre Batcheff connaît l'art de nouer une cravate' ('Pierre Batcheff knows the art of wearing a tie'); there is a statement in the text pointing to 'nos sympathiques Jean Murat, André Roanne, Pierre Batcheff à l'élégance dégagée, jeune et de bon goût' ('our likeable Jean Murat, André Roanne, Pierre Batcheff with their casual, youthful and tasteful elegance'; d'Ahetze 1930: 7).

Along with other stars, Batcheff's views were sought for spurious and superficial surveys, such as the one, occasioned by *Gentlemen Prefer Blondes* (Malcolm St Clair, 1928), on whether blondes were preferable to brunettes. Unlike the other respondents for this instalment of the survey (*jeune premier* Eric Barclay and filmmakers Alberto Cavalcanti, Donatien and Jacques Feyder), whose responses are serious, Batcheff responds humorously, saying that one cannot tell the difference most of the time because of the way cameramen use the lighting, and that in any case he prefers wigs (Lenoir 1928a: 419).

Batcheff's dismissiveness extends to his own films. A 1928 star portrait tells us that he hates his own films, and that his screen character 'lui reste indifférent, et il le voit vivre et s'agiter, sans lui porter autrement d'intérêt' ('remains indifferent to him, and he watches him live and bustle about without having the slightest interest in him'; Lenoir 1928b: 534). A few months later, fans were reminded: 'Je ne vais jamais au cinéma, – surtout quand on donne un film dont je suis' ('I never go to the cinema, especially when it's one of my

Year	Refs
1924	2
1925	1
1926	2
1927	3
1928	58
1929	44
1930	30
1931	26

Figure 2.2   References to Batcheff in *Ciné-Miroir's* 'On répond' column

films'; Kolb 1929: 12), a statement which is all the more telling given that there is plenty of evidence that Batcheff was an avid cinema-goer, as affirmed by Denise Tual, for example, who also pointed out that Batcheff particularly liked the films of Clair and Renoir (interview, November 1994).

Similarly, one of the more interesting features of Batcheff's intersection with fan culture is his attitude to fan mail. In the same interview with Jean Kolb to which we have just referred, Batcheff apologises for not answering fan mail, saying that he rigorously classifies all the letters sent to him but that he is too busy to respond, and promising that he will employ a secretary to deal with his correspondence. Figure 2.2 shows the number of references to Batcheff in the readers' column, 'On répond', from a single magazine, *Ciné-Miroir*. As we can see, the data confirm his sudden leap to stardom in 1928; but they also show a declining number of references thereafter, when we might have expected them to increase. Not only that, but the tenor of the interventions changes over time.

In the references from 1924–5, the issue of mail is hardly mentioned. But from summer 1928, the references are frequently complaints that he is not answering mail, such as this example from 20 July: 'Je ne sais pas si Pierre Batcheff répond, car plusieurs lectrices se plaignent de son silence' ('I don't know whether Pierre Batcheff answers, as several women readers have complained about not hearing from him'), with many more complaints of this kind in 1929, such as this rather damning advice from 31 May: 'Inutile d'écrire à Pierre Batcheff, il ne veut pas répondre, ce serait un timbre gâché' ('Pointless writing to Pierre Batcheff, he doesn't want to answer, it's a waste of a stamp'). Indeed, there was even an editorial piece in the magazine by Jean Vignaud that year focusing on stars who did not respond and singling Batcheff out, with Vignaud quoting a presumably fictional reader, 'Mademoiselle Myosotis' ('Miss Forget-me-not'): 'Voulez-vous me dire si Pierre Batcheff répond ordinairement aux lettres qu'on lui adresse? Je vous charge de lui donner une bonne "tirée d'oreilles" de ma part, car il ne m'a pas encore répondu depuis un mois que je lui ai écrit' ('Can you tell me whether Pierre Batcheff usually answers his letters? I would like you to box his ears for me, because he hasn't answered the letter I sent him a month ago'; Vignaud 1929: 35). By 1931, however, there are no longer any complaints of this kind, and the indications are that he appears to have started responding again: 'Oui, Pierre Batcheff et Nils Asther répondent aux lettres' ('Yes, Pierre Batcheff and Nils Asther are answering letters'; 27 March).[10] As we have not been able to find any record that he employed a secretary to deal with his fan mail, as suggested above, it is likely that Batcheff himself decided to put right his failure to respond during the key years 1928–30, when he became the equivalent of a superstar, and tried to change his image by working with the avant-garde and comedy. We can only surmise that this may well have had something to do with nervousness in the transition to sound cinema, and the need to maintain a fan base so that he could subsidise his scriptwriting with an active career as a film star, no matter how distasteful the idea of the typecast *jeune premier* might have been for him.

That distaste is clear in the discussion with Kolb concerning fan mail. Kolb asks him what he thinks about women who write to him because they are clearly besotted with him. His answer: 'Elles me troublent, car, pour chacune d'elles, je me dis: "Est-elle sincère ou se moque-t-elle de moi? . . . Est-ce à l'artiste que s'adressent ces jolis mots ou au personnage représenté?" Et, finalement, le premier devient très jaloux de l'autre' ('I find them disconcerting, because for each of them I have to ask myself: "Is she sincere or is she making fun of me? . . . Are all those pretty words addressed to the artist or to the character the artist represents?" And in the end the one becomes jealous of the other'; Kolb 1929: 12). Emerging from this brief comment is a key issue: the double, the man split into two, the man watching himself act, the man outside himself, irremediably 'othered'. It had already surfaced a few years earlier in one of the few articles directly written by Batcheff, the first in what was to be a series for a newspaper based in Avignon. In that article he contrasted cinema and real life, saying that life was an 'infiniment plus attrayant spectacle dès l'instant où l'on possède la faculté de se muer en spectateur de sa propre comédie' ('an infinitely more attractive spectacle from the moment when you have the ability to turn yourself into the spectator of your own comedy'; Batcheff 1926).

There are several aspects to this 'otherness': Batcheff's Russianness, which we can parallel with Valentino's; the concomitant reification of the star as pin-up; and, finally, a more general interest by the surrealists in particular during the 1920s and early 1930s with doubling and distancing.

BATCHEFF, VALENTINO AND 'OTHERNESS'

As we saw in Chapter 1, in 1926 Batcheff could have, if he had wished, taken up where Valentino left off. There are many parallels between the two stars. Most, if not all, of the social conditions Miriam Hansen identifies as key to the emergence of Valentino obtained in France. Shifting gender relations in the aftermath of the Great War had given women more independence as more of them joined the workforce, and had led to a redefinition of femininity and a 'liberalisation of sexual behaviour'; as a result, there was a questioning of 'standards of masculinity, destabilising them with connotations of sexual ambiguity, social marginality, and ethnic/racial otherness' (Hansen 1986: 7). Hansen shows by careful analysis of mise en scene how Valentino is positioned as the object of the gaze, and that this leads to a 'systematic feminisation of his persona' (Hansen 1986: 13), which is motivated in various ways through the narrative (he can be a dancer, for example) or through aspects of mise en scene ('feminine' costume). She also discusses the masochism which underpins Valentino's persona, as well as the shades of incest in on-screen relationships (Hansen 1986: 20). She briefly considers Valentino's 'otherness' as Latin Lover, and its relationship to institutionalised racism in American society, the fear of the immigrant, and by extension the fear of the Black man. His exotic roles, especially as the Sheik, Hansen argues, displaced fears of miscegenation for American audiences (Hansen 1986: 23–4).

Not only are many of the socio-economic conditions in France clearly similar to those in the USA during the 1920s, but the features of Valentino's persona raised by Hansen are also all features of Batcheff's persona. We find, as we shall see in following chapters, the same feminisation, incestuous relationships on screen, masochism (although interestingly without the sadism that Hansen also identifies in Valentino's characters) and otherness. Where this last is concerned, there are interesting modulations. While Batcheff's characters are frequently exoticised, not least in his final incarnation as Si Hamed in *Baroud*, his otherness is associated not with the Southern European, as was the case with Valentino, but, given his Russian origins, with the Slav. There are frequent references in the popular press to these origins, and it is more than likely that his films for the Russians of Montreuil, Films Albatros, would have intensified this association. There were likely to be 'oriental' touches as well, given that in the popular imagination the Russians were considered in the same bracket as the Chinese and Indochinese, a feature reinforced by Batcheff's birthplace in Manchuria, frequently commented on in star portraits. Manchuria is a region bordering Russia and North-East China. Outer Manchuria had been invaded by Russia in the mid-nineteenth century. Batcheff was born in Harbin, in Inner Manchuria. Although much more obviously Chinese as an area, Harbin had been established by the Russians in 1898 as the base for the construction of the Chinese Eastern Railway. It was also a haven for Russian Jews escaping from persecution. Following the defeat of the Russians in the Russo-Japanese War of 1904–5, it had become a bustling international centre with no less than sixteen consulates; it is likely that Batcheff's father, as a Jewish businessman (the nature of whose business we do not know), would have gone to Harbin to protect himself and his family, and been part of this expansion.

Schor's sketch of French attitudes to the Russians brings out a feature that we shall find in Batcheff: 'Ils étaient tour à tour ascètes et jouisseurs, fatalistes et entreprenants, tendres et violents; le regard de ces êtres déconcertants, plein d'une exquise délicatesse, pouvait être traversé par des éclairs de sauvagerie asiatique. C'était là que résidait tout le mystère et le charme de l'âme slave' ('They were both ascetics and hedonists, fatalists and enterprising, tender and violent; the eyes of these disconcerting beings, full of an exquisite sensitivity, could be shot through with flashes of Asiatic savagery. This was why the Slav soul was so mysterious and charming'; Schor 1996: 114; see also Lequin 1992: 388). One of his interviewers describes Batcheff's well-bred elegance, Romantic appearance, and especially 'ses yeux admirables où se jouent toute la sensibilité slave et les reflets d'une intelligence sans cesse en éveil' ('his wonderful eyes with their Slav sensitivity and glimmers of an alert and intelligent mind'; Sannier 1930: 665). Denise Tual frequently talks of his fantastical nature and 'Russian atavism' (see, for example, Tual 1987: 112, 132).

It is worth recalling that immigration in 1920s France was significant and that its attendant problems were very publicly discussed. The French population increased very slowly during the post-war years, but what increase there was could be said in large measure to be due to immigration. The greatest number of incomers were Italian and Polish, the Italians representing 28 per cent of all immigrants in 1931, and the Poles 17.5 (Schor 1996: 60); treaties had been signed with both countries in 1919. There were approximately 1.5 million immigrants in 1921, or 4 per cent of the total population, rising to 2.4 million in 1926 or 6 per cent (Sirinelli 1993: 89). Given that the Polish immigrant community was one of the largest in France during the 1920s,[11] as well as being one of the better organised (Schor 1996: 96–7), it is also likely that Batcheff would have been a vehicle for the working out of fantasies and fears relating to the frontiers of 'North Europeanness', just as Valentino was for 'South Europeanness'. This would have been all the more the case given, first, nervousness in relation to the possible 'Bolshevik' leanings of the Russian immigrants, and, second and more generally, the financial crisis of 1926 and the xenophobic discourses it generated (see Schor 1996: 65).

PIERRE BATCHEFF
DANS
" L'Ile d'Amour"

JRPR.
PARIS
112

Figure 2.3 Batcheff as pin-up in *L'Île d'amour* (1928)

There is a major difference between Valentino and Batcheff, however. If Valentino's Europeanness was construed as slippery and dangerous, Batcheff's Russianness supported and intensified the distance that is associated with the star as static pin-up.

BATCHEFF AS PIN-UP

Gaylyn Studlar's work on Valentino emphasises 'transformative masculinity', which she defines as 'masculinity as a process, a liminal construction, and even as performance' (Studlar 1996: 4). She argues that Valentino's persona must be transformed from what we might call the sado-macho to the more tender, attentive and nurturing masculinity that allows for the 'reconciliation of masculinity with feminine ideals' (Studlar 1996: 172). Studlar's Valentino is more markedly different from Batcheff, given that she focuses tightly on Valentino as a dancer, exploring the dangers that the dancing male or 'tango pirate' could pose for the unwary female. By contrast, we would argue, Batcheff's persona is considerably less fluid and mobile. He is rarely a dancer, oddly, given his well-attested love of dancing; indeed, he adopts static poses in many of his films. Moreover, although he may be constructed as erotic object of the gaze, particularly in the more static poses, unlike Valentino, little is done in his films to help him escape from objectification, such as, for example, the consistent use of whips by Valentino to signal the man in control. On the contrary, as we shall show in the chapters that follow, a persistent trope for Batcheff's characters is the passive suffering male, drooping Pietà-like in a woman's arms. Indeed, his standard posture involves a droop combined with a stoop as well, as was commented on in the film press; in the readers' column of *Ciné-Miroir* for 11 May 1928, for example, we read: 'Je ne sais pas pourquoi il a une tendance à porter le cou en avant' ('I don't know why he tends to droop his head forwards'). And, unlike Valentino's highly erotic 'hot-hip' tango in *The Four Horsemen of the Apocalypse*, Batcheff's contact with his female partners on screen is curiously distant; not only does he not dance, as we noted above, but also another persistent trope in his star performance, as we shall see, is the faraway or downcast look, even as he sits (or, frequently, lies incapacitated) close to the woman he loves.

Richard Dyer has shown how the distant or downcast look of the male pin-up functions as a disavowal of objectification. The faraway look is almost literally an escape, a spatial displacement from the passivity and commodified objectification of the spectator's gaze; the male pin-up's look off (what we are calling the distant look) 'suggests an interest in something else that the viewer cannot see – it certainly doesn't suggest any interest in the viewer' (Dyer 1992: 104). Dyer also points out that there are pin-ups who stare straight at the camera, and that their gaze to some extent reasserts masculinity by its 'penetrating' nature (Dyer 1992: 109). Batcheff's gaze is hardly ever straight to camera, however. His gaze is not only looking away or off; it is literally vacant. He is there without being there; or, rather, he is there, somewhere else, rather than being here. Batcheff is an absent presence.

The distant look is also a disavowal of the femininity incorporated within that objectification; as Solomon-Godeau says of the nineteenth-century pin-up, the ephebe, he combines 'the edifying and culturally sanctioned universe of male *vertu* and beauty, but leavened (. . .) with a femininity contained, interiorised, and incorporated' (Solomon-Godeau 1997: 175). Femininity is inscribed within the pin-up as the giving-up of the body we see, while the distant look vacates the passive shell of the body; what is 'pinned up' is a feminine-connoted residue, an abandonment. Masculinity as exemplified by Batcheff cannot be pinned up or pinned down; it is never there where you look because it has always already drifted somewhere else, evacuated. As Dyer has pointed out in relation to what he calls the Sad Young Man in popular culture: 'The sad young man (. . .) is (. . .) not yet a real man. He is soft; he has not yet achieved assertive masculine hardness (. . .) The sad young man is a martyr figure [and] embodies a mode of sexuality we might now label masochistic' (Dyer 1993a: 42). He relates this historically both to the Romantic poets (whom we have seen are a constituent part of the French ephebe), as well as to Christian traditions of (male) martyrdom, particularly that of Saint Sebastian (Dyer 1993b: 77–8). Moreover, we have just seen how Batcheff's characters frequently lie prone and suffering, drooping, passive objects in pain, 'looking off' in more ways than one.

We established above that Batcheff might well have functioned as a source of anxiety. In this section we established that this would have been at least partly because, like Valentino, he was as feminine as he might have been masculine. We have argued that, as was the case with Valentino, the combination of masculine and feminine in Batcheff should not be construed as the uneasy splicing of two antipodes, but an indeterminate and often perplexing fluidity, ungraspable and unlocatable because of what we have called Batcheff's 'vacancy'. We would like to go one step further, and position that 'vacancy' within the concerns of surrealism.

BATCHEFF AS A SURREALIST STAR

Batcheff's 'vacancy', as we have called it, is for us a sign of critical distance combined with rejection of the insipid *jeune premier* roles he hated. It is in our view clearly linked to a shift in surrealist thinking in 1928–9, evident in the work of André Breton, as well as in the work of Dalí, in the form of paranoia-criticism, and also linked to Artaud's attempt to reconceive cinema language in the mid- to late 1920s.

In the second manifesto of surrealism, which appeared in the same number of *La Révolution surréaliste* as the filmscript of *Un Chien andalou*, Breton lamented the fact that automatic writing, seen in the first manifesto of 1924 as one of the main vehicles for achieving the surreal, had in a few short years led to clichés. The reason for this, he suggested, was that those who practised automatic writing had not maintained a sufficient critical distance; aspiring surrealist writers 'se satisfirent généralement de laisser courir la plume sur le papier sans observer le moins du monde ce qui se passait alors en eux – ce dédoublement étant pourtant plus facile à saisir et plus intéressant à considérer que celui de l'écriture réfléchie' (Breton 1988: 806; 'were generally content to let their pens run rampant over the paper without making the least effort to observe what was going on inside themselves, this disassociation being nonetheless easier to grasp and more interesting to consider than that of reflected writing'; Breton 1972: 158). We can see how the issue of Batcheff's 'vacancy', which we articulated as a key component of gender indeterminacy above, can be seen as a broader ontological imperative, as a means of detachment in the sense used by Breton. Breton distanced himself from the persona adopted as a writer, with a view to bypassing the rational mind, so as to ensure the authenticity of the verbal flux. Batcheff, in a parallel move, distanced himself from the clichéd commercial roles he performed – both in his comments about them, and in the vacant look we have identified as a marker of disconnection from the performance itself – so as to ensure something more authentic, as he himself kept on saying in his star interviews, something closer to (his conception of) the real.

Dalí was an important figure for the surrealists in the period 1929–34, and his paranoiac-critical method, which Breton suggested could be applied to all the arts including cinema (Breton 1992: 255), adds another layer to the issue of distance and disassociation. The paranoiac-critical method, best illustrated in paintings by Dalí such as *Métamorphose de Narcisse* (1937, Tate Modern), consists in replacing one image by its transformed or anamorphic double; but in principle, doubling is infinite (Dalí 1930: 10). An example of the process in *Un Chien andalou* is the sequence of dissolves (ants emerging from the hole in the hand, a woman's armpit, a sea urchin, the head of the androgyne). The images thus created are called simulacra by Dalí, and his view of their relationship to 'reality' is close to Baudrillard's simulacra, a key notion of postmodernism: not copies of the real, but the real itself, a dizzying circulation of always-already transformed images. We would like to argue that the *jeune premier* role is a simulacral image, all the more so in that there is no original image, only a constant circulation of variants of already existing images, performed by others as well as Batcheff. This is well exemplified by the illustration to one of Batcheff's star portraits (Figure 2.4), where we see a number of his roles pictorialised, neatly disposed in a circle, suggesting the circularity of simulacra.

Figure 2.4 'Leurs visages' (*Mon ciné*, December 1928)

Artaud's trajectory was very similar to Batcheff's, although there is no evidence that they knew each other. He worked with Charles Dullin in L'Atelier (earlier than Batcheff) and with Georges Pitoëff (later than Batcheff); he took opiates like Batcheff; they both knew Dr Toulouse, as we saw in Chapter 1; he used the cinema to support himself while lamenting its commercialism, like

Batcheff (see Artaud 1961: 110); he wrote film scripts, and like Batcheff, had one of them, *La Coquille et le clergyman* (1928), made into a film.[12] He also acted in a number of films, most famously as Marat in Gance's *Napoléon*, as had Batcheff in the role of General Hoche, but also in *La Passion de Jeanne d'Arc* (Carl Theodor Dreyer, 1928), and in films by directors with whom Batcheff had also worked: *L'Argent* (Marcel L'Herbier, 1929) and *Tarakanova* (Raymond Bernard, 1929).

In the course of 1927–8 Artaud wrote a number of pieces concerning *La Coquille et le clergyman*. For Artaud, there are three sorts of cinema (Artaud 1961: 21–2). The first is narrative cinema based on rudimentary psychology, a translation of literary procedures to the screen. The second is pure cinema, which, in common with other surrealists, he dislikes for its formalist lack of emotion.[13] The third type, he claims, is announced by *La Coquille et le clergyman*. Artaud does not abandon psychology, associated with narrative cinema, but claims that the new cinema will show human behaviour in its 'barbarity' (Artaud 1961: 23), where desire is more important than convention. The comments he makes concerning the circulation and disruptive nature of desire are close to Dalí's paranoiac-critical paradigm where an image is anamorphised into a succession of simulacra impelled by desire: 'La femme étale son désir animal, a la forme de son désir, le scintillement fantomatique de l'instinct qui la pousse à être une et sans cesse différente dans ses métamorphoses répétées' ('The woman displays her animal desire, she has the shape of her desire, the ghostly sparkle of her instincts that force her to be the same but ever different in her repeated metamorphoses'; Artaud 1961: 76).

A second, and rather more difficult notion to understand is Artaud's attempt to create a new language where images are disconnected from clear referents, 'images issues uniquement d'elles-mêmes et qui ne tirent pas leur sens de la situation où elles se développent mais d'une sorte de nécessité intérieure' ('images which emerge exclusively from themselves, and do not draw their meaning from the situation in which they develop but from a sort of powerful inner necessity'; Artaud 1961: 23). The aim is to do for cinema what Breton had defined as the goal of surrealism in the first manifesto: to find 'le travail pur de la pensée' ('the pure work of thought'; Artaud 1961: 78). Indeed, Artaud suggests that images are redundant in this endeavour; cinema can express thoughts not through images, but 'avec leur matière directe, sans interpositions, sans représentations' ('with the matter that they are made of, without anything coming in between, without representations'; Artaud 1961: 80–1). It is clear, however, that 'pure thought', however abstract and difficult to grasp it may be, in these circumstances can only be achieved by the kind of doubling and critical distancing that we have already seen in both Breton and Dalí. Artaud writes that spectators will only really understand his film if they are prepared to 'regarder profondément en soi' and to engage with an 'examen (. . .) attentif au *moi* interne' (Artaud 1961: 82; 'look deep into themselves'; 'an attentive examination of the inner self'; Artaud 1972: 67).

Artaud was very quickly to lose faith in the cinema. His 1933 article 'La Vieillesse précoce du cinéma', emphasised its static nature; once fixed on celluloid, images are frozen forever, and not amenable to the kind of work to which we have just referred (Artaud 1961: 95–9). None the less, his scenario *Les Dix-huit Secondes* (Artaud 1961: 11–15) where 'one futile identification follows another, as the actor's centerless self goes from double to double' (Williams 1981: 29), shows how Artaud was grappling with individual identity as the principal problem in the accession to 'pure thought'. As Williams points out, and this reflects our view of Batcheff's work more generally, 'the actor has finally hit upon an identification with the actor in himself – with an aspect of himself that is perpetually the reflection of the Other' (Williams 1981: 29).

We would like to suggest that Batcheff is a surrealist star: indeed, the only one, given that Artaud's relationship to the cinema was rather different. This might seem like the baldest of truisms. By common consent, there are very few 'surrealist' films, and the fact that Batcheff, one of the major commercial stars of the 1920s, acted in one of those very few films – indeed, one of the even fewer that are labelled 'surrealist' – by definition makes of him a surrealist star in ways that Gaston Modot was not. Although the latter was the hero of Buñuel and Dalí's next film, *L'Âge d'or* (1930), he was no more than a key second player of the French cinema throughout his career. Batcheff, on the other hand, mixed with the surrealists, and not just Buñuel and Dalí; Denise Tual reports that she and Batcheff were close friends of Robert Desnos (interview, November 1994). Moreover, as Tual points out in the same interview, Batcheff wrote copiously, and in a surrealist mode, both in terms of the speed with which he wrote (an essential for surrealist automatic writing), making it difficult sometimes to read what he had written (as we ourselves have discovered working on his manuscripts), and in terms of the scripts' content: 'Il écrivait. Mais c'était très mystérieux, illisible du reste (. . .) Il écrivait beaucoup, oui, des scénarios, disons surréalistes si vous voulez' ('He wrote. But it was all very mysterious, usually illegible (. . .) He wrote a lot, scenarios that were surrealist').

In more theoretical terms, Batcheff's critical distance from the roles he played parallels the distance from oneself promoted by Breton in the effort to discover what lies beneath the masks of identity, or as Breton puts it neatly in the first few lines of *Nadja*, to discover whom I haunt (Breton 1988: 647). The roles he played are for him no more than Dalí-esque simulacra, simulations hiding an emptiness. An unwilling star, he disconnects from these roles. We have defined his persona as an absent presence, where masculine and feminine

coalesce and fuse, these two sets of binaries articulating at least partly the reconciliation of opposites in Breton's 'point of the mind' in the second manifesto. But more actively than this, he chose to star in two films that were very
different from the others in his portfolio, both of which are clearly part of the
surrealist zeitgeist in 1928–9.

Un Chien andalou combines Dalí's obsessive simulacral images with Artaud's
proposals that pure thought could in some sense percolate in between images,
which themselves needed to transgress convention to reveal the violence of
affect. Humour is the link between *Un Chien andalou* and *Les Deux Timides*, as
it is between Batcheff and the surrealists. It is striking that the films the surrealists kept on returning to as their ideal were comedies. As early as 1918, Louis
Aragon published poems on Chaplin in Louis Delluc's *Le Film* (18 March
1918) and Pierre Reverdy's *Nord-Sud* (May 1918) (see Virmaux 1976: 119–20),
and the surrealist group famously published a diatribe to support Chaplin in
his 1927 divorce.[14] Buñuel wrote admiringly on Keaton in 1927 (Buñuel 1927).
In 1932, Artaud published a piece on the Marx Brothers in which the epithets
he uses to characterise their work are tragic, hallucinatory and anarchic, claiming that their films demonstrate intellectual freedom (Artaud 1964: 165–8).
Even in 'La Vieillesse précoce du cinéma' the following year, signalling his disillusion with the cinema, Artaud wrote that one of the few things he none the
less values about the cinema is the destabilising effects of comedies (Artaud
1961: 99). And long after the cinema had ceased to interest them, other surrealists evoked film comedies above all as the films that interested them most;
for example, Breton recalls Mack Sennett, Chaplin and Picratt (the French
name for Al St John) in 1952 (Breton 1999: 903).

Similarly, we have seen how Batcheff frequently mentioned American
comedies in his star interviews. Keaton, as Denise Tual reminds us, was a particular favourite, and Batcheff modelled his rejected filmscript *Émile-Émile* on
Keaton's comedies (Tual 1987: 115). In a 1928 interview, Batcheff rates Keaton
rather more highly than Chaplin: 'Buster Keaton a quelque chose d'angélique,
et Chaplin, quoi qu'il exploite trop le sentiment de pitié, est supérieurement
intelligent' ('Buster Keaton has something angelic about him, and Chaplin,
although often too sentimental, is supremely intelligent'; Frank 1928: 9).
Indeed, another interviewer, commenting on Batcheff's wish to direct a
Keaton-esque comedy, saw a physical resemblance between Batcheff and
Keaton: 'L'acteur qui nous fait le plus rire, Buster Keaton, n'a-t-il pas, comme
lui, un visage long, maigre, une bouche sérieuse et un regard dramatique?' ('The
actor who makes us laugh the most, Buster Keaton, like him has a long thin
face, a serious mouth and dramatic look in his eyes'; Doré 1930: 647).

We proposed at the end of Chapter 1 that Batcheff was a forerunner of
Poetic Realism. This chapter has shown us how he was caught as a performer

in the major debates of the period where cinema was concerned, with one foot in commercial cinema and the other in avant-garde cinema. He embodies the tensions between these two broad poles, figured most aptly in his look. On the one hand we have the vacant look we have identified as 'absent presence', and that we could see as the vacuity of the commercial cinema; on the other, we have, as its anamorphic negative, the rolled-up eyes of *Un Chien andalou*, signalling ecstatic and hysterical desire. At a key moment in its history, the moment when French cinema was to turn to sound, Batcheff – 1920s *jeune premier*, consciously deconstructing his persona with anarchic avant-garde work and Keaton-esque comedy, and foreshadowing the realism of the 1930s – is the star who best encapsulates that critical moment. The following chapters trace these permutations through his films.

Notes

1. Richard Abel gives a succinct overview of the film-related press in the 1920s (Abel 1988: 195–9 and 321–4). See also Gauthier 2002.
2. He is questionably 'French', however, given that he went on in 1922 to work in the USA under the name Charles De Roche, mainly for Famous Players-Lasky, before returning briefly to French productions in 1930.
3. *Cinéa Ciné pour tous*, 134, 1 June, p. 31.
4. Rogers's first film was the appropriately titled *Fascinating Youth* (Sam Wood, 1926). His appearance in this list is perhaps mainly due to the fact that his best performance was in the film that won the first 'Best Picture' Academy Award in the 1927–8 season, *Wings* (William A. Wellman, 1927).
5. Van Duren had starred in *Mon Paris* (Albert Guyot, 1927) and *La Princesse Mandane* (Germaine Dulac, 1928). He starred as Figaro in the film of the same name (Tony Lekain and Gaston Ravel, 1929), and committed suicide in 1930.
6. He is 'sur la lisière' (on the edge of adolescence), perhaps because he had been born in 1899, and was in 1928 almost thirty. The article goes on to argue that he has some of the features of a full-grown man.
7. In similar vein, André Breton wrote in 1951 about the attraction of the cinema, whose forte is to 'concrétiser les puissances de l'amour qui restent malgré tout déficientes dans les livres, du seul fait que rien ne peut y rendre la séduction ou la détresse d'un regard' ('make concrete the power of love which books in spite of everything are less good at, simply because they cannot render a seductive or a helpless look'; Breton 1999: 904).
8. We find a similar trope used for Valentino, whom we shall consider in more detail below: 'What a woman really wants to do for Rodolf [sic] is to bandage his wounds; comfort him; stroke that well-brushed hair; spank him; proudly show him off' (newspaper clipping quoted in Hansen 1991: 263).
9. Angelo died in 1933 at the age of 58, but Murat had starring roles in the 1930s, his career extending into the mid-1960s. Roanne, on the other hand, fell back on

non-starring parts in the 1930s, his career none the less extending into the mid-1950s. Petrovitch pursued a long career in German cinema into the late 1950s. Préjean had starring roles until the late 1940s, many of these being with major directors such as André Berthomieu, Marcel Carné, Christian-Jaque, Henri Decoin, Julien Duvivier, Carmine Gallone, Georg Wilhelm Pabst, Robert Siodmak and Jacques Tourneur.

10. Danish-born Nils Asther had a long career in film, beginning in 1916 in Sweden and Germany before moving to the USA where, at the end of the 1920s, he had played opposite Joan Crawford in *Our Dancing Daughters* (Harry Beaumont, 1928) and *Dream of Love* (Fred Niblo, 1928), as well as Greta Garbo in *Wild Orchids* (Sidney Franklin, 1929) and *The Single Standard* (John S. Robertson, 1929).

11. See Ponty 1988 for Polish immigration in the 1920s.

12. The writing of filmscripts was one of the ways the surrealists arguably compensated for the difficulty they had in making films. See Virmaux and Virmaux 1976: 64–75.

13. As Abel points out, the debate around 'pure cinema' was one of the major debates of the 1920s; see Abel 1988: 329–32 for a summary of the main positions.

14. 'Hands off love', *La Révolution surréaliste*, 9–10 (1 October 1927), pp. 1–6.

CHAPTER 3

Beginnings

In this chapter, we consider Batcheff's very first films. Extraordinarily, his first film in a role other than that of an extra is a starring role, as the virginal young lover. In his second film, he plays a major role opposite one of the major actresses of the early 1920s, Natalie Lissenko, although his part is that of the dissolute youth, contrasting markedly with his first film. In the third film we consider in this chapter, *Feu Mathias Pascal*, he has a small part, the starring role being taken by one of the major actors of the 1920s, and Natalie Lissenko's partner, Ivan Mosjoukine. We have devoted considerable analysis to each of these three films, even to *Feu Mathias Pascal*, because they establish the beginnings of a complex star persona combining innocence and deviousness, that deviousness shading off into madness in *Feu Mathias Pascal*.

CLAUDINE ET LE POUSSIN, OU LE TEMPS D'AIMER (JANUARY 1924)

Batcheff's first film role was a substantial one as the young lover playing opposite Dolly Davis, a well-established comic actress who would go on to star in a number of films by well-known directors.[1] Marcel Manchez was an unknown director, however, who only went on to make two or three films (one of these being the following year, *Mon frère Jacques*, again with Dolly Davis). The reaction of critics is perhaps all the more unusual; *Claudine et le poussin* was well received, seen by many as a minor masterpiece.[2] The film was sufficiently popular to have a book based on it by the popular novelist Jean d'Agraives, writer of adventure novels, and who very quickly published his *Le Temps d'aimer* (the sub-title of the film) under the auspices of one of the film magazines, *Mon ciné*.[3] Six months after the film's release, *Mon ciné* was extravagantly comparing the book of the film to one of the great classical texts from the second century, calling it 'une réplique moderne du fameux *Daphnis et Chloë* de Longus' ('a modern reply to the famous *Daphnis and Chloe* by Longus'; Petitbeau 1924: 22).

For French critics, its virtue was mainly that its light comedy was resolutely un-American and quintessentially French. The reviewer for *Cinéa-Ciné pour tous* wrote this typical comment: 'C'est du pur style français et cela nous repose des comédies burlesques qui nous viennent d'Amérique et n'ont d'attrait, le plus souvent, que par leur excentricité, mais sont dépourvues de ce qui fait, depuis Molière, une des gloires de notre pays' ('It has a pure French style, a welcome relief from the American burlesques whose only attraction is often their eccentricity, but lack what since Molière is one of the glories of our country'; Vernes 1924: 32). He and others pointed out that this 'glory' is the light but perfectly formed comedy: 'Ni l'humour anglais ou américain, ni la joliesse italienne, à plus forte raison le colossal allemand, n'ont pu approcher de cette légèreté qu'on a voulu blâmer trop souvent parce qu'on nous l'enviait' ('Neither English or American humour, nor Italian prettiness, and even less the heavy German humour can touch this lightness that people reproach us for because they envy it'; d'Herbeumont 1924: 193). Reviewers similarly placed the film in a literary context, citing amongst others the playwrights most famous for their romantic comedies; the reviewer of *Cinéopse*, for example, wrote that the film 'évoque irrésistiblement cette grâce particulière à nos productions françaises. On y trouve ce quelque chose de joli et de fin qui de Marivaux passa chez Alfred de Musset' ('conjures up irresistibly the grace that is the hallmark of our French productions. It has that pretty and delicate quality that Marivaux had and passed on to Alfred de Musset'; d'Herbeumont 1924: 193).[4]

The mise en scene of the film is cleverly if simply constructed to suggest the constriction of interior spaces, representing the stifling bond between mother and son, and the freedom of exterior spaces. At the start of the film Claude is frequently shown flanked by his mother and tutor, such as the shot of the three of them, standing at the gates of the château, behind the gate's iron bars. Claudine, on the other hand, is freer; she flings open the window of her room, takes her dog out and wakes everyone up (sticking her tongue out at the servant who tells her off). Claude will gradually emancipate himself with Claudine's help, and this is figured by subtle shifts in the mise en scene. Initially flanked by family, he ends up on the outside of the group of three (such as when they play chess). Once Claudine has opened her window, we frequently see Claude at his bedroom window (Figure 3.1). Similarly, we see him smoking a few shots after we see Claudine smoking.

The two of them are at their freest by the river, a commonplace location of pastoral idylls in French literature. It is here that they exchange kisses as the priest dozes, and bathe in the spot where Claude normally fishes, watched over by the priest. And it is outside in the woods that Claude can be seen carrying his shotgun, whose phallic connotations are evident (Figure 3.2).

However, as the word 'poussin' (a chick, but used figuratively to designate under-elevens in sport) in the title makes clear, Claude is not just dominated by his mother, but also by Claudine; the parallel names underline both closeness, necessary for them to be attracted to each other, but also Claudine's

Figure 3.1 *Claudine et le poussin*: Claude at his bedroom window (Collection Roche-Batcheff)

control of Claude, whose name is neatly contained and circumscribed by hers. Batcheff plays the 'spoilt rich kid' character boyishly, with pouting lips; but he also exploits the erotic potential of costume and mise en scene to the full. So, for example, in Figure 3.1, he is very much Juliet to Claudine's Romeo, posing

Figure 3.2   *Claudine et le poussin*: the phallic gun (Collection Roche-Batcheff)

for her gaze. So too, Figure 3.3, the lovers by the river, shows how he lets himself be mothered by his lover, while at the same time exposing his neck for the gaze of the film's spectator in the pose of the ephebic boy. It is the passive melancholy of the male pin-up, of what Richard Dyer calls the Sad Young Man, the soft, feminised masculinity of the youth waiting to become a 'harder' man (Dyer 1992). The absence of a father figure is in this sense telling (the bumbling priest is a stock figure of fun in French culture, and does not remotely come into play as a father figure); it is as if there were a role waiting for Claude to step into. Coincidentally, Batcheff's personal situation, as the 'man' of the family in the absence of his father and surrounded by women (his mother, sister and aunt), corresponds to his situation in this film, as does the arrival of Denise Tual in 1926.

Batcheff's second film, *Princesse Lulu* (February 1925), reprises the role of the young lover. In it he plays a Prince Charming who rescues the poor Lulu, lusted after by her father's employer. Trévise considers him less effective in this role than in his first film: 'Pierre Batcheff est un prince charmant un peu nerveux et gauche (. . .) (et) ne retrouve pas le succès de son début: *Claudine et son Poussin*' [sic] ('Pierre Batcheff is a rather nervous and clumsy Prince Charming (. . .) who has not matched the success of his first film, *Claudine et le poussin*' (Trévise 1925b: 27).

Figure 3.3 *Claudine et le poussin*: the lovers by the river (Collection Roche-Batcheff)

As we shall see in later sections of this book, Batcheff chooses to maintain the Sad Young Man character we see by the riverside in *Claudine et le poussin* in many of his films, always poised on the edge of masculinity, closer to Marcel L'Herbier's favourite actor Jaque Catelain than to other *jeunes premiers* of the period, such as Albert Préjean.

Le Double Amour (June 1925)

We see the Sad Young Man again in his fourth film, with the neatly evocative title – given the way in which the Sad Young Man faces two ways, back to childhood and forwards to adulthood – *Le Double Amour*; the mother is again a dominating character, but this time we find a father. *Le Double Amour* also reprises a character played by Batcheff in his third film, *Autour d'un berceau* (premiere March 1925; general release May 1925), where he plays a minor role as an 'élégant noceur' ('elegant debauchee'; *Cinématographie française* 1925b: 7) with gambling debts who steals a large sum of money from his best friend and flees the country. The same magazine comments on aspects of his performance that we will see returning throughout his career: 'le charmant Pierre Batcheff est, malgré ses ridicules moustaches, aussi séduisant, nonchalant et racé' ('Pierre Batcheff is charming, and despite his ridiculous moustache,

Figure 3.4   *Autour d'un berceau*: Batcheff's 'ridiculous moustache' (Courtesy of the Bibliothèque du Film, Paris)

attractive, nonchalant and distinguished'; *Cinématographie française* 1925c: 17) (Figure 3.4). As Batcheff commented in his notebook, adumbrating a theme that he was to return to frequently, the film was 'insignifiant; éternel manque d'argent' ('insignificant; perennial lack of funds').

Jean Epstein's *L'Affiche* (April 1925) had been a great success, which he and Films Albatros tried to replicate in *Le Double Amour* a few months later, with the same actress and writer. As one reviewer put it, the character played by Lissenko in both films is 'l'amante passionnée qu'on délaisse; puis, la mère pour qui l'enfant devient l'unique raison d'être' ('a passionate lover abandoned, and then a mother for whom her child becomes her only reason for living'; Trévise 1925a: 27), to which we should add that in both films, she is reunited with the contrite father of her child at the end of the film. One of the more startling features of *Le Double Amour* is its melodramatic décor.

Two aspects of décor – created by one of Epstein's regular collaborators, Pierre Kéfer – stand out in this respect, both in the Art Nouveau style. The first is a motif that dominates the family drawing room in the shape of a fan, similar to the canopy of Hector Guimard's famous gate to the Porte Dauphine metro (1899), although resembling a spider's web rather more than the very regular 'petals' of the Guimard design. We see it (at the start of the second reel) behind Laure as she recalls her former glories as a singer and social celebrity, the past being superimposed on her rather more mundane and impoverished domestic present as we see her here darning her glove. Later in the film (at the start of the third reel), we see her and the character played by Batcheff, Jacques Maresco, framed by the motif as he lies in her arms and pleads with her to save him from the dishonour of having stolen gaming chips. The point being made by the décor is one of entrapment; she is trapped by poverty, he is trapped by his uncontrollable urge to gamble at the expense of probity. But this is somewhat tempered by another aspect of the motif, which, like Guimard's canopy, protects the mother and her son in their domestic space; indeed, the resemblance to a spider's web noted above emphasises this aspect of the décor. The strong bond between mother and son is further emphasised by a bedroom scene in which she kisses the baby in his cradle (reel 2), the next shot showing the young man's clothes laid out on his bed as she questions him about his gambling debts; the reason we mention this scene is also because it is replayed in *Un Chien andalou* a few years later.

The second motif is a more obviously floral design on the walls of the family apartment, with boldly painted aloe-like leaves. We see this motif in the bedroom scene we have just mentioned, where Batcheff stands slouching, framed by a door to his right and the aloe motif on the wall to his left, a characteristically distant look in his eyes. The design of the décor suggests that he is caught between the domesticity implied by the motif, and the wish to escape it (indicated by the door to his right), by indulging his atavistic urge to gamble, inherited from his father. The motif returns most vividly at the end of the film, in the police station, where Jacques's father has impugned himself to save his son from dishonour. Jacques and his mother are framed against the aloe motif, mother protecting the son (although Batcheff again has a distant look in his eyes), as an accusing intertitle saying 'a thief' intervenes. There follows a complex choreography for the mise en scene. In a first shot, there is a reprise of a previous mise en scene, with Jacques/Batcheff standing framed by a door to his right and the aloe motif to his left, the domestic value of the motif being more evident here as it frames his mother in the foreground, while the escapist value of the door is in turn made clear by the foregrounding of his father (who had left the country in dishonour and made his fortune in the USA) to the right of it (see Figure 3.5). This is followed by a shot of Jacques slumped head down on the table, and a final family shot of Jacques at the table framing his father to his right and his mother to his left, with the aloe motif in the background (see Figure 3.6).

The message of this mise en scene, with its cleverly inverted triangular structure, is very clear; the atavistic urges displayed by Jacques have been contained and domesticated by the return of his father, who has brought back the law to the family group. In so doing, the character played by Batcheff has been

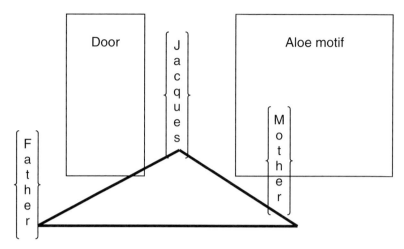

Figure 3.5   *Le Double Amour*: the family triangle

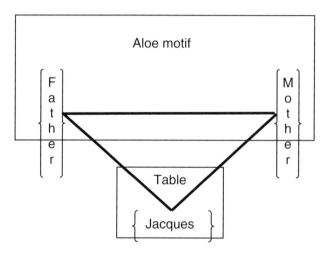

Figure 3.6   *Le Double Amour*: the inverted family triangle

returned to the status of the son, the young feminised man, 'adolescent inquiet' ('anxious adolescent'; Derain 1925a: 15), 'délicat et vibrant' ('delicate and vibrant'; Trévise 1925a: 27), whose urges to escape, urges we saw in *Claudine et le poussin*, have been blocked, and who is dominated, as so many of Batcheff's characters, by a strong woman, in this case his mother. That blockage is articulated through an excessive mise en scène, as Geoffrey Nowell-Smith pointed out in relation to melodrama. Recalling that the function of melodrama is to work out the problems of patriarchal normalisation, Nowell-Smith points out that this acceptance of castration by the otherwise rebellious

Figure 3.7 *Le Double Amour*: Batcheff's character dominated (Courtesy of the Bibliothèque Nationale, Paris)

son can only be achieved at the expense of repression, and that repression always resurfaces in melodrama as hysterical excess (in the Freudian sense) in relation to its attempt to conform to the patterns of realism (see Nowell-Smith 1977: 117). The hallucinatory quality of the scenes just described points

Figure 3.8 *Le Double Amour*: a characteristic stare into the distance (Courtesy of the Bibliothèque Nationale, Paris)

precisely to excess, an excess of emotion predicated on the rejection of constraint and convention, the fulfilling of deeply felt desires at odds with domesticity and yet in thrall to those familial structures.

Jacques's urges to disentangle himself from domestic constraints are manifested in two other distinct ways, one of which is an issue of star performance, the other one of narrative. We have already mentioned the faraway look in Batcheff's eyes. This was already evident in *Claudine et le poussin*: for example, in the scene where Claude lies in Claudine's arms by the river (see Figure 3.3). In *Le Double Amour*, it is much more prevalent, as we have noted. Batcheff stares into the distance not just when his mother questions him about his gambling debts, or in the final scenes when he is labelled a thief by the intertitle, but also when he is gambling, as can be seen in a characteristic shot in Figure 3.8. He maintains the distant look when, shortly afterwards, he rises abruptly from the gaming table, bumping into the people around him. It can even be seen in a relatively minor prop, the locket that his mother opens, one side of which has his mother 'looking' at the photograph in the other half, which is of Jacques, staring away from his mother into the middle distance.

Second, one of the scenes commented on favourably by several reviewers is the one where Jacques is in prison. A member of the public – later the scriptwriter of one of Batcheff's films, *Le Perroquet vert* – sent in a long appraisal of the film to *Cinéa-Ciné pour tous*, commenting in particular on this scene:

> Enfin, il y a une chose presque unique, je crois, au cinéma, un passage comme j'en vis bien rarement : celui de la Prison. Il faut être un bien grand artiste pour avoir trouvé ce tableau étrange, qui devient vite hallucinant : La solitude nette et noire du cachot, le mandoliniste privé de son instrument et dont les doigts jouent d'une mandoline imaginaire, la petite souris blanche, l'expression de Jacques, et la ronde extraordinaire, le rêve tourbillonnant qu'a inventé Epstein, rêve où tournent mandoline, souris et jeux de cartes. (Casembroot 1925: 35)

> (There is something nearly unique in the cinema, a scene I have rarely seen: that of the Prison. You must be a truly great artist to have imagined this strange tableau, which quickly becomes hallucinatory: the dark solitude of the cell, the mandolinist deprived of his instrument and whose fingers play an imaginary mandolin, the little white mouse, Jacques's expression, and the extraordinary whirling dream invented by Epstein, a dream where mandolin, mouse and packs of cards whirl around.)

This is one the very few 'subjective' shots of the film. As Jacques sits in expressionist semi-darkness, shots of the fanlike design in the apartment and a card game are superimposed, suggesting to us the two poles of his life: the domestic space and the space of desire. But it is the surreal collocation of Jacques in his tuxedo and a mandolin player playing an imaginary instrument, accompanied by a pet mouse, that strikes us more in this scene. Whereas in *L'Affiche*, such subjective shots were associated with the character played by the mother, here they are associated with the son. The almost uncanny nature of this particular mise en scène is one we will meet again in Batcheff's films; he is increasingly associated with the strange, the bizarre, the hallucinatory. This is the case in his next film, where he plays a minor role, but a role that will show how a set of connotations are gradually coalescing and hardening around his star persona.

Feu Mathias Pascal (July 1925)

Feu Mathias Pascal is one of Marcel L'Herbier's most celebrated silent films, according to Noël Burch (Burch 1973: 23).[5] But it has been overlooked in favour of *L'Inhumaine*, perhaps because it has been difficult to view in a clean and complete copy. That said, *Feu Mathias Pascal* is one of the few films with Batcheff that has been commented on significantly in an academic context, and for that reason we shall dwell on the arguments before proposing a focus on Batcheff.

According to Burch, *Feu Mathias Pascal* is more coherent than *L'Inhumaine*, but this coherence is principally due to the fact that the film is no more than the illustration of an anecdote. Twenty years or so after Burch's rather negative account of the film, Richard Abel's more positive view still underlines the film's coherence, basing his analysis on the film's major narrative technique of doubling (Abel 1984: 415–21). Our view is that the film is far more incoherent than would appear, and that this incoherence can be located in Batcheff's character, through whom a variety of surrealist preoccupations are linked, principally the notion of the double.

L'Herbier describes the production of *Feu Mathias Pascal* in his biography (L'Herbier 1979: 114–18). He saw Pirandello's play, *Six Characters in Search of an Author*, in Paris in April 1923, then again a year later in March 1924. Anxious to adapt something by Pirandello to the screen, he read the novel *The Late Mathias Pascal*, which had been published in 1904 and translated into French a few years later in 1910 (Pirandello 1904, 1910). A contract with Albatros Films was signed on 24 October 1924, so that he could use their star Ivan Mosjoukine,[6] and production spanned December 1924 to February 1925. The film was premiered on 29 July 1925 at the Marivaux cinema, and went on general release in February 1926.

The story follows Pirandello's novel closely. Some elements are lost in the general tightening up of the plot, such as a secondary character, the Spanish man whom Mathias meets in Monaco and who resurfaces in Rome; Mathias's travels around Italy and his stay in Milan; the philosophical discussions on theosophy with Anselmo Paleari. L'Herbier added artistic embellishments, such as the dream of the young lovers, considered by the influential critic Émile Vuillermoz to be a work of art, or Mathias's fantasised attack on the villain Papiano. The only substantial difference from the novel is the ending. In the book, Mathias leads people to believe that Adrien has committed suicide in Rome, and stays in his village to write the novel we have just read. In the film, he returns to Rome to live with Adrienne. The ending can be interpreted ironically, however; we see Mathias and Adrienne framed in a canted wedding photo and walking towards us, preceded by a shot of Mathias saluting his own grave.

The film was well received by the critics, partly because they expected it to be more obscure, given that it was based on work by Pirandello, who had a reputation as a difficult and highly intellectual writer; and partly because it was a film by L'Herbier, whose *L'Inhumaine* had broken new ground in filmmaking (Derain 1925b: 27). *Feu Mathias Pascal* was 'complètement original' ('completely original'; *Cinématographie française* 1925d: 12), but 'plus normal' ('more normal'), 'moins dangereusement spécial' ('less dangerously special'; Derain 1925b: 27), with 'moins de stylisation, plus d'humanité' ('less stylised and more human'; Tedesco 1925: 8) than the previous film. L'Herbier seemed to be becoming more commercial, and trying to 'toucher simultanément l'élite et le grand public' ('to reach not just an elite public, but a much broader public'; Croze 1925b: 1). The *Gazette de France* considered the film to be L'Herbier's best (Pigasse 1925), while *Cinéa-Ciné pour tous* was full of praise for L'Herbier's technique, 'jamais plus précise, plus sure, plus lumineuse' ('never more precise, sure-footed, luminous'; Épardaud 1925: 11).

Those critics who did not like the film tended to focus on the second half. The following is a typical view, setting out a contrast between the coherence and order of the first half, and the incoherence of the second:

> La seconde partie est moins parfaite, plus relâchée, et séduit moins le regard, comme elle intéresse moins l'esprit. Seule la fin charmante rachète les parties 'spirites' des scènes de Rome. Et puis, M. L'Herbier a succombé à son esprit impulsif, qui l'a entraîné dans un rêve curieux mais pas harmonisé avec la première partie d'un avant-gardisme classique et mesuré. Le presque cubisme de cette scène est d'ailleurs facilement oublié dès qu'on repense aux féeries lumineuses de la première partie du film. (Derain 1925b: 27)

> (The second half is less perfect, looser, visually and intellectually less attractive. Only the charming conclusion manages to redeem the 'spiritualist' Roman scenes. L'Herbier has yielded to impulsive in this curious dream, which is quite out of kilter with the classically avant-gardist and considered first half. Thankfully, the near-cubism of this scene is easy to forget when one remembers the luminous fairytale of the first half of the film.)

The scenes praised by critics nearly always came from the first half of the film, such as the village fete: 'Certaines scènes comme la fête au village et la mort de la mère et de l'enfant sont des scènes inoubliables par la beauté rare de leurs éclairages, et l'ambiante folie, ou tristesse de leur atmosphère augmentées de poésie' ('Certain scenes, such as the village fete and the death of the mother and child, are unforgettable because of the rare beauty of the lighting, the prevailing sense of madness or sadness imbued with the poetic'; Derain 1925b: 27). While only citing one scene from the second half – Mathias and his double – *Cinéa-Ciné pour tous* cites several from the first in its list of 'best scenes': 'Feu Mathias Pascal invoquant son double et le prenant à parti, la fête populaire de San Gimignano, la scène de jeu, formidable page cinégraphique qui est un des chefs-d'œuvre de Marcel L'Herbier (. . .), la bibliothèque livrée aux rats' ('The late Mathias Pascal calling up his double and arguing with it, the village fete, the gaming tables, one of Marcel L'Herbier's works of art (. . .), the rat-infested library'; Épardaud 1925: 10–11). Émile Vuillermoz also speaks of a work of art when commenting the scene of the village lovers, which for him sketches in a few brushstrokes 'le poème douloureux de la grande illusion humaine' ('the painful poem of human illusion'; Vuillermoz 1925a), and in a passage quoted by L'Herbier in his biography, Vuillermoz alludes even more to the metaphorical nature of L'Herbier's shots when describing the shots of rails as the train takes Mathias away from the village, rails that 'se rapprochent, s'unissent, se séparent et bifurquent au gré des aiguillages avec la rigueur mécanique des destinées humaines' ('come closer together, unite, separate and fork away as the points come and go, as harshly mechanical as human destiny itself'; Vuillermoz 1925b). But as L'Herbier says, what Vuillermoz could not forgive was that such sublime scenes were embedded in a banal story, a view echoed by Burch some fifty years later.

Noël Burch shows how the film has a variety of styles, much like *L'Inhumaine*, amongst them the intimism of the rural *Kammerspiel*, burlesque fantasy and an expressionist comedy of manners. But unlike *L'Inhumaine*, these divergent styles come together thanks to the beauty of the décor (by Alberto Cavalcanti and Lazare Meerson). The film is even more coherent because of Mosjoukine's performance: 'il ne s'agit à chaque plan que de trouver une nouvelle astuce pour mettre en évidence le personnage de Mathias-Mosjoukine, à chaque séquence de trouver un nouveau style qui reflétera la prochaine étape de l'histoire' ('Each shot tries to find some way to highlight the character Mathias-Mosjoukine, each scene tries to find a new style that will reflect the next stage of the story'; Burch 1973: 26). And Burch then formulates his well-known criticism of the film, that it is regressive compared to *L'Inhumaine*, because it demonstrates how 'la mise en scène (est) au service d'une anecdote' ('mise en scene has been put at the service of an anecdote'; Burch 1973: 26).

Richard Abel focuses much more on doubling procedures. The two halves of the film echo each other, because in each of them four similar events occur: Pascal seeks freedom; his money is stolen (by the lawyer, then by Scipion); the family is threatened by an unscrupulous trickster (the lawyer first, then Papiano); and last, Pascal wins a wife (Romilde in the first half, whom he steals from Pomino; Adrienne in the second, whom he steals from Papiano). In addition to this macro-narrative level, Abel shows how the narrative is regularly disturbed by morbid or fantastic elements, and how this contributes to doubling procedures. First, Pascal has to cope with the double death of his mother and his daughter. Second, he wins in the casino, but the shots of the gaming tables are intercut with shots of his gaming table neighbour's suicide. In both cases, then, death is involved, a double death in the first case, and a doubling in the second where life and death are inextricably linked. In the part of the film which interests us most, the Paleari household, Mathias doubles himself on two separate occasions. In the first, he imagines himself courting

Figure 3.9 *Feu Mathias Pascal*: expressionist corridors (Courtesy of the Bibliothèque du Film, Paris)

Adrienne, but the fantasy becomes a nightmare when his double appears, only to mock him. Then he imagines himself teaching Papiano a lesson when he believes that Papiano is threatening Adrienne, leaping through the air as if in a dream. A further element of doubling is the loss of his money during the séance, this paralleling negatively his wins in Monte Carlo. By identifying these structural and visual doublings, Abel underlines the extreme coherence of the film. The two halves echo each other, emphasising a philosophical theme related to the double: man believes himself to be free, but that freedom is an illusion.

Our rather different view is that the film is incoherent, but that this is part of the point. Abel's analysis obscures a fundamental difference between the two halves of the film, a difference of which contemporary spectators were aware. The doubling of the main character, accompanied by a false identity, only takes place in the Paleari sequence. This part of the film is very different in its mise en scene, 'cubist' according to *La Cinématographie française* (Derain 1925b: 27), in all probability due to the *Caligari*-like corridors and expressionist lighting of the Paleari flat, a labyrinthine and fantasmatic space, linked to spiritualism and madness. In this sequence, we come across the doubling between reality and dream, between long never-ending corridors and claustrophobic enclosed spaces, between extreme close-ups and ensemble shots; these tensions and uncanny repetitions jostle together, emphasising the surge of desire and its incompatibility with reality. How can we explain, rather than explain away this difference between the two halves?

We could argue that the double is a very Pirandellian theme. Doubling is linked to disillusion and pessimism; Pirandellian man is but a shadow of himself, as is shown by an extraordinary passage from the novel in Chapter 15 where Mathias tries to stamp out his shadow. We could equally allege that the frankly comical elements of Mathias's doublings correspond rather neatly to Pirandello's philosophy of *umorismo*, a version of Hegelian irony. We could also link the theme of the double to Mosjoukine, who played ten or so characters in his own film, *Le Brasier ardent* (1923), a particularly incoherent film which Abel explains by showing how it is a synthesis of a variety of national cinematic traditions (Abel 1984: 368).

There is a further doubling, as Mosjoukine is shadowed by another actor of Russian extraction, Batcheff, who plays Scipion, a character himself doubled, not only by virtue of pretending to be someone else, an hysteric, but because in so doing he becomes like Mathias, a character who masquerades. And just as Mathias is haunted by death, so too Scipion is haunted, but by madness. Batcheff introduces elements which would not have been apparent in 1926, but which soon became considerably more so by his association with members of the surrealist group and his starring role in *Un Chien andalou*.

In all likelihood, Batcheff came to L'Herbier's notice in 1924, probably as a result of his starring role in *Claudine et le poussin*. In his biography the director describes Batcheff as an 'extremely promising actor', saying that he had wanted to promote him in *Feu Mathias Pascal*, as well as having ideas for future major roles:

Figure 3.10 *Feu Mathias Pascal*: the haunted look of Scipion the hysteric (Courtesy of the Bibliothèque du Film, Paris)

J'avais naguère contribué à faire son mariage avec Denise Piazza, fille du grand éditeur d'art. Et je n'ai pu oublier le dîner de fiançailles où, assis non loin d'Henri de Rothschild homme par excellence de théâtre, je me présentai comme un homme de simple cinéma qui souhaitait donner au futur époux de Denise l'occasion (cadeau de noces) de briller dans un film tiré de *L'Idiot*. J'en avais acheté les droits à son intention et dans ce héros de Dostoïevski son languoureux slavisme aurait pu rivaliser par anticipation avec la phénoménale ambiguïté de Gérard Philipe. (L'Herbier 1979: 210)

(I had helped arrange his marriage to Denise Piazza (. . .) I shall never forget the engagement dinner where (. . .) I presented myself as a man of the cinema who wished to give Denise's future husband the chance, as a wedding present, to show his mettle in a film based on *The Idiot*. I had bought the rights with him in mind, and as Dostoyevsky's hero his languorous slavism could have rivalled the phenomenal ambiguity that Gérard Philipe was later to display.)

In Pirandello's novel, Scipion is presented as an 'epileptic', a term used by L'Herbier in his screenplay: 'Scipion, le frère, crétin et épileptique, n'était ni tellement crétin ni tellement épileptique. Il l'était pour passer inaperçu, pour écouter toutes les conversations et les rapporter à son frère' ('Scipion, the brother, an epileptic cretin, was neither cretinous nor epileptic. He only appeared to be, so that he could circulate freely and listen to people's conversations so as to relay them back to his brother').[7] However, in many accounts of the film in the trade press, the term 'hysteric' is used, a subtle but important difference. It is the case with *La Cinématographie française* (*Cinématographie française* 1925d: 12) and *Hebdo-Film*, which talks of 'Batcheff, visage de lazzarone brun et beau dans Scipion l'hystérique' ('Batcheff, with the face of a tanned and handsome *lazzarone* in the role of Scipion the hysteric'; *Hebdo-Film* 1925). Suicide, spiritualism and hysteria: all of these were key preoccupations of the surrealists in the 1920s.

Suicide had already appeared as a theme in L'Herbier's work, in *L'Inhumaine*, even if it was in reality the false suicide of Einar Norsen (played by Jaque Catelain). But suicide was a major preoccupation of the French intelligentsia in the years following the Great War. We can recall the powerful attraction of Jacques Vaché for André Breton, the key theorist and leader of the surrealist movement. Vaché had died of an overdose of opium in 1919, and Breton had edited Vaché's war letters the same year (Vaché 1919), recognising his influence in the first surrealist manifesto, published in November 1924, just before the shooting of *Feu Mathias Pascal*, and in the same year as *L'Inhumaine*'s release. One month later, the first number of *La Révolution surréaliste* carried short news stories of suicides;[8] this was followed by the questionnaire, 'Le Suicide est-il une solution?' ('Is Suicide a Solution?', in the second issue of January 1925,[9] while L'Herbier was shooting in Italy.

Spiritualism was for Breton one of the solutions to the problem of authenticity in the key surrealist practice of automatic writing (see Breton 1922: 3). Breton had become disillusioned with automatic writing because of the incursion of conscious elements, as we saw in Chapter 2. He was equally disillusioned with accounts of dreams, another key surrealist practice, because of the incursion of memory. Although he refused to admit the possibility that the dead might be able to communicate with the living, none the less the results of séances, particularly those with the poet Robert Desnos, made him write that he and his fellow surrealists 'demeurent confondus, tremblants de reconnaissance et de peur, autant dire ont perdu contenance devant la merveille' ('remained staggered, trembling with acknowledgement and fear, [their] composure shaken when faced with the marvel'; Breton 1922: 3). Jean Starobinski has shown the extent to which Breton was influenced in his thinking by the parapsychological and mediumnistic strand of the psychiatric tradition (Starobinski 1968).

Madness was related to this interest, and was a major preoccupation of the surrealists during the 1920s. Breton proclaimed in the first surrealist manifesto that 'ce n'est pas la crainte de la folie qui nous forcera à laisser en berne le drapeau de l'imagination' ('fear of madness would not force [the surrealists] to keep the flag of the imagination flying at half-mast'; Breton 1988: 313). Artaud published his 'Lettre aux médecins-chefs des asiles de fous' ('Letter to the Insane Asylum Head Doctors') in *La Révolution surréaliste* of April 1925 (Artaud 1925). Louis Aragon and Breton celebrated a particular form of madness – hysteria – three years later in the same journal as the 'moyen suprême d'expression' ('supreme means of expression'; Aragon and Breton 1928), and Breton celebrated the power of madness in his autobiographical text *Nadja* in the same year (Breton 1928). By the end of the 1920s, 'madness' for the surrealists was specifically associated with the feminine; as we shall see in later chapters, this is important for the way in which Batcheff's star persona developed.

We are not suggesting that L'Herbier was directly influenced by surrealist preoccupations. After all, Robert Desnos singled out L'Herbier in 1929, the year of *Un Chien andalou*, as the representative of an avant-garde cinema that he rejected, in terms recalling those of Burch for *Feu Mathias Pascal*: 'L'utilisation de procédés techniques que l'action ne rend pas nécessaires, un jeu conventionnel, la prétention à exprimer les mouvements arbitraires et compliqués de l'âme sont les principales caractéristiques de ce cinéma' ('Technical processes not solicited by the action, conventional acting, and the pretence of expressing the arbitrary and complicated movements of the soul are the principal characteristics of this kind of cinema'; Desnos 1966: 189/Desnos 1978: 36). And for L'Herbier too, *Un Chien andalou* left much to be desired. He was to write much later in his biography that *Un Chien andalou* had left its mark on him; he said he was 'foncièrement passionné' ('deeply fascinated') when it was first released, but that his view changed later, and that he believed that 'cette apothéose de la dissolution n'était faite que pour combler des instincts dissolus' ('this apotheosis of dissolution was good only for dissolute minds'). The film remained for him 'splendidement marginal' ('splendidly marginal'; L'Herbier 1979: 177–8), despite his admiration for Batcheff, whom he praised for his 'superbe duplicité d'intentions et de regards' ('superb duplicity of intentions and gazes'; L'Herbier 1979: 117–18).

None the less, *Feu Mathias Pascal* is shot through with traces of surrealist thematics, as the preoccupation with death, madness and the parapsychological might well have suggested. This makes of it a peculiarly incoherent film. Burch proposes that Mosjoukine guarantees unity for the film, but our view is that his presence cannot achieve this. On the contrary, Mosjoukine's performance is unstable and changing; he uses a range of registers, just as the style of the film, as Burch rightly points out, juxtaposes rather than synthesises a variety of genres. *La Cinématographie française* used the word 'cubist' to describe the fractured nature of the film. Given that the surrealist group had yet to make its mark in the years following the publication of the first manifesto, it is understandable that this word should be used; the Cubists were a well-established avant-garde movement, and could therefore serve as a reference point, a convenient shorthand, for those wishing to distinguish between low culture and a more difficult high culture.

Our contention is that the film exemplifies a transition from an older avant-garde to a newer one. Whereas *L'Inhumaine* exemplified a fascination with technology and the power of machines to shape the environment – a fascination shared by the Italian Futurists, the Cubists and Dada – *Feu Mathias Pascal* shows a shift to darker preoccupations with the nature of identity. While we could argue that Mosjoukine's protean performance harks back to a 'cubist' representation of personality, there are elements of the narrative that suggest something that, we would contend, only Batcheff's Scipion manages to convey.

The novel poses a question about the nature of freedom; it is the title of the book being written by Mathias, and a major preoccupation for Pirandello. Freedom in Mosjoukine's performance is the possibility of acting out a variety of roles and identities, which, given Mosjoukine's reputation as a spectacular actor, 'a Protean master of disguise' (Abel 1984: 367), suggests that there is a controlling consciousness able to choose from that range of possibilities. In such bravura performances, Mosjoukine remains Mosjoukine, the puppet-master who acts out whatever identities are required. He is essentially free to choose his identity, as the subtle change to the novel's ending indicates; rather than return to an old identity and write a book philosophising on the illusion of freedom, in the film Mathias returns to the new identity.

Batcheff, however, gives us a different view of identity from Mosjoukine. His character slips eerily from the shifty to the hallucinated, head dipped with cunning eyes peering out, to head raised and eyes bulging hysterically. Where Mosjoukine is 'mercurial' (Abel 1984: 367), Batcheff is ghostlike, helped by the 'languorous slavism' L'Herbier was to write about later. The fact that his character is supposed to be epileptic only increases the sense of unease. He is an uncannily spectral character, popping up in corridors and behind doors almost supernaturally. His character corresponds much more than Mosjoukine's to the rhetorical question posed by André Breton two years later in the first lines of *Nadja*: 'Qui suis-je?' ('Who am I?'), to which Breton answers by rephrasing the question: 'Qui je hante?' ('Whom do I haunt?'; Breton 1988: 647).

The sense of a cultural transition which we are indicating is also helped by another advantage of retrospective analysis: the transition from an older star, Mosjoukine (who in 1926 was 37), to the younger Batcheff, whose career corresponded more or less exactly with the high point of surrealism (1924–35). In February 1927 Mosjoukine was tempted by Universal's Carl Laemmle to go to Hollywood. When his film for Universal, *Surrender* (1927), performed poorly, he returned to Europe to make films for the Germans, never quite achieving the same star status he had in France during the first half of the 1920s.[10] The late 1920s were to be Batcheff's.

In this chapter, we have seen how Batcheff's persona was quickly established in the early 1920s. Emerging from the long tradition of ephebic youths in French post-Revolutionary painting, his persona is to some extent calqued on that of Jaque Catelain, whom he resembles physically. But Catelain was more straightforwardly the *jeune premier*, whereas Batcheff from the start not only has a dreamier appearance, but is also associated with the strange and the uncanny, if not with the criminal and the insane. He is also, by virtue of his contract with Albatros and his origins, more Other than Catelain, and his 'Russianness' only serves to emphasise his 'foreignness', his enigmatic, alien quality. These qualities are played on and deepened in the next group of films we shall be considering, in which he plays variants of the Lover.

Notes

1. Dolly Davis (1896–1962). She has more than fifty films to her credit from 1920–38, including René Clair's *Le Voyage imaginaire* (1926), as well as films by Jacques de Baroncelli and Henri Chomette.
2. A word used by Edmond Épardaud (1924: 16), and by Émile Vuillermoz (1924); a 'joyau' ('jewel'), according to Louis d'Herbeumont (1924: 194).
3. d'Agraives (1924). He published eight such volumes in the 1920s, several of them for *Mon ciné*, including Eric von Stroheim's *Foolish Wives* (1922), and, for other publishers, the Jackie Coogan vehicle *Little Robinson Crusoe* (1924) and Victor Sjöström's *He Who Gets Slapped* (1926).
4. See also de Mirbel (1924), who writes of the film's 'exquis marivaudage' ('exquisite *marivaudage*').
5. The film earned 1,219,026 francs, although surprisingly only about a third of this was earned in France (information from original documents in the private collection of Marie-Ange L'Herbier).

6. English language texts sometimes adopt the spelling 'Mozzhukin'; we have, in common with Richard Abel, kept the French spelling.

7. Private collection of Marie-Ange L'Herbier, Scenario number 2, p. 9. Scipion does not appear in the first version of the film script (12 pp long), but he is in the second version (13 pp long).

8. 'Le Suicide par persuasion' ('Suicide by Persuasion', *La Révolution surréaliste*, 1 (1 December 1924), p. 16; 'Les Désespérés' ('Desperate People', ibid., p. 20; 'Drame dans un escalier' ('Drama in the Stairwell', ibid., p. 21; 'Suicides', ibid., p. 32.

9. *La Révolution surréaliste*, 2 (15 January 1925), pp. 8–15.

10. Mosjoukine's star status can be seen in their respective fees. His fee was 60,000 francs, while Batcheff's was 1,200 francs (private collection of Marie-Ange L'Herbier).

CHAPTER 4

Historical reconstructions

The four films we shall be exploring in this chapter fall into the historical reconstruction genre as defined by Richard Abel (Abel 1984: 160–205). In none of them does Batcheff play a major role, but the roles he plays articulate a persona that is very clear in his starring roles, predicated on a static and often masochistic masculinity. We might argue that the historical epic is more than likely to lead to a more static performance, given the decorative value of sets and more particularly costumes that constrain action. But this does not seem to affect the leading men in these films, who thrust and parry while Batcheff looks on, slightly bemused by it all, lost in his 'look off', semi-detached from what action there is.

Abel has shown how the French came to the historical reconstruction genre rather later than many other national cinemas, with the Italian cinema dominating the genre before the First World War. But by the mid-1920s, the French cinema had caught up. Two directors were key in this development, and both of them are represented in the films we shall be exploring in this chapter: Henry Roussell,[1] whose *Violettes impériales* (1924) was, according to Abel, one of the three films that defined the new genre (Abel 1984: 171); and Raymond Bernard, director of the Société des Films Historiques, whose *Le Miracle des loups* (1924) was voted best film of 1925 by the readers of *Cinéa-Ciné pour tous* (Abel 1984: 175–9). Batcheff had second roles in two of these directors' later films: Roussell's Napoleonic *Destinée* (1926),[2] and Bernard's *Le Joueur d'échecs* (1927). He also had a small part in what is perhaps the best-known historical reconstruction of this period, Abel Gance's *Napoléon vu par Abel Gance* (1927). And, finally, he had a second role in Henri Fescourt's *Monte-Cristo* (1929).

Napoléon vu par Abel Gance and *Le Joueur d'échecs* have had significant work done on them. This is particularly the case for the first of these two, which has had considerable attention paid to it over the years, either in general studies of Gance's work or in work specifically devoted to *Napoléon* (see Kramer and Welsh 1978, Brownlow 1983, Icart 1983, King 1984, King 1990, Kaplan 1994, Véray 2000, Turim 2004, Véray 2005). We shall therefore focus on Batcheff's role in these films, before turning to the relatively unknown

Monte-Cristo,[3] where Batcheff is the main focus of an extended fantasy sequence in the Count's hide-away on the island of Monte Cristo. The major point emerging from these films is that they confirm Batcheff's masochistic persona, which, as we shall see in future chapters, is developed in subsequent films. In *Destinée*, he is wounded and visited in hospital by his lover; in *Napoléon* and *Le Joueur d'échecs* he loses the woman he loves to a rival; and in *Monte-Cristo*, where he plays the son of Monte-Cristo's enemy, he is tricked by the Count.

DESTINÉE (DECEMBER 1925)

Destinée, scripted by Roussell, mixes history and fiction, running two love affairs in parallel:[4] 'Sa matière historique n'est là que pour envelopper un admirable drame humain dont l'amour est le ressort' ('history acts as the frame for an admirable human drama motivated by love'; *Cinéa* 1925b: 33). In the first affair, the young Bonaparte courts Josephine de Beauharnais; in the second Bonaparte's fictional aide-de-camp, the Marquis Roland de Reuflize, played by Batcheff, courts a young Italian woman, Floria (Isabélita Ruiz). Roland and Floria's love affair develops, even though she is promised to another, when Roland is asked to teach her French (Figure 4.1). Roussell claimed contemporary relevance for the film, suggesting that the period of the Directoire was very similar to the post-war 1920s: 'La France souffrait en 1795 du même malaise dont elle se plaint aujourd'hui: désir effréné de jouissance, agiotage, situation financière difficile, luttes acharnées entre les fractions politiques' ('France was suffering the same malaise in 1795 as today: the frantic pursuit of pleasure, speculation, a difficult financial climate, relentless political infighting'; Bonneau 1926: 414). Batcheff, more than any other character, represents the 'frantic pursuit of pleasure', corresponding to the role of the *jeune premier* as a reaction to the Great War that we explored in Chapter 2. He is very much the pin-up; we see him in a variety of costumes, principally the colourful striped costume of fashionable Directoire youth, his hair worn long, followed by the equally colourful uniform of the hussars, his hair in long braids.

But it is less the passive side of the pin-up that anchors him in the stereotype of the careless youth, than his almost dizzying mobility. He is, until he is wounded at the Battle of Lodi, 'fougueux', as one reviewer called him ('enthusiastic' or 'animated'; Bonneau 1926: 418). The first time we see him, he jumps up excitedly after spotting Floria, and spends most of the opening Jardin des Tuileries scene literally running after her in energetic fashion. Once he has caught up with her in David's studio, he is still agitated, his face extremely mobile with wide eyes and wide mouth, all smiles, his arms frequently arcing in expansive gestures; as Brownlow points out, Batcheff 'is directed to give an

Figure 4.1 *Destinée*: Roland teaches Floria French (Collection Roche-Batcheff)

ebullient performance, so unlike the calm gravity of his General Hoche in *Napoleon*' (Brownlow 1984: 5).

Batcheff's character conveys a certain shallowness, partly because of this excitable animation, but also because of his sudden change of political allegiance. He is teaching Floria French in David's studio, and they write an anti-Revolutionary statement: 'Détestons les hommes de la Révolution' ('Hate the men of the Revolution'); Napoleon spots this and changes the word 'hate' to 'honour', followed by a terse speech in support of the Republic, as a result of which Roland unexpectedly leaps up and asks Napoleon if he can serve in his army. This role may well be unlike that of Hoche in Gance's film, but in one respect it is similar: the almost homoerotic closeness between Batcheff's character and Napoleon. Indeed, the only extreme close-up of the film (in the version we have seen) is that of Roland and Napoleon's faces, side by side, when Floria reveals to them that the Austrians only have 10,000 men and that Napoleon will win if he surprises them. The incipient feminisation of Batcheff's character as shallow pin-up in Napoleon's shadow is extended by the decline of his mobility in the film.

There are several large set pieces in the film, much admired by reviewers, the most common description of them being that they were like historical prints come to life (see, for example, Derain 1925c: 18, Trévise 1925c: 27).

During one of these, the Battle of Lodi, Roland is wounded and Floria tends him at his hospital bedside, introducing the trope of the masochistically passive martyr figure reprised and developed in *La Sirène des tropiques*, *L'Île d'amour* and *Vivre* in 1927–8, as we shall see in Chapter 5, and whom we also find in *Monte-Cristo*.[5] We find the usual epithets for Batcheff, underlining the feminisation of the *jeune premier*, as we discussed in Chapter 2: 'Le charmant et élégant Pierre Batcheff séduira bien des yeux féminins (. . .), délicieux de finesse et de séduction' ('Pierre Batcheff is charming and elegant, and will seduce many women (. . .), deliciously sensitive and seductive'; Derain 1925c: 18). One reader commented that Batcheff was 'un peu mièvre pour un officier de l'époque, mais bon tout de même' ('a bit vapid for an officer of the time, but good none the less'; *Mon ciné* 1926: 21). The fact that Floria dresses as a man to gain access to Roland as he lies in hospital only emphasises the femininised passivity of Batcheff's character. And, as we shall see, what is in this film only hinted at, a vaguely homoerotic slant to his relationship with Napoleon, will be developed in Gance's film, as will the less mobile, more understated acting style Batcheff uses for the hospital scene.

A comment by Batcheff in his notebook suggests that he might well have been resistant to Roussell's wishes, as it indicates the development of an understated acting style more consonant with the passive martyr figure. Roussell is reported to have complained about Batcheff's acting: 'Mais jouez, jouez donc!! Vous ne faites rien' ('But act, act for heavens sake! You're not doing anything.') Batcheff notes in his diary: 'Je fais une chose qui n'est pas faite pour les gens myopes ou pour ceux qui ont l'amour des gestes théâtraux poussés à l'extrême: on appelle cela du *Cinéma*' ('I am doing something which is not aimed at those who are blind or those who like extreme theatrical gestures: it's called *Cinema*'; Collection Roche-Batcheff). This statement, assuming that it is a comment by Batcheff on his own ideal acting style, makes his performance in *Napoléon vu par Abel Gance* all the more understandable, but raises interesting questions for what was seen as a very mannered performance in *Le Joueur d'échecs*.

As Abel points out, *Destinée* suffered from the release of Gance's film in 1927 (Abel 1984: 195), although its re-release in 1928 (flagged in *Cinémagazine* 1928c: 323) might well have been to capitalise on Gance's success. Moreover, the period covered by *Destinée* formed only a small part of Gance's film, which was considerably more ambitious in its historical scope as well as in its formal preoccupations. Roussell's film had been enthusiastically received when it first came out; by 1928 when it was re-released, the tone was more one of slightly grudging respect: 'Même après Napoléon, tout ce qui touche à la légende de l'Empereur est intéressant' ('Even after [Gance's] *Napoléon*, everything relating to the legend of the Emperor is interesting'), reads the short account of the re-release in *Cinémagazine*, finishing laconically – 'Bon film' ('Good film'; *Cinémagazine* 1928c: 323). Brownlow, viewing it some fifty years later, also thought it an effective historical epic, if 'permeated by a slightly theatrical atmosphere, and a hint of operetta' (Brownlow 1984: 7). Curiously, the two parallel love affairs of *Destinée*, Napoleon and Josephine on the one hand, and Roland and Floria on the other, come together in Gance's film, with Napoleon, Josephine and General Hoche (played by Batcheff), forming a love triangle.

NAPOLÉON VU PAR ABEL GANCE (APRIL 1927)

Gance's film generated a vigorous debate; as Jean Tedesco, director of the avant-garde film theatre Le Vieux-Colombier 1924–34, put it, 'après un hiver d'indifférence qu'aucun film nouveau, hors *Metropolis*, ne dégela, voici enfin un peu de chaleur, un peu de fièvre' ('after a winter of indifference that no film apart from *Metropolis* was able to thaw, here at last there is some heat, a bit of a fever'; Tedesco 1927: 9). The debate pitted radical form and regressive ideological content against each other, an opposition neatly encapsulated in Marxist critic Léon Moussinac's two 1927 articles for *L'Humanité*, translated in King's volume on Gance (King 1984: 34–41), in which there is an extended discussion of the debate. The first of Moussinac's articles was a withering attack on the politics of the film, the second an admiring appraisal of many of the spectacular effects, such as the three-screen split or triptych.

The film was a roll-call of some of France's best-known actors: Suzanne Bianchetti (Marie-Antoinette), who had acted in Roussell's *Violettes impériales*, had played the Empress in another Napoleonic film, *Madame Sans-Gêne* (Léonce Perret, 1925), and was to play the Empress Catherine in another historical reconstruction later in 1927, *Casanova* (Alexandre Volkoff); Philippe Hériat (Salicetti), who had acted in no less than seven of Marcel L'Herbier's films as well as in *Le Miracle des loups*; Nicolas Koline (Tristan Fleury), familiar from several films by Viktor Tourjansky and from Alexandre Volkoff's *Kean* (1924); Henry Krauss (Moustache), who acted alongside Batcheff in *Le Bonheur du jour*, due out a couple of months after *Napoléon*; Gina Manès (Josephine de Beauharnais), who was familiar from Jean Epstein's films (*L'Auberge rouge* and *Cœur fidèle*, both from 1923); Max Maxudian (Barras), who had acted in a number of films directed by Roger Lion in 1923–5, as well as Gance's well-known *La Roue* (1923) and Roussell's *La Terre promise* (1925); and, finally, Edmond Van Daële (Robespierre), who had acted in Epstein's *Cœur fidèle* and *6½ × 11* (1927), and Louis Delluc's *L'Inondation* (1924).

Many of these were well-established actors. Batcheff, by contrast, was still only nineteen years old at the time of the premiere in April 1927, with only two films to his name as first-billed star: *Claudine et le poussin* (1924) and *Le Secret d'une mère* (1926). *Éducation de prince*, his third major star billing, was premiered two months after *Napoléon*'s premiere (although they both went on general release in November that year). In Brownlow's 1980 reconstruction of 5 hours and 13 minutes, Batcheff appears for approximately 12 minutes or 4 per cent of screen time as 'le séduisant Hoche' ('the seductive [General] Hoche'; Derain 1927b: 25). None the less, his narrative significance is key, as he introduces Napoleon to Josephine de Beauharnais, and his performance plays into the politics of the 'mediating look', as discussed by Norman King (King 1984: 191–7). He appears in three scenes in the second epoch, which function together to set up the Napoleon/Josephine relationship. Moreover, as we shall see, Batcheff's performance introduces interesting ambiguities that complicate King's view of the function of the look in the film.

In the first of the three scenes, approximately 10 minutes into the second epoch,[6] Hoche comforts Josephine in Carmes prison, where they are both incarcerated. People are summoned for execution, and the announcer calls out 'De Beauharnais!' However, Josephine's ex-husband is also there and he gallantly offers to go, because, as the intertitle has it, the jailers 'only need one head' with the name De Beauharnais. Josephine faints in Hoche's arms as her ex-husband is led away to the guillotine. In the second scene, at approximately 30 minutes, the two are released; there is a temporal ellipsis to a year later, and we see Napoleon asking Hoche's advice about the revolt in the Vendée, which Napoleon has been asked to lead. Hoche leaves the room to talk to Josephine, and it is clear that the two are romantically involved; Napoleon brushes past them, staring intently at Josephine. The third scene is the most important (and longest) of these three, as Josephine will transfer her affections from Hoche to Napoleon. It starts at approximately 1 hour with the Victims' Ball at Carmes prison in Paris, and the scene shifts to a chess game between Hoche and Napoleon, with Josephine present (Figure 4.2). It soon becomes apparent through the cutting and the focus on competing intense gazes that the game is about Josephine, as Napoleon's intertitle makes clear: 'Take care, I am about to take your Queen.'[7] Once Hoche has lost his queen to Napoleon's knight, he stands up and almost apologetically exits, with a shrug.

The most striking aspect of this final scene is the intensity of the looks, combined with Batcheff's enigmatic smile. This is slowly built up over the three scenes. In scene 1, Hoche observes Josephine from afar before introducing himself, and apart from the section of the scene where they focus on the roll-call of condemned prisoners, Hoche spends much of the time looking at her, generally with medium or occasional medium-close shots. In scene 2, Hoche and Josephine, arm in arm and in medium shot, stare in a long-held shot at Napoleon as he walks away, a hint of a smile playing on Batcheff's lips.

Figure 4.2 *Napoléon vu par Abel Gance*: the chess game (Courtesy of the Bibliothèque Nationale, Paris)

Although he and Josephine talk, there is no intertitle to explain what is being said; the audience assumption, we would suggest, is that it is likely to be expressions of admiration for Napoleon, although Batcheff's knowing smile suggests something additional, but impossible to interpret. It is in scene 3, the Victims' Ball, that the gaze, combined with smiles from all three characters, both in variety and in intensity, are fully explored, with a large number of close-ups focusing on the three characters' faces, and especially their eyes.

The scene as a whole is principally about seeing and being seen. In that respect, it is not only a scene that plays into one of the generic tropes of the human condition, but, partly because of that and partly for other reasons, it is a scene that is much more about the present (the 1920s) than about the 1790s, as King points out, writing that it is:

> The most visually actual of the whole film. It presents a society which is stylish, elegant, innovatory, exciting – and effete. A decadent world of the 1790s and of the 1920s, subject to the whims of a Barras or a Josephine, to mediocre politicians and to cartels. A world which merges past and present even in the flimsy costumes worn by the dancers. (King 1990: 31)

We would wish to push the historical analogy further by pointing out that the scene can be viewed as a metaphor for stardom itself. In that respect, the actors' looks compete for the gaze of the diegetic crowd and of the film spectators, and the tussle at a metaphorical level is that between the intensely melodramatic performance by Dieudonné and the more understated performance by Batcheff, signalling, as we saw from the comment in Batcheff's notebooks concerning *Destinée*, a shift in performance styles.

Napoleon is the major attraction, as saviour of France, although the crowd's attention then switches to the 'three women who have bewitched Paris' (Josephine, Madame Tallien and Madame Récamier). Napoleon impassively watches Tallien and Récamier enter the ball, a smile appearing when Josephine is announced. She beams and nods at the crowd, her gaze eventually lingering in Napoleon's direction. Hoche tries to arrest her gaze, with a close-up shot of him from her point of view greeting her and staring up at her as she stands on the steps leading into the room. Josephine moves into the crowd, who follow her; there is a shot of two older men staring in her direction, the issue of the gaze being made very clear as one of them holds up an elaborate pair of glasses, while the other holds a monocle to observe the scene. Napoleon and Hoche shake hands, and Napoleon moves off in pursuit of Josephine, observed intently by Hoche, with a faint smile on his face. Hoche follows them, and stretches his hand out to Josephine, who looks at him but stops smiling. Hoche seems to understand that she is transferring her affections and looks down (and downcast), jerking his head up to look at her from below his eyebrows. Josephine smilingly tells Napoleon that it was here that she was summoned to the scaffold. The three of them are then seen together in a medium-long shot, Napoleon at the bottom of the triangle, Hoche on the first step to Napoleon's left, and Josephine higher up to Napoleon's right; the triangular mise en scene is important, as it will recur later in the chess game (see Figures 4.3 and 4.4). The triangle establishes a stable configuration. Napoleon looks at the crowd; Josephine looks at Napoleon; Hoche looks at Josephine looking at Napoleon. Moreover, during this part of scene 3, as well as later in the chess game, there is a remarkable stability in the three gazes. Josephine tends to look down, either at the crowd or at the two men from her position on the steps, or when she stands over them in the chess game; Napoleon tends to gaze levelly; Hoche looks up, because of his position below them or because Batcheff looks from under his eyebrows.

Hoche makes a second attempt to hold on to Josephine by pointing out the exact location where he held her in his arms, complete with flashback, Josephine looking discomfited at this recollection of their intimacy and her dependence on him. Meanwhile, Hoche looks intently at Napoleon, oddly toying with what looks like a piece of string with his teeth, something to which we shall return. Josephine moves away from them and Napoleon follows her. Hoche is left looking at the two of them, leaving him in a close-up shot.

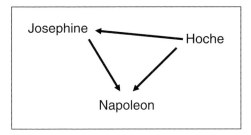

Figure 4.3 *Napoléon vu par Abel Gance*: the triangle on the steps of the Victims' Ball

In the first part of this scene, then, a context of public gazing has underpinned a battle of private gazing whose purpose is the domination of Josephine, articulated subtly by the position of the actors and by close-ups of their intense gazes and smiles as Hoche tries to prevent Josephine's gaze from being absorbed in Napoleon's intense stare. As was the case in scene 2, Batcheff smiles faintly, and it is difficult to interpret his smile, not least when compared with the smiles of the other two main characters. Napoleon's equally faint smile is clearly one of desire, responding to Josephine's brasher open-lipped smiles, intended to attract him.

There follows what can be construed as an interlude as we see shots of people enjoying themselves, under Napoleon's disapproving glare. He moves off to play a chess game with Hoche, in which the triangle set up in the first part of the scene returns. The triangle formed by Napoleon, Hoche and Josephine dominates the screen. Josephine is again at the apex, standing; this time the two men have changed position at the base, with Napoleon to her left and Hoche to her right (Figure 4.4). Napoleon's gaze switches from the chessboard, to Josephine and to Hoche in turn. Josephine gazes at Napoleon. Hoche also gazes at Napoleon and at the chessboard, but not at Josephine. Gance cleverly prefigures the metaphor of Napoleon taking Hoche's queen by having Hoche look at the group in the mirror, effectively inverting the triangle, his by now well-established enigmatic smile playing on his lips.

The chess game sequence therefore brings together the two strands running through the whole of scene 3: space and the look. It focuses and concentrates them both concretely and figuratively in a metaphor that expresses shifting relationships of power. In so doing, it plays into the dynamics of the gaze as explored by King, who makes two major points about the look in the film. The first concerns Napoleon's look on others, which 'directs and authorizes [our] responses' (King 1984: 193), the context making it clear whether we are supposed to approve (Rouget de Lisle) or disapprove (the depravity evidenced by the Victims' Ball) of what others are doing. The second concerns the gaze of others on Napoleon, keeping him at a respectful distance for us,

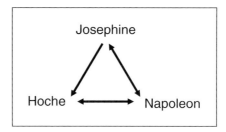

Figure 4.4 *Napoléon vu par Abel Gance*: the triangle during the chess game

and in so doing turning him into unattainable spectacle: 'Bonaparte is constructed as object of desire, as realisation of what we cannot attain, leaving us as inferiors (. . .) The look, passing through intra-diegetic spectators, is constituted in such a way as to construct the hero as spectacle' (King 1984: 196–7). Josephine and Hoche's repeated gazing at Napoleon constructs him as spectacle along the lines indicated here by King. However, with both of these characters, there are interesting complications.

In the case of Josephine, it is what follows the chess game that introduces retrospective complexities. Once Hoche has left, she sits down opposite Napoleon and waves her fan, rhythmically obscuring her gaze. She asks him pointedly what weapons he fears most, to which he replies 'Fans, Madame.' In a fairly obvious way, the metaphor of military combat has shifted from the men's game of chess to one based on a female-connoted accoutrement. It is clear that Josephine dominates and controls events, and has done so ever since her entrance into the Victims' Ball; in the fan sequence, she has six close-up shots to Napoleon's three, and the movement of her fan is echoed by two shots of two scantily clad women on a swing, the shots emphasising the sexual undertow of what Josephine is doing with her fan. But more importantly, unlike the gazes of so many other characters on Napoleon, Josephine's gaze asks for reciprocation, and her actions with the fan construct her as spectacle as much as they do Napoleon. It is as if she might be saying: 'I will give you my gaze to make you a spectacle, but only if you give me yours to make me a spectacle for you.'

What we have noted in relation to Josephine also complicates Hoche's gaze. His faint smile, when combined with his gaze, renders his position relative to Napoleon ambiguous, difficult to interpret. Is it the barely contained smile of anger and rivalry, the subdued and languid smile of resignation, the subtle smile of the politician, or the tender smile of support for his leader? In terms of King's argument, is Hoche's character helping to construct Napoleon as spectacle? Or is he surreptitiously undermining Napoleon by having a gaze that resists Napoleon as spectacle, and/or a gaze that protests Napoleon's magnetic power over 'his' woman?

When we place Hoche's enigmatic gaze and smile in relation to Josephine's, it becomes yet more complicated and ambiguous. The symmetry we have observed in the first triangular relationship places Hoche in the same position as Josephine, at the base points of an inverted triangle (see Figure 4.3). This is, we would argue, supported by the odd detail we noted above: Hoche playing with what looks like a string between his teeth, partially obscuring his mouth but occasionally revealing it as he toys with the string. It is quite unclear why he does this on the narrative level; maybe it is intended to signal a certain nervousness on his part. An unintended effect, however, particularly when placed alongside Josephine's seduction of Napoleon, is that Hoche looks as if he is also attempting to seduce Napoleon, almost as if he might be saying: 'Josephine may have beautiful eyes and a beautiful smile; but look at my mouth which I am opening for you, look at my eyes, they are just as beautiful.' We would wish to argue that Hoche pursues Napoleon as much as he does Josephine, and that he uses the same corporeal tactics. The homoerotic nature of their relationship is further emphasised by a brief sequence immediately preceding the chess game. We see a drunken sans-culotte sitting next to what he assumes to be a woman, but who turns out be another sans-culotte in drag, much to his surprise; immediately after this cameo involving two men, we see the intertitle setting up both the intimacy and the resemblance between two men, Hoche and Napoleon: 'A game of chess was bound to attract two strategists like Bonaparte and Hoche.'

The triangular spatialisation of the three characters' relationship returns, as we noted above, in the chess game. Here, however, it is Josephine who is at the apex of the triangle, with the two men facing each other at the base; and Hoche no longer looks at Josephine (except tangentially in the mirror), all of his attention being focused on Napoleon, thereby emphasising even more the intense homoerotic nature of the relationship. And, as if to compensate for the lack of mouth-play we saw earlier, sexual attraction is displaced on to Madame Tallien's bare legs, constantly present to the right of the frame (see Figure 4.2). Batcheff is, of course, constrained by the necessities of historical authenticity to wear a tight-fitting uniform, quite unlike the open-necked silk shirts we have seen him wear in other films, while Madame Tallien was famous for her outrageous outfits. In the absence of historical support for a camp dishabille, Batcheff uses all the resources of his face – eyes, lips, mouth, tilt of the head – in ways that contrast both with Napoleon's rather dour intensity and with Josephine's exuberant simperings.

Batcheff's performance may be enigmatic and touched with the homo-erotic; it is certainly understated, conforming to the comment made in relation to *Destinée*, as it is in the next film we shall consider.

LE JOUEUR D'ÉCHECS (JULY 1927)

Bernard's film was partly filmed in the same studio and at the same time as Gance's (Brownlow 1990: 2). The film was a great success. Although some reviewers thought it overly complex and sometimes fragmented (for example, Derain 1927a: 24), it was praised by audiences and critics alike. Épardaud, the reviewer for *Cinéa-Ciné pour tous*, for example, relates how the audience spontaneously applauded at the end of the first part of the film, crying 'Bravo Bernard!', and considered that no film since Gance's *La Roue* four years earlier had enthused audiences as much (Épardaud 1927: 15). His review singles out the scene where Sophie sings the Polish Hymn of Independence superimposed on shots of the Russian cavalry, pointing out that it is not just strikingly original, but rousing and moving, as the audience reaction shows. As Abel says in his caption to a frame from this scene, the shot 'turns the defeat of the Polish insurrection into a stunningly imagined vision of victory' (Abel 2005: 360), and in so doing, as Épardaud wrote, 'donne une forme matérialisée à ce rêve impossible' ('materialises the impossible dream') of independence (Épardaud 1927: 16). Abel has devoted considerable attention to the film, both in his 1984 volume (Abel 1984: 190–3) and in the more recent article in a special number of *Film History* on the year 1927 from which we have just quoted. This dispenses us from a detailed consideration of its merits, not least amongst which are its spectacular and complex set designs (see Abel 1984: 190–1), so that we can concentrate on Batcheff's performance.

Batcheff played opposite Édith Jehanne, with whom he also starred in *Le Perroquet vert* the following year. She had previously had small parts in two films by Bernard, *Triplepatte* (1922), and *Le Miracle des loups* two years later.[8] Reviewers were fulsome in their praise of her in *Le Joueur d'échecs*, calling her a 'révélation' ('revelation'; Derain 1927a: 24; Épardaud 1927: 16). Batcheff, by contrast, fared rather poorly. While Derain, clearly a supporter of Batcheff more generally, found him 'racé et charmant' ('distinguished and charming'; Derain 1927a: 24), and the same journal thought him 'séduisant et émouvant' ('seductive and moving'; *Cinématographie française* 1926b: 93), Épardaud complained about his mannered acting (Épardaud 1927: 16). To our mind, his performance is no different to his performance in *Napoléon vu par Abel Gance*; as we shall see, Batcheff has similar mannerisms in the two films. What is different, however, is the way he is shot and the length of shots, which may well have affected the way someone like Épardaud viewed his performance.

Batcheff is on screen for much more of the film than was the case for *Napoléon vu par Abel Gance*, approximately a quarter of the running time of 133 minutes. In the first half of the film, entitled 'The Song of Independence',[9] his role consists in the establishment of his character's relationship with

Figure 4.5 *Le Joueur d'échecs*: the confrontation. A film by Raymond Bernard. (© Gaumont, 1926)

Sophie, and him being forced to accept that he cannot maintain it across political rivalries. In the second half, entitled 'The Great Deception', his role consists of him betraying his political allegiance to Russia to save Boleslas and sacrificing his love for Sophie not just to the Polish cause, as was the case in part one, but also to Boleslas. We shall see a similar conflict between love and duty in *Éducation de prince*, which we shall consider in the next chapter.

In the first half of the film, Batcheff has two significant scenes. In the first of these, lasting about two and half minutes, we see Serge painting Sophie (the association with painting is repeated in *Éducation de prince*), and then offering her a necklace as a token of his love for her. In the second, much more significant scene, lasting sixteen minutes, Serge is at Kempelen's house helping prepare for Sophie's birthday celebrations (although Batcheff is not on screen for all of that time as the birthday celebrations are intercut throughout with images of the Polish rebellion); we see the two of them dancing a stately minuet, and then talking in the gardens. The scene is intended to build to a parallel climax. On the one hand there is the love scene, whose climax is an extreme close-up of the two lovers' faces, cheek to cheek, indicating deep emotion; on the other, there are the intercut shots of the Polish rebellion, which are increasingly violent. The two come together when a bloodied and defeated Boleslas spies on the lovers and confronts them, telling Serge to leave.

The effect of the parallel narrative strands is to undermine and isolate Batcheff's character, who appears to be sealed off in a world of artifice and inconsequential sentimentalism in comparison with Boleslas's macho heroism. Serge paints and looks decorous, while Boleslas stands up to face what is characterised as Russian tyranny. Not only does Serge paint while political rivals play chess (a metaphor for military and political power) and end up brawling, and he holds a lapdog for Sophie; both scenes also undermine him by having a master–servant parallel narrative strand as Serge's clumsy aide-de-camp mimics Serge's love affair in comic mode by chasing Sophie's maid. Although this parallel relationship carries on into the second half, it is to some extent mitigated by Serge's role in helping Boleslas and Sophie in part two of the film. But the second half reprises some of the basic situations of the first. So, for example, we again see the two lovers sitting in a long, sentimental scene, again spied on by Boleslas, who is hiding in the automaton, and who therefore overhears Serge articulate the conflict between love and duty: 'What a terrible dilemma I would be in – to have to hand him over – I who love him like a brother.' We again see Serge dancing, this time at the masked ball, his frivolity and mobility strongly contrasted with the staring eyes of Boleslas. It is true that the masked ball is used as a smoke-screen to smuggle Boleslas away from harm; but the echoes with the first half of the film strongly cast Batcheff's character in the light of the frivolous and useless noble. This is only partly redeemed by the melodramatic scene at the end of the film where Serge persuades Boleslas not to give up the fight; they shake hands, and Boleslas says 'How can I ever forget what you have done for me?', to which Serge replies, sacrificing himself: 'I would do it again. Be happy . . . you and Sophie.'

Serge's surname may be relevant in this respect, as it may well be an indirect reference to Oblomov (or Oblomoff, as the Thames Silents restoration spells his name, and as Oblomov is sometimes spelled; the name in the film is in fact Oblonoff, but the error is telling). Oblomov is the hero of Ivan Goncharov's 1858 satirical novel of the same name, which gave rise to the term 'Oblomovism', a reference to the slothful inactivity of the hero who spends most of his time in bed and cannot muster the energy to attend to more or less anything. The novel is usually seen as a satire of the Russian nobility.

This underlines Serge's relative uselessness as the sentimental lover. Batcheff's character in the film is redundant, rather like Oblomov was as a metaphor for a waning social class. Serge's role in the plot is wholly subsidiary; we could remove the love affair between Sophie and Serge, and it would not change the basic plot line of Poles fighting for their independence.[10] Lucien Wahl was well aware of this in his brief review of the reprise of the film in late 1929, as was Épardaud before him, pointing out that the film's 'véritable sujet (. . .) est l'effort que fait, à la fin du dix-huitième siècle, la Pologne pour secouer le joug de la Russie' ('the true subject is Poland's late-eighteenth-century attempt to throw off the Russian yoke'), and he lists the Batcheff sub-plot and the sub-plot revolving around the automaton as the main elements leading to an over-complicated plot (Wahl 1929e: 5).

Serge's 'Oblomovism' is all the more paradoxical when we consider that one view of the social and ideological significance of this film, like others based in Russia, is that it can be seen as a reflection by the Russian émigré community on Soviet Russia and their nostalgia for a lost Czarist Russia (Abel 1984: 182; Abel 2005: 353).[11] If we accept this view, then Batcheff's position becomes crucially fractured. His Russian-sounding name and his associations with Albatros would suggest that, rightly or wrongly, he might well have been seen as belonging to that émigré community; and yet in this film he is on the side of the oppressors, who are by displacement the Bolsheviks and their supporters.

Everything about Batcheff's character, therefore, conspires to show him up as ineffectual, slightly comical and tangential to the real action, eccentric in the strictly etymological sense of the word, fractured and dislocated. This is no doubt one reason why, when this is combined with long scenes of swooning lovers, that a reviewer such as Épardaud could complain about Batcheff's mannered acting; Batcheff is almost literally de trop. But in fact, Batcheff's acting is no different from his acting in Gance's film; indeed, one of the more obviously actorly mannerisms, unlikely to be dependent on the director, is one we also see in Gance's film (it is unlikely to be dependent on the director precisely because we also find it in Batcheff's previous film): the sudden jerk of the head upwards when he is rejected. In *Napoléon vu par Abel Gance*, it was when Hoche realises that Josephine is transferring her affections to Napoleon; in *Le Joueur d'échecs*, similarly, it is when Boleslas refuses to acknowledge Serge as his friend at the end of the birthday celebrations when Serge is waiting for his hat to be brought out from the house. Serge moves toward Boleslas, looking at him pleadingly, just as happened in the scene from Gance's film. The two friends end up bowing stiffly to each other before Batcheff walks off, shoulders stooped, sent off as peripheral to the real action.

In our analysis of the film, we have identified what amounts to an eccentric space for Batcheff's character. In the next film, we will find that this space of difference and dislocation is even more firmly worked through his character.

Figure 4.6   *Le Joueur d'échecs*: the isolated and ineffectual Serge (© Photoplay Productions)

MONTE-CRISTO (MAY 1929)

Alexandre Dumas's adventure story has frequently been adapted for the screen. Prior to 1929, there had been a large number of American versions, not least Emmet J. Flynn's version for Fox starring John Gilbert (1922). In France, there had only been one version, serialised in fifteen episodes by Henri Pouctal for Pathé (1917–19), although several other Dumas adaptations had appeared, amongst them an adaptation of *The Three Musketeers* by Pouctal with André Calmettes (1912), adapted a second time by Henri Diamant-Berger in 1921, and *Kean* by Volkoff, as mentioned above. There had also been two versions of *La Dame de Monsoreau*, one by an unknown director (although often wrongly attributed to Maurice Tourneur) in 1913, and another, starring Gina Manès (who played Josephine in *Napoléon vu par Abel Gance*) by René Le Somptier in 1923. Fescourt had started making films in 1912, and by the time of *Monte-Cristo*, 'the last silent superproduction' (Fescourt 1959: 348), had made 73 films, 60 of them before 1918. His major achievement had been one of the big films of the 1925–6 season, a four-part 32-reel adaptation of *Les Misérables* (see Abel 1984: 130–2).

In other words, both director and story were dependable, and the film was roundly praised. Lucien Wahl's strapline for his review is typical in this respect: 'De la variété mais pas d'excentricité, de l'unité mais pas de monotonie'

('Variety but not eccentricity; unity but not monotony'), and he went on to praise the way the film, despite being an adventure film, refused to pander to spectacular action sequences; Wahl 1929d: 7). Others praised the essential coherence and balance of the film, combined with a well-judged lyricism (Pierret-Marthe 1929: 570–1). Boris Bilinsky's set designs were singled out for praise, especially the evening at the Opera (Pierret-Marthe 1929: 571) and Monte-Cristo's palace done using scale models and trompe-l'œil (*Cinéa* 1929: 27);[12] he had been the costume designer for Albatros's *Le Lion des mogols* (Jean Epstein, 1924), *Le Prince charmant* (Viktor Tourjanksy, 1925) and *Casanova*. Actors were also praised, Batcheff being singled out by one review for his remarkable acting in the scene where he is provoked by Monte-Cristo (Olivet 1929c: 920).

The film is divided into two epochs, the first covering chapters 1–30 of Dumas's novel, the second the remaining 87. As was the case with *Le Joueur d'échecs*, Batcheff's role is confined to a few major scenes, all in the second part; indeed, the second part opens with Albert's visit to the island of Monte-Cristo, lasting just over six and a half minutes, this being immediately followed by Albert's introduction of Monte-Cristo to Paris society at the Opera. Batcheff subsequently appears in two related scenes, the first being the evening at Monte-Cristo's palace where Fernand's betrayal of Haydée's father is revealed in a theatrical sketch, leading to Albert's fury in the 'provocation scene' referred to above (about 50 minutes into the second half). This leads, ten minutes later in the film, to a duel, where Albert, having been told by his mother of his father's betrayal, refuses to fight the Count.

The adaptation is faithful, although many minor events are omitted;[13] and there is some compression of characters and events, all of which relate in one way or another to Albert. A major character and his family are omitted: Danglars, the purser of Dantès's ship, *Le Pharaon*. This is important because, in the novel, Albert is the fiancé of Eugénie, Danglars's daughter, whereas in the film he does not have any key relationship, other than with his parents and Monte-Cristo. Similarly, while in the novel there is a long section where Albert and his friend Franz visit Rome, during which it is Franz who visits the island of Monte-Cristo, in the film Franz is omitted, as is all of the Roman section (involving a carnival, bandits, catacombs and gruesome executions), and it is Albert who visits the island, a scene which is foregrounded by opening the second half of the film. The various events in the film leading up to the provocation of Albert (opera, palace and theatrical sketch) are kept apart and what goes on within these scenes in the film is scattered across a number of locations in the novel.

The effect of these changes foregrounds Albert, giving him much more narrative substance, while at the same time disentangling him from the extremely complex network of relationships so important to the novel. This, we might argue, is to some extent remedied by the final 'family scene' where all the remaining 'good' characters are reunited under the distant but watchful eye of Edmond. Additionally, in this scene Albert is dressed as a soldier just like Maximilien, the ship-owner's son, and they are represented as a result more like brothers than the good friends their handshake is clearly intended to convey. This rather sentimental scene does not redress Albert's tangential and isolated status, however. It is very much out of kilter with the final scenes of the novel, where resolution for the characters is ascertained as part of couple relationships. The Count meets Albert and his mother in Marseille, with Mercédès sighing nostalgically for the past she has lost rather than (as in the film) the future; he then takes Maximilien to the island, where he will be reunited with Valentine. Ultimately, Albert is, like so many of Batcheff's characters, isolated and distanced.

Nowhere is this clearer than in the island sequence which opens the second part of the film, corresponding to Chapter 31 of the novel (Dumas 1981: 331–57). It is the only scene of the film which is clearly designed architecturally to be unrealistic, an orientalist fantasy, and it therefore seems almost like a parenthesis for the action. It is narratively motivated by allowing Monte-Cristo to be introduced into Paris society, but there are other ways in which this could have been done; and in any case, as we have explained, the corresponding passage in the novel has nothing to do with Albert, and is even more free-standing.

There are other reasons why Albert seems isolated and distanced from us. We see him in a boat agreeing to a suggestion from his guide that they should stop off at the island. He is drugged (in the novel Franz is blindfolded once on the island), and wakes up in a vast cavern supported by a multitude of abstractly plant-like pillars sparsely furnished with a few cushions and a coffee table,[14] with the Count dressed as a pasha with an ostentatious turban sitting next to him.[15] Haydée is introduced to him, and he sips hashish, drifting off into a dream, the décor and the characters within it going in and out of focus to reflect his intoxication, and waking in surprise in a field on the Italian coast.

Apart from the reference to drugs, which we shall encounter again in *Vivre* in the next chapter, this sequence reaffirms the trope of the ephebic youth we first encountered in Batcheff's very first film, *Claudine et le poussin*: the Sad Young Man, as defined by Richard Dyer, a representation that is developed in many of his subsequent films. The homoerotic nature of the sequence is made clear right at the start when Albert, casually reclining in the bottom of the boat, wearing an open-necked shirt and tartan slacks, his hair ruffled by the wind, is serenaded by two sailors playing their guitars. He is served drugged wine, and falls into the passive posture of the helpless young man,

Figure 4.7 *Monte-Cristo*: Albert and the pasha (Courtesy of the Bibliothèque du Film, Paris)

which we shall find repeated in many of the films analysed in the next chapter, and a posture repeated throughout the sequence: when he wakes up in the cavern, when he drifts off into his drug-induced dream, and when he wakes up in the field. But whereas in the novel, the account of his dream state is suffused with orgasmic sensuality, statues coming to life and embracing him fully on the lips (see Dumas 1981: 356–7), in the film there is a rather more conventional kaleidoscope effect for the pillars and musicians to suggest little more than intoxication of a purely mechanical kind. The sensuality conveyed by Dumas's florid prose is inscribed purely in Batcheff's ecstatically passive pose. This minimises our identification with his experience, while isolating him as pin-up.

Unusually for a Batcheff character, his next major scene, the provocation scene admired by reviewers, shows a rather more aggressive and angry character. Albert leaves Monte-Cristo's house with his outraged parents, after the theatrical representation impugning Fernand. Albert returns, clearly intent on causing trouble. He enters the ballroom in a (for this film an unusual) sweeping backwards travelling shot and confronts the Count. His anger is conveyed in subtle, almost imperceptible movements – a narrowing of the eyes as he sees the Count ahead of him, followed by very slightly raised eyebrows, a tightening of the lips, a faint shudder of the upper body when he confronts him – his understated performance vindicating the admiration of reviewers. But any sense that this activity might counterbalance the morbid passivity of the Sad Young Man established in the island sequence is dissipated by the ensuing duel, where Albert refuses to fight the Count. And we find yet again the space of isolation in which Batcheff's characters operate. In the novel, Albert's explanation of his refusal to fight divulges his father's double betrayal of Haydée's father and of Edmond Dantès before that, and he shakes the Count's hand (Dumas 1981: 1116–17). In the film, only the Count understands what is at issue, and the two bow stiffly to each other, just like Serge bowed stiffly to Boleslas in *Le Joueur d'échecs*, like the Count, his friend.

Batcheff's characters in the historical reconstructions are rejected by their friends and by their lovers; they are drugged or become ill; they lie passively, but also erotically, for our consumption as melancholic objects. While Batcheff's characters in these films are secondary, the tropes we have identified are naturally more prominent in the films where he stars as the leading man in the role of the lover. It is to these films that we now turn.

Notes

1. His stage name was Henry-Roussell. Both 'Henry Roussel' and 'Henry Roussell' (unhyphenated) are found in documents of the period; most seem to have the double 'l', and it is as such that he is listed in the database of the Bibliothèque du Film.

2. Some documents from the period list the title as *Destinée!*, others without the exclamation mark; the Bibliothèque du Film lists it without, and we have adopted this version.

3. The film was restored by Lenny Borger for ZZ Productions. It was premiered at Cannes on 20 May 2006 and screened on TV for Arte's series 'Le Muet du mois', 23–4 September 2006.

4. The film appears to have been extremely long, at least in its first version. Lucie Derain commented after the press preview (9 December 1925) that 'quelques coupures seront nécessaires (. . .) Trois heures et quart de projection sont suffisantes pour nous, elles seraient excessives pour les spectateurs payants' ('some cuts will be necessary (. . .) Three and a quarter hours are enough for us, but they would be far too much for paying spectators'; Derain 1925c: 40). The version we have been able to consult is an abridged Pathé-Rural 17.5mm copy, 66 minutes long, owned by David Wyatt, London. As far as we know, this is the only surviving version of the film.

5. There is an illustration of this scene in Bonneau 1926: 417. The whole of this number is devoted to the film.

6. We are using the Brownlow version of the film, broadcast on Channel 4 on 22 and 23 July 1989.

7. The intertitles are in English in the Brownlow version of the film.

8. She also starred in a film by Georg Wilhelm Pabst the same year, *Die Liebe der Jeanne Ney*, and in another film by Bernard, *Tarakanova* (1930), where she plays the eponymous heroine in yet another Russian period piece involving the Empress Catherine II (see Abel 1984: 193–4).

9. As was the case with *Napoléon*, we are using the Brownlow version of the film with intertitles in English.

10. Other interpretations are, of course, valid. Kevin Brownlow has suggested in a private communication that 'the reason Serge is in the story is to defuse nationalism; Sophie is the symbol of Polish independence, and yet she loves a member of the hated enemy'.

11. It should perhaps be said that Abel also suggests that this particular film could just as well be seen as a displacement for the French Revolution: 'The film's celebration of Polish independence from the Russian monarchy in a period just prior to the French Revolution tempts one to read it as a displacement of the one onto the other' (Abel 1984: 192).

12. See Abel 1984: 194–5 for a brief historical account of the film along these lines. Figure 99 on page 194 shows the *maquette-plastique* for Monte-Cristo's shooting gallery alongside the finished shot.

13. For example, we know about the secret of Benedetto's birth much earlier in the film than in the novel, and he is apprehended in Paris, whereas in the novel he escapes and is caught in an inn; Caderousse dies while trying to rob Monte-Cristo's palace in the novel but not in the film, where he returns in the showdown at the trial; Valentine is not poisoned in the film; Edmond does not return to visit his cell in the Château d'If, as he does at the end of the novel.

14. In the novel, the count's living space is not open-plan, but made up of a variety of chambers, each of which is richly furnished with tapestries, carpets, animal skins and tables laden with food.

15. In the novel, the count is dressed in a Tunisian costume, complete with a fez; here he is dressed to look considerably more oriental.

CHAPTER 5

The lover

In this chapter, we will present seven films in which Batcheff starred during a very busy three-year period (1926–8) when ten films appeared. In these seven films he is always the Lover (as he is in all his films), often a foreigner (Russian, Corsican, 'Silistrian') or placed in a foreign location (the 'tropics', Africa), usually from the upper class (aristocrat, baron, prince) or highly successful in his career (an engineer, an aviator, a famous artist). He discovers that he is an illegitimate son in three of these films, subsequently rejecting his family; in two of them he even falls in love incestuously with his half-sister. We can see a consistent narrative emerging from the films he chose to star in during this period; he tries to be a lover within a family structure that is in his eyes oppressive, and as a result escapes, becoming other or alien. We will dwell in particular on two films, *Éducation de prince* and *La Sirène des tropiques*, partly because they are easily consultable, but mainly because they exemplify the problems of otherness.

LE SECRET D'UNE MÈRE (JULY 1926)

Le Secret d'une mère is based on a best-selling novel, melodramatically entitled *Abandonné!*, published two years before by Eugène Barbier (Barbier 1924). Barbier, a popular novelist, was very much in the public eye. One of his earlier novels, *Le Dernier des Capendu*, had been adapted for the screen in 1923, directed by Jean Manoussi, and both films had had a 'book of the film' published in Tallendier's cinema series, copiously illustrated with photographs from the films themselves (Laumann 1926, 1927). In *Le Secret d'une mère*, Batcheff plays an artist who feels doubly abandoned; he has learnt that his recently deceased father was in fact his stepfather, and that he had been placed in an orphanage when young. He has met a girl studying at art school like him, but he discovers that she is his half-sister. He rejects his biological mother, and goes off to Rome where he marries someone else, winning a prestigious prize for a painting of his wife and son, called 'Maternity'. At the end of the film, deemed highly 'moral' by some reviewers, some semblance of order is restored when he returns to see his sick mother with his stepmother, the film ending on his acceptance of both mothers.

ÉDUCATION DE PRINCE (JUNE 1927)

Éducation de prince reprised one of Batcheff's standard roles, already seen in *Autour d'un berceau*, but much more obviously in *Le Joueur d'échecs* six months earlier: that of the sophisticated aristocrat. Henri Diamant-Berger was one of the major directors of the 1920s. By the time of *Éducation de prince* he had twenty films to his credit as director, some of them made in the USA, such as *Lover's Island* (1925) and *The Unfair Sex* (1926). He was best known for the first film version of *The Three Musketeers*, a serial released over three months in 1921–2 and one of the most successful films of the decade (see Abel 1984: 21, 164–6). *Éducation de prince* was based on a well-known play by Maurice Donnay, published in 1895 (Donnay 1895), with two successful runs, the first at the Théâtre des Variétés in March 1900, the second at the Théâtre du Vaudeville in November 1906. Donnay had been elected to the Académie Française in February 1907. Another of his plays, *Oiseaux de passage* (1904), had been adapted for the screen in 1925, directed by Gaston Roudès for Grandes Productions Cinématographiques, and this was no doubt one of the motivating factors for Diamant-Berger's film version of *Éducation de prince*.

The film had mixed reviews. While most admired the fact that Edna Purviance had been secured for the role of the Queen, there was a general feeling that the film was an incoherent mixture of French sensibility and American adventure film. The reviewer for *Cinémagazine*, for example, pointed out how the first part of the film corresponded to the witty repartee for which Donnay was known, but that the second part seemed to be a completely different film, 'ne faisant plus penser à Maurice Donnay mais à Tom Mix et à Buck Jones' ('no longer making you think of Maurice Donnay but of Tom Mix and Buck Jones'; Bonneau 1927: 585). Lucie Derain similarly complained about the generic pot-pourri, going 'du drame au burlesque, en côtoyant le ridicule maintes fois' ('from drama to burlesque, bordering on the ridiculous'; Derain 1927c: 30), suggesting that the latter part of the film should be cut by half for its distribution in the USA.

The structure of the film is important for Batcheff's star persona, as we shall see below. Batcheff's character, Prince Sacha, is that of the inexperienced youth, as is emphasised by his stepmother who says to Cercleux: 'Il sait l'histoire, les sciences, la politique, tout ce qui peut s'apprendre dans notre pays . . . mais il ne connaît rien des femmes. Je veux que Sacha devienne un homme accompli' ('He knows history, the sciences, politics, everything that can be learnt in our country, but he knows nothing about women. I want Sacha to become a man'). Cercleux takes Sacha in hand (Figure 5.1), and there follows a whirl of parties, or, as one of the intertitles has it, 'le tour de Paris en 24 sourires' ('the tour of Paris in twenty-four smiles'), the idea of the tour

Figure 5.1   *Éducation de prince*: Cercleux takes Sacha in hand (Collection Roche-Batcheff)

exemplified by shots of women smiling. Batcheff's role echoes that of Claude in *Claudine et le poussin*, not least because Sacha, like Claude, will meet an 'artiste' who, with Cercleux, will endeavour to educate him sentimentally, and because he is, like Claude and Jacques in *Le Double Amour*, controlled by a mother figure: his stepmother, the Queen. And as was the case with *Le Double Amour*, a slightly dubious father figure enters his life, to be instated as a real father (or stepfather in the case of *Éducation de prince*) at the end of the film when the Queen and Cercleux agree to marry.

As was the case with *Le Double Amour*, mise en scene supports Sacha's dependency on parental figures. When the Queen arrives unannounced in Sacha's Paris apartment, we see Batcheff wearing a morning jacket with a curious zigzag motif, echoing a balalaika hanging on the wall behind him. The Queen later plays this instrument, strongly suggesting the interconnection between her and her stepson. Much later in the story, in a key scene for the development of Batcheff's persona which we will analyse below, the throne on which he sits is a simplified inversion of the zigzag motif, suggesting that the moment has come for him to throw off his dependency and to make decisions for himself as an all-powerful monarch. This is, of course, an important difference from the two previous films.

Interestingly, however, the imbalanced structure of the film commented

on by so many reviewers works against the escape from dependency, in spite
of a magnificent central scene focused both literally and figuratively on Sacha.
At the key moment of the narrative, when Sacha must decide whether to flee
the revolutionaries, there are three medium close-up shots of Batcheff sepa-
rated by intertitles. He faces the camera with what was by now the trademark
distant look in his eyes, trying to make his decision, the three shots between
them lasting more than thirty seconds. He is surrounded by shadows, allowing the key lighting on the right side of his face to emphasise his body as spectacle for our consumption; as one reviewer said, 'Batcheff est un jeune prince
séduisant' ('Batcheff is a seductive young prince'; Villette 1927: 10), the long
set of shots emphasising that spectacle as one of the more important aspects
of his seductive power. Dramatic intertitles break up the shot: 'Sire, il faut
partir!' ('Sire, you must leave!'), 'C'est le sort de cette dynastie qui se joue' ('The
fate of your dynasty is in the balance'), 'Des hommes sont là-bas prêts à
mourir pour vous, Sire. Les abandonner serait une lâcheté' ('Men are out there
ready to die for you, sire. It would be cowardly to abandon them'). His dramatic immobility during these shots is finally broken when he slowly nods,
articulating the difficult passage from the insouciance and inexperience of
youth to the heavy responsibility of the man who is king. As a result, the film
focuses sharply on Batcheff's character, and we might be forgiven for thinking that the transition from youth to manhood is about to be developed. There
are subjective point-of-view scenes that seem to be leading to such a development, such as when Sacha is told that he must marry Princess Hermine,
daughter of their powerful neighbour, the King of Illyria. A miniature version
of Raymonde dressed in a tutu dances out of the inkwell on the desk in front
of him, Sacha's reverie being literally punctured when his Minister dips the
pen into the inkwell, killing Raymonde, a 'scène très "cinéma"' ('a very
"cinematic" scene'; Derain 1927c: 30).

But the gravity of Sacha's rite of passage and the focus on his development
is quickly dispelled, in a variety of ways. First, the star as spectacle takes over,
eliminating anything other than the star body as seductive surface. When he is
warned of the plot against him, he is dressed in an open-necked white silk
shirt, set apart from the actors around him. We are cued in to the importance
of his costume in an oddly displaced comment later by the General in the
scene on the supposedly inappropriate clothes worn by another character: 'Je
trouve la tenu du capitaine Hersch indécente pour se présenter devant son roi'
('I think that what Captain Hersch is wearing is indecent in the presence of his
king'). Figure 5.2 shows Batcheff in his silk shirt earlier in the scene. It is a pro-
foundly troubling mise en scene, showing two couples: one, the Queen and
Cercleux, mutually seducing each other as Sacha's parental figures; the other
consisting of Sacha, strongly colour-contrasted and costume-contrasted with

Figure 5.2   *Éducation de prince*: Batcheff's silk shirt (Collection Roche-Batcheff)

his tutor, Ronceval. Batcheff's posture, however, when placed in the context of the heterosexual couple mutually seducing each other, suggests more than obviously the ephebic feminised youth, flaunting his body passively as a compensation for action.

A second way in which Batcheff's star persona is blocked is, paradoxically, given what we have just noted, the sudden incursion of action sequences: the escape in a sleigh, the snowstorm, the return to the castle in a hijacked tank.

A third procedure is the use of comedy, noted by reviewers. For example, Cercleux is mistaken for the traitorous pretender to the throne and taken prisoner, leading to much jollity on the part of other characters when they discover who the 'traitor' is. Moreover, the humorously sentimental ending diffuses any sense of maturity for Batcheff's character. Sacha says he will break his engagement to Hermine, and his tutor Ronceval says he should consult the Queen, whom they discover kissing Cercleux. The final shot is of Sacha kissing Raymonde, while trying to cover Ronceval's eyes (Figure 5.3). The final title signalling 'the end' is decorated with a Cupid, which says it all, as we return to the sentimental whimsy of the start of the film, but without the witty repartee or sense of the risqué.

Finally, Batcheff's star persona cannot develop beyond the dependency of the ephebic youth caught in the display of his body as spectacle for another

Figure 5.3 *Éducation de prince*: the final whimsical shot (Collection Roche-Batcheff)

reason. He is resolutely in between cultures, neither one nor the other, but both while being neither. This is suggested neatly by the traditional tussle between love and duty (see Figure 5.4), located in two very different cultures: Paris, associated with pleasure, Raymonde and the playboy Cercleux; and the pedestrianly named capital of Silestria, Bojaz, associated with violence, traitors and the irritatingly pedantic Ronceval. Batcheff's in-betweenness is encapsulated in a curious scene where the Queen berates Cercleux in her supposedly native language. The intertitle reads 'Vestora retibsco ver tagri yourotu tronia coulverto viripourche Chosko!'; this is translated by Sacha, caught between stepmother and future stepfather, between the traditional and the sophisticated: 'Anathème sur toi. Tu es issu de requins et que ta sœur soit couverte par un bélier!' ('Anathema on you. You are the son of a shark, and may your sister be covered by a ram!').

LE BONHEUR DU JOUR (JULY 1927)

Le Bonheur du jour reprises, exactly a year later, the same situation as *Le Secret d'une mère*. And as with *Le Secret d'une mère*, it is based on a successful text, this time a play by Edmond Guiraud, which had opened on 22 November 1926 at the Théâtre de l'Odéon and had run for two full seasons (1926–9), the

Figure 5.4   *Éducation de prince*: love versus duty (Collection Roche-Batcheff)

film version being released so as to capitalise on the play's success. The director, Gaston Ravel, had become something of a specialist in adapting stage
plays to the screen: a Sardou play, *Rabagas*, in 1922, followed by a hardy
favourite in 1924, Musset's *On ne badine pas avec l'amour*, and several others
before *Le Bonheur du jour*, including *Fräulein Josette, Meine Frau* by Pierre
Gavault and Robert Charvay in 1926, starring Dolly Davis, Batcheff's co-
star in his very first film. The title of *Le Bonheur du jour* refers to a writing
desk in which a letter reveals to Batcheff's character, the aristocratically
named Jean Plessiers de Chavignac, that the man he thought was his father
had married his mother when she was pregnant by another man, making him
in his eyes an illegitimate child. As was the case with *Le Secret d'une mère*, we
find the same theme of the rejected child. In the first film he rejected his
parents and ran away to Rome; in this one he rejects them and runs away to
Africa. In both of these films, Batcheff's performance was singled out as
one of the highlights, but more particularly in this second film; Lucie Derain
comments that his performance in the scene where he reads the letter revealing his parentage is full of 'belle et sobre émotion' ('deep and simply
expressed emotion'), praising his facial expressions more generally in the
film as one of *La Cinématographie française*'s 'éléments favorables' ('favourable
elements'; Derain 1927d: 38).

Figure 5.5 *Le Bonheur du jour*: Batcheff's 'simply expressed emotion' (Courtesy of the Bibliothèque Nationale, Paris)

LA SIRÈNE DES TROPIQUES (DECEMBER 1927)

As was the case with *Éducation de prince*, Batcheff's character in *La Sirène des tropiques* also finds himself caught between two cultures, connoted as sophisticated and primitive respectively, the place of the less sophisticated mother in *Éducation de prince* being taken by the music-hall star Josephine Baker. Baker was the star of La Revue Nègre, which had taken Paris by storm for a few short weeks in October and November 1925. This was due in large part to Baker, whose more than half-naked body gyrated and jerked in what appeared to be a combination of carefully worked out dance steps and expansive, loose movements, accompanied by comical contortions of her facial features, including the trademark crossing of her eyes.[1] She was one of the most iconic figures of the 1920s, synthesising 'Americanism, dance-mania, hedonism, feminism' (Klein 1990: 371). Much has been written about Baker, but few capture the electrifying nature of her performance better than the eyewitness account of American poet e e cummings:

> She enters through a dense electric twilight, walking backwards on hands and feet, legs and arms stiff, down a huge jungle tree, as a creature neither infrahuman nor superhuman but somehow both: a mysterious unkillable Something,

> equally non-primitive and uncivilised, or beyond time in the sense that
> emotion is beyond arithmetic. (Hammond and O'Connor 1988: 411)

After a brief European tour, she signed up in 1926 at the Folies-Bergère. Part
of the Folies-Bergère performances had been captured on film and was
released at the same time as *La Sirène des tropiques*, but *La Sirène des tropiques* was
the first of three feature films starring Baker.[2] In each of these a simple plot-
line imitated Baker's meteoric rise, featuring 'protagonists that long for love
but get stardom instead of domestic bliss' (Francis 2005: 829), or, as Phyllis
Rose less charitably put it, 'an innocent girl from the tropics goes to Paris,
where she dances and is transformed into an elegant woman by beautiful
clothes' (Rose 1989: 120);[3] indeed, the film incorporates part of her Folies-
Bergère routine. It is also one of her best, according to a recent commenta-
tor, because she was able (at least partly) to improvise, articulating a very
personal gestural space quite at odds with those of her time and close in its
specificity to a ritual: 'Cet aspect sauvage, presque mécanique, ses grimaces
enfantines, le côté chaplinesque de son personnage donnent à sa danse
l'étrangeté d'un rituel, dessinent une brèche dans la rigidité de la gestuelle et
des comportements de son époque' ('Her almost mechanical savageness, her
childlike grimacing, the Chaplinesque side of her character, gave her dancing
the strangeness of a ritual, sketching out a radical break in the body language
and the behaviour of her time'; Bensard 1995: 6).

Baker was such an unusual performer that she overshadowed both the story-
line and the other actors, not helped by a conventional plot which was criticised
by one reviewer for not being more adventurous: 'Le scénario (. . .) manque
parfois de nouveauté, et nous aurions voulu des péripéties plus inattendues'
('The script is somewhat predictable, and we would have liked to see more unexpected twists'; Orta 1928: 31). The reviewer for *Le Figaro* commented that he
'could only remember Mademoiselle Josephine Baker', who was for him 'une
véritable révélation (. . .) vivante, attendrissante et si véritablement amusante,
qu'un rire inextinguible agitait la salle' ('a real revelation (. . .) vivacious, touching and so amusing that the audience were shaken by uncontrollable laughter';
Spa 1927). For *Cinémagazine*'s reviewer, the whole point of the film was Baker's
astonishing performance: 'Tout l'intérêt de l'interprétation réside évidemment
dans le jeu très personnel de Joséphine Baker (. . .) Elle étonne et ravit' ('The
whole point of the film is Josephine Baker's very personal performance (. . .)
She astonishes and delights'; Farnay 1927: 588).

La Revue Nègre played into an early twentieth-century fascination with
'blackness'. This had started with painters such as Picasso prior to the Great
War, and had extended into the other arts, with jazz and dance being the focus
in the mid-1920s (see Klein 1990: 373–4; Sweeney 2004: 11–33). Much of the

Figure 5.6 Publicity still for *La Sirène des tropiques* (Courtesy of the Bibliothèque du Film, Paris)

discourse focusing on blackness tended to contrast nature with culture, blackness being seen as a marker of the primitive. As a modern American woman, however, Baker's exotic primitivism faced both nostalgically backwards, as well as utopianly forwards, offering 'a reconnection with the past, while pointing out a path through to the future' (Sweeney 2004: 20).

This complex ideological and temporal layering of Baker's persona, no less than the radical break that her performance marks in contemporary acting, clearly impacts on Batcheff's persona, who was similarly connoted as 'other' through his similarly exotic 'languorous' Slavism. Underlying this section on *La Sirène des tropiques*, then, is the question: what happens when two very different 'others' work in the same imaginary space? The best example of this in the film is the sequence occurring after the apprehension of Alvarez, when André and Papitou search Alvarez's office. Papitou sits on Alvarez's bookcase throwing documents away haphazardly, while André finds the letter from Sévéro asking Alvarez to kill him. They occupy very different parts of the set, Batcheff at the desk, Baker higher up perched on the bookcase. But this contrast is far less marked than the principal contrast between very different geographical locations.

The film is structured in such a way that the 'tropics' (as the intertitle has it) and everything they represent are contrasted with Paris. There are three broad sections lasting about twenty minutes each: twenty minutes establishing the two locations and the plot; twenty-eight minutes in the tropics; twenty-four minutes in Paris, with a comic transitional fourteen-minute section devoted to Papitou's transatlantic voyage prior to this last section.

There are clear and stereotypical echoes between the two locations. Both have their lecherous villain who attempts to rape the damsel in distress (Sévéro in Paris, his henchman Alvarez in the tropics). Both have a communal space: the village in the tropics, and the Place de la Concorde in Paris, where in both cases we see Papitou with children. Both have performance spaces in which Papitou dances, the difference between them being one of spaciousness; the village performance space is small and crowded, while the Olympic Palace is airy, with serried ranks of seats. Finally, both locations have a violent confrontation between André and the forces of evil: Monte Puebla in the tropics, and the park where the duel takes place, in both of which Papitou is an observer.

Such parallels serve to emphasise the deeper binary between nature and culture on which the film appears to rest. Parisian spaces are large and airy, with straight lines. The Sévéro apartment has tall columns used as framing devices together with door frames, and panelling has distinctively straight lines and sharp angles. The tropics, on the other hand, are dominated by circular or natural lines, such as the round village huts, or the S-shaped tree in which Papitou plays before going to the river to bathe.

The purpose of the section of the film located on the transatlantic liner serves to link the two locations in the most obviously geographical sense, but equally to disturb the distinction between culture and nature. The liner itself, as the word suggests, follows a linear trajectory across an unbounded ocean. Papitou's antics make the travellers mill around anarchically through the liner's ordered spaces; moreover, what might have seemed a relatively conventional slapstick routine blurs the boundaries established by the colour of skin, and functions to parody the sophistication of white westerners. Papitou over-determines her blackness by rolling in coal, only to whiten herself with flour in a reversal of black-face, before emerging from her bath like Botticelli's Venus. What began as a simplistic binary between nature and culture therefore turns into a more complex set of relations as a result of this transitional sequence.

We might wish to argue that Papitou is being punished for her attempt to take away André from Denise, and in addition for attempting to become a more sophisticated westernised woman, thereby to some extent betraying Rousseauesque and Orientalist stereotypes of the Noble Savage, not least by her parody of 'whiteness' in the transitional sequence on the liner. While both of these arguments are quite plausible, we would wish to argue that her punishment is directly related to issues of performance and agency, and that these

Figure 5.7 *La Sirène des tropiques*: Papitou cares for the wounded André (Courtesy of the Bibliothèque du Film, Paris)

are connected to her relationship with Batcheff. Put simply, she is punished for taking control of the gaze, in two senses: first, she draws the audience's gaze from Batcheff to herself, thereby weakening Batcheff as object of the gaze; second, she turns Batcheff into an even weaker object of the audience gaze by dominating him in terms of the narrative and the mise en scene.

Baker draws the gaze away by being more 'other' than Batcheff; she is black rather than white, and her acting style – by turns excessively comical or excessively tragic – is completely at odds with Batcheff's considerably more understated style. She is also more obviously active; she thus neutralises his exoticism as the languorous Slav. She constantly moves, darting to and fro across the set, nimbly shinning up trees and furniture, effortlessly scaling rocks; she is protean (parodically white with flour as well as over-determinedly black with coal). Batcheff, on the other hand, is relatively static; we tend to see him sitting (with Denise, with Sévéro, at Alvarez's desk), watching (Papitou dancing, Alvarez stealing). He is vacantly statuesque when contrasted with Baker's sinuously mercurial kinetics. One exception is the Monte Puebla sequence, although here his laboured movements across the rocks, due to his injuries, are pointedly contrasted with Papitou's lithe agility. Batcheff is 'other' by his passive immobility, which turns him into the fetishised pin-up. Baker is

Figure 5.8   *La Sirène des tropiques*: Papitou stands over André (Courtesy of the Bibliothèque du Film, Paris)

'other' by excessive mobility, and also, crucially, by her ability to shift across multiple boundaries so as to play into fetishisation while at the same time interrogating it: for example, in the coal and flour sequence.

Not only does Baker draw the gaze away from Batcheff through aspects of her performance; she also dominates him in the narrative and the mise en scene. Papitou controls André; she cares for him when he is hurt on Monte Puebla (Figure 5.7), in a masochistic-submissive trope repeated in Batcheff's next two films. She stands over him again when she promises to help retrieve the compromising situation at the end of the film (Figure 5.8), and she, rather than André, shoots Sévéro in the duel. These events conspire to undermine Batcheff's agency, who comes across as impotent and not infrequently effeminate. When he arrives in the tropics, for example, he uses a lady's fan because of the heat; in the fight with Alvarez in the caves of Monte Puebla, André ends up on the floor, saved in the nick of time by the mounted police; and, most tellingly, at the end of the film, when Papitou shoots Sévéro from her hiding place in a tree, the last we see of André is his comical incomprehension that he has shot Sévéro while shooting his gun in the air.

Finally, by having two 'others' working against each other, Baker emphasises not just Batcheff's effeminacy but more crucially his status as passive melancholic anchored in post-war trauma. While 'Baker represented the unfettered frenzy of libidinal urges breaking through the nihilism of despair' (Sweeney 2004: 50), a supremely mobile and indeed upwardly mobile reaffirmation of life after the 1.38 million dead of the Great War, correlatively Batcheff's Sad Young Man, static in the face of Baker's 'frenzy', is caught, much more obviously than he would otherwise have been, in masochistic melancholia. Her 'blackness' emphasises his 'whiteness' so that it becomes more than white; it becomes drained, lifeless, the pallor of a ghost, death contrasted with Baker's spontaneous and frenzied vitality.

We might argue that Batcheff is no more than a pin-up in some of his commercial films. By being placed next to Baker, he becomes a representative of all Sad Young Men dead on the battlefields, and those alive but shell-shocked, the alienated and traumatised younger generation – in a word, survivors.

L'ÎLE D'AMOUR (FEBRUARY 1928)

L'Île d'amour was Batcheff's thirteenth film, and was made for the same company as *Le Bonheur du jour* six months earlier, Franco-Film. It was based on a novel by a minor popular novelist (Saint-Sorny 1922), later to be remade by Maurice Cam with the same title and with Tino Rossi in Batcheff's role in 1944. Batcheff was praised for his performance, described variously as 'excellent' (Jeanne 1928), acting 'avec esprit' ('wittily'; Farnay 1928: 425), 'avec tact' ('tactfully'; Wahl 1929c: 5), and the word that constantly returns is seductive: 'Sa transformation en homme du monde pour être un peu rapide n'en est pas moins séduisante' ('His transformation into a man of the world is perhaps rather precipitate, but he is still seductive'; Trévise 1928: 28). One reviewer considered it one of his best films to date, writing that 'Rarement Pierre

Figure 5.9   *L'Île d'amour*: Bicchi learns sophistication (Collection Roche-Batcheff)

Batcheff s'est montré aussi adroit comédien que dans ce film qui lui doit une bonne partie de ses qualités' ('Rarely had Batcheff been as skilful as in this film, which owes much of its qualities to him'; Berner 1928). The film's release was overshadowed by the suicide of the film's female star, Claude France, a month before the film's release, on 3 January 1928;[4] some reviewers found the film's release so close to her death in poor taste (for example, Jeanne 1928). Her role as Xénia, an American heiress, reprised one aspect of her star persona, the well-to-do foreign traveller, usually American or English, which she had played in *L'Abbé Constantin* (Julien Duvivier, 1925) and *La Madone des sleepings* (Marco de Gastyne and Maurice Gleize, 1927). In *L'Île d'amour* she plays the bored and unfulfilled niece of an American tycoon, whose superior status allows Batcheff's character to develop from uncultured but passionate rustic, to a level of sophistication appropriate for Xénia's status (Figure 5.9).

Batcheff's role as a son of the Corsican soil legitimises considerable baring of the chest, as can be seen in a publicity still for the film (Figure 5.10). Batcheff was never more a pin-up than in this film, and Durand films him lovingly, with many close-ups of his face. The pin-up we see in Figure 5.10 is paradoxical, however, as it contains within it the two poles of his character as it develops through the film: on the one hand, he is the Noble Savage, with vital urges, and very active; on the other, his love for Xénia will lead him to

Figure 5.10 *L'Île d'amour*: Batcheff as pin-up (Collection Roche-Batcheff)

quieten down and become more sophisticated, to become even more of a pin-up, even more an object of Xénia's adoring gaze.

Bicchi begins the story as nothing in social terms; as he says to Xénia when she asks him who he is, 'je ne suis rien' ('I am nothing'). His low social status is indicated by his clothes, his violent brawling with Bozzi (who stole his fiancée from him, and for whom he nurtures a deep-seated hatred) and Batcheff's animated performance; he swings his body about, and uses his arms expressively in ways that we rarely see in his films, doing so particularly when offered what are for Bicchi enormous sums of money by Xénia and her uncle. Once he has fallen for Xénia, however, Bicchi's clothes increasingly cover more and more of his body as he wears suits and eventually dress suits, and the animation we see at the start of the film turns into sophistication, finishing with a dance at the gala opening of the poorhouse. Towards the end of the film, when he knows that he has been invited to the gala, he sits significantly by a caged songbird as he wonders how he will manage to appear sophisticated enough, suggesting the gradual taming of more natural urges, and echoing an earlier scene where he struggles out of his hospital bed to sing a love song under Xénia's window.

Bicchi's desire to be worthy of Xénia leads him to dine in an up-market hotel-restaurant with the intention of observing the clientele eat so that he can improve his manners. The scene is frankly and unusually comical for Batcheff, hinting at the more developed comedy of *Les Deux Timides* at the end of that year. Seeing customers use their knives and forks to skin pears, he tries, inappropriately, to do the same thing with a chicken leg; he ends up using his knife and hands to skin the meat, and lifting the whole leg up to his mouth.

The Noble Savage returns here in comic mode, but he also returns in a more repressed form. A short dance routine is inserted into the gala opening for Xénia's poorhouse, entitled 'A Fantasy in Black and White', with the music-hall star Mistinguett and the black entertainer Harry Flemming. As one reviewer pointed out, the routine added nothing to the action (Berner 1928), its purpose being mainly, as hinted in the pressbook, to attract a wide range of audiences, given that Mistinguett had not appeared on screen since 1917. None the less, it functions at another level as a mise en abyme of the relationship between Bicchi and Xénia, whom we will see dancing together, although less boisterously than Mistinguett and Flemming, shortly afterwards. The fact that Mistinguett's partner is black plays into the familiar trope for Batcheff of the mysterious and potentially 'savage' foreigner; but the fact that the two of them dance in a quietly sophisticated manner in stark contrast to the performers also signals the taming of the Noble Savage he was at the beginning of the film.

That taming involves the masochistic diminishing of the previously animated ephebe. Bicchi is injured when he saves a young boy from being run over by the tycoon's car. Injury reduces him to the passive etiolated object of Xénia's gaze, as can be seen in the bedside scene of the hospital in Figure 5.11, where she ends up spoon-feeding him. Later, as mentioned above, he leaves the hospital to sing an impassioned love song below her balcony, his shirt open at the neck and the wind ruffling his hair, the epitome of the Lover. His effort

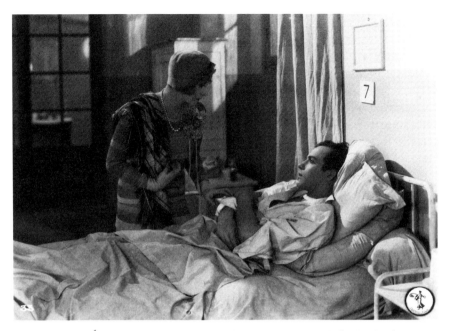

Figure 5.11 *L'Île d'amour*: Batcheff as object of the woman's gaze (Collection Roche-Batcheff)

causes him to collapse into a coma, at death's door for many days, emphasising the inevitable reality for so many of Batcheff's *jeune premier* roles; the young lover must remain passive, emptied, and he must suffer in his immobility so that a woman can gaze at him and care for him. The injured suffering lover cared for by a beautiful woman is a trope we first encountered in *La Sirène des tropiques*, and which we encounter once more, but with more sinister overtones, in *Vivre* a few months later.

VIVRE (JULY 1928)

Vivre exacerbates this new aspect of Batcheff's persona as the sophisticated but enfeebled hero. He plays Baron Derozier, stricken by tuberculosis, who falls in love with the wife of the doctor who might be able to save him, and who eventually commits suicide by an overdose of cocaine when he realises that his love is not returned. The film marked the return to the screen of Robert Boudrioz, whose *Tempêtes* (1920) for Albatros had starred Nathalie Lissenko and Ivan Mosjoukine (see Gaillard 1923). His atmospheric 'peasant' film *L'Âtre* (1923) was much praised by René Clair (see Abel 1984: 111–14), and had been followed by the less successful studio spectacular *L'Épervier* (1924; see Abel 1984: 207). Boudrioz had stated his intention of developing the 'psychological' film (Lebreton 1928b). The dramatic intensity of the film pleased some reviewers – 'Enfin, voici du cinéma intelligent! (. . .) un film humain, profond' ('At last an intelligent film! (. . .) human, profound'; Lebreton 1928b) – a sentiment echoed in a variety of trade magazines. On the other hand, *L'Écho* thought the story, adapted from a play, inappropriate for the screen, too theatrical: '*Vivre* ferait un roman magnifique, une pièce théâtrale admirable' (*Vivre* would make a magnificent novel, an admirable play'; *Écho* 1928). Another found the story artificial (Wahl 1929a: 5). Batcheff was deemed 'remarquable' ('remarkable'; Lebreton 1928b), 'charmant' ('charming'; Robin 1928: 102), and the reviewer of *Matin* wrote that he played the role 'avec beaucoup d'élégance, de délicatesse et un romantisme qui ne déplaît pas. Voilà un jeune premier qui a de la race' ('with considerable elegance, delicacy and a pleasing romanticism. This is a matinee idol who has breeding'; Frantel 1929). These are key words for Batcheff's star persona: charm, elegance, breeding, associated with upper-class characters, but tempered by passivity which could lead in its extreme form to suicidal tendencies, life imitating art four years later.

LE PERROQUET VERT (OCTOBER 1928)

Le Perroquet vert was adapted from a novel by the well-known socialite, Princess Marthe Bibesco (Bibesco 1924). In it, Batcheff, once more playing opposite Édith Jehanne, is a renegade Bolshevik, who falls in love with Natacha, the daughter of the man who gave his life to save him, only to discover that Natacha is his half-sister, his mother having been the lover of Natacha's father. Natacha goes into a convent, so the Batcheff character, ironically called Félix but far from happy, loses both his father-substitute and his half-sister. The feeling of a very Slav doom-laden fatality permeates the film. Jehanne's eyes are more heavy-lidded than they were in *Le Joueur d'échecs* seventeen months earlier; the first reel consists of her husband's sudden death and an extended flashback to her tragic childhood with a dead brother and a haunted father; the witch-like 'aïeule' ('grandmother'), all dressed in black, shows Natacha the family crypt, recounting how their forebears fell in love with their siblings, and because they could not pursue the relationship, 'moururent jeunes ou perdirent la raison' ('died young or went mad').

It was the young director Jean Milva's only released film,[5] and was generally seen as derivative in its style, being 'nettement influencé par le souvenir de Fritz Lang et de Jean Epstein' ('clearly influenced by Fritz Lang and Jean Epstein'; Marguet 1928: 163), another magazine mentioning *Das Cabinet des Dr Caligari* (Robert Weine, 1920) and the more recently released *La Chute de la maison Usher* (Jean Epstein, 1928), 'et autres productions qui constituent les romantiques de l'écran' ('and other Romantics of the screen'; Lebreton 1928a). The set was designed by Géa (Georges-Charles Augsburger), the Swiss-born satirist/caricaturist, who also plays a character in the film, and the comments refer principally to Natacha's account of a worrying dream, 'futuriste et logique en même temps' ('both futurist and logical'; Kolb 1928: 17), with a street full of Expressionist angles in the style of *Das Cabinet des Dr Caligari* and *Metropolis*. Equally, the set for the crypt where the ancestors lie, but which also serves as the meeting place for the rebels, is Epsteinian, with strategically placed shafts of light.

Batcheff was clearly suited to the part of the rebellious Russian by his origins, and he received considerable praise for what was seen as a refreshing departure from the star persona that had been forming over his previous films, that of the etiolated matinee idol: 'Nous avons vu cette fois un nouveau Batcheff, non plus un jeune premier joli, mais un homme, un partisan plein de vigueur' ('We have seen a new Batcheff, no longer the pretty *jeune premier*, but a man, a partisan full of vigour'; Marguet 1928: 163). Indeed, the first time we see him, at the beginning of the second reel,[6] he may well have his shirt open at the neck in the typical pin-up pose, but he is rushing down some stairs very energetically, his hair tousled, his mouth open and smiling, his nostrils flaring. And in much of what follows, which includes a fierce struggle between the rebels and the Bolsheviks, Batcheff runs frantically, a major departure from the much more static performance style of his previous films, even crawling up a chimney and precariously walking along the rooftops, before crawling into sewers to hide from his pursuers.

Oddly, however, all this changes in the final reel. He escapes to Nice with Natacha, and, rather as had happened in *L'Île d'amour* earlier that year, we see a transformation in his character. He wears a suit, his hair is slicked back, he walks calmly along the streets of Nice, and looks off when hugging Natacha, reverting to the performance style of his previous films. He also reverts to the static pin-up; for example, in one of the scenes where he is relaxing with his friends and Natacha, we see him against a slightly S-shaped tree, his body sinuously following the tree's contours, while the others frame him against it. The feeling of isolation this shot conveys is considerably more pronounced in one of the final scenes, where the grandmother comes like the wicked witch to spoil the lovers' wedding by announcing that they are siblings. Batcheff, unlike any of the other characters in the crowded wedding scene, is shot against a black background, the right side of his face key-lit; there follow a rapid-cut series of shots of his stricken face and the face of the parrot, representing Fate, even though at the start of the film, the point of view had been Natacha's. The end of the film, therefore, reasserts Batcheff's previous persona of the tragic Slav, carrying the burden of history and loneliness.

In the next two chapters, we turn to the films for which Batcheff is more often than not remembered, and which mark not just the apogee of his career, but also a transition in his star persona.

Notes

1. 'The cross-eyed, goofy, stereotypically blackface grin would become a kind of signature, even when – most effectively when – she was glamorously dressed, so that it seemed a parodic comment on her own beauty, on conventions of beauty, on the culture that had made her famous' (Rose 1989: 15).
2. See Ezra 2000 for a post-colonial analysis of Baker's two 1930s films, *Zouzou* (Marc Allégret, 1934) and *Princesse Tam-Tam* (Edmond Gréville, 1935). *La Sirène des tropiques* was co-directed by the veteran Henri Etiévant, and Mario Nalpas; the two of them had co-directed *La Fin de Monte Carlo* in 1926.
3. It may be worth noting that Rose's brief summary of the film inverts two sequences, the village dance and the attack on Batcheff's character in the hills; Rose did not have access to the reconstituted version. Her view of the film is that of Denise Tual's: namely, that it was 'silly' (Rose 1989: 120). She reports Tual's anecdote about Baker refusing to act unless a fur coat was bought for her (see Tual 1987: 98).
4. France began her career in L'Herbier's *Le Carnaval des vérités* (1920; see Abel 1984: 140–1). She had major roles in *Le Bossu* (Jean Kemm, 1925), *L'Abbé Constantin* (Julien Duvivier, 1925) and *Lady Harrington* (Hewitt Claypoole Grantham-Hayes, Fred LeRoy Granville, 1926), prior to *L'Île d'amour* and *La Madone des sleepings* (Marco de Gastyne and Maurice Gleize, 1927).
5. Milva was Brazilian, which worked against him in the quota system introduced in 1929: 'Parce qu'étant brésilien, Milva voit ses films frappés d'un régime défavorable: ils ne donnent au producteur que trois licences et demie (. . .) d'importation. Alors que si Milva était français, ses films vaudraient sept licences, donneraient droit à son éditeur d'introduire sept films étrangers en France' ('Because he's Brazilian, Milva's films are at a disadvantage; they only give producers three and a half import licences. If he had been French, his films would have allowed his distributors to bring seven foreign films into France'; Berner 1929: 4). There are records of a second unreleased film, *Deux Balles au cœur*, made in 1929 and co-directed with Claude Heymann. This starred the English actor Jack Trevor, and Henri Debain, who was to play Caderousse in Fescourt's *Monte-Cristo*, considered in Chapter 4.
6. The film preserved in the Cinémathèque Royale de Belgique consists of three reels.

CHAPTER 6

Comedy: Les Deux Timides *(December 1928)*

Batcheff had been the lead in two films before 1927: *Claudine et le poussin* in 1924 and *Le Secret d'une mère* in 1926. He was the lead in no fewer than six films in the two years running from June 1927 through to June 1929: *Éducation de prince*, *Le Bonheur du jour*, *La Sirène des tropiques*, *L'Île d'amour*, *Les Deux Timides*, *Un Chien andalou*. These consolidated his status as one of the leading *jeunes premiers* of the decade. The last two of these are not just the best of them; they are also closely linked, in a number of ways. They are comedies, and thereby introduce a new facet to Batcheff's skills and persona. They are by two of the great directors of European cinema, both of whom were innovators. Both films can be seen as parodies of commercial cinema. They brought Batcheff closer to what he really wanted to do: engage with cinema as an art rather than the venial commerce that had led him to despise his own status as a (reluctant) film star. Finally, in both of them the masochistic elements liminally present in so many of the films we have so far considered – illness, madness, criminality, suicide, self-sacrifice – are foregrounded. *Les Deux Timides* and *Un Chien andalou* display a troubled masculinity very different from that of many other *jeunes premiers*, not least because in these two films it is shot through with playfulness, like rays of light emerging through stormclouds.

Contemporary reception

During the second half of the 1920s, the French comic film was undergoing a renaissance, largely thanks to Albatros (see Abel 1984: 223–4); in 1924 Tourjansky made *Ce Cochon de Morin* and Volkoff *Les Ombres qui passent*. The latter film had starred Mosjoukine, who a year earlier had released *Le Braiser ardent*, to which we referred in Chapter 3. René Clair was a key figure in this renewal, making two films in particular for Albatros, after his earlier fantasy comedy shorts, *Paris qui dort* (1923) and *Entr'acte* (1924). The latter film was scripted by the Dada poet Francis Picabia, and starred amongst others Picabia and other Dada artists such as Marcel Duchamp and Man Ray, as well as composers (Erik Satie and Georges Auric). It has often been labelled 'surrealist', suggesting Clair's engagement with an avant-garde sensibility that we clearly see in Buñuel and Dalí's *Un Chien andalou*. The two Albatros films were *Un Chapeau de paille d'Italie* (1927) and *Les Deux Timides* (1928).

Albatros, originally focused on the Russian expatriate community, had decided to employ French directors early on (see Albera 1995: 12), amongst them Marcel L'Herbier, who had directed *Feu Mathias Pascal* for them (see Chapter 3). Albatros's Alexander Kamenka and Clair signed a contract for two films in May 1926 (Vezyroglou 2000: 124), leading to *La Proie du vent* which went on general release a year later. Meanwhile, Clair bought the rights to a farce by the mid-nineteenth-century playwright Eugène Labiche (1815–88), *Un Chapeau de paille d'Italie* (published in 1851), from L'Herbier early in 1927. The film premiered in July and went on general release in January 1928. It was enormously successful, partly because it satirised French bourgeois society at the end of the nineteenth century, the golden years prior to the shock of the Great War; it therefore played with a sense of nostalgia for a period of stability, but not so remote as the mid-nineteenth-century setting of Labiche's farce. Clair's contract with Albatros was renewed in October 1927, leading to a second Labiche adaptation from 1860, *Les Deux Timides*.

Unlike Clair's *Un chapeau de paille d'Italie*, this film's action is transposed into the present. Although it was popular with critics, it seems to have been less so with audiences (Vezyroglou 2000: 134). Indeed, Clair himself later disparaged the film, and is reported to have said that it was no more than a game for him (McGerr 1980: 60), an opportunity 'to render speech through images rather than sound – because it was precisely at this time that the silent era was coming to an end' (Samuels 1972: 88, cited in McGerr 1980: 60). Many commented on how 'French' the film was (e.g. Derain 1928: 37, and a piece in *Filma*, both mentioned in Vezyroglou 2000: 134). This reflected, as had *Un chapeau de paille d'Italie* before it, both nostalgia and a sense of national identity. *Cinémonde*'s reviewer wrote that Clair had delivered 'une comédie bien française d'accent, d'expression, de sujet, et ses personnages nous semblent délicieusement "avant-guerre" avec tout le regret que ce mot peut comporter' ('a very French comedy, in its tone, its means of expression, its theme, and its characters seem deliciously pre-war with all the regret the word conjures up'; Olivet 1929a: 440). It also reflected the anxiety of the French film industry in the face of the well-developed and extremely successful American comedy. *Cinéa-Ciné pour tous*'s reviewer, for example, makes this quite clear, opening his review as follows: 'Nous nous désespérâmes longtemps de ne pouvoir opposer aucune œuvre originale aux comédies américaines. L'esprit devait-il rester l'apanage des réalisateurs d'Hollywood ? . . . "Enfin René Clair vint . . ."' ('We despaired that we would ever be able to hold up a truly original work to the American comedies. Were American directors going to have the monopoly over wit? . . . "At last, came René Clair . . ."'; Épardaud 1928: 24;

see also Vezyroglou 2000: 134). One reviewer goes part of the way to explaining why the film might have struck many as quintessentially French, commenting on the film's tone: 'Il y a en lui quelque chose de gai, d'ironique et de voilé, une fantaisie un peu mélancolique et qui se moque de soi, qui l'apparente à Musset, à Gérard de Nerval, aux conteurs d'entre le dix-huitième siècle et le romantisme' ('There's something gay, ironic, hidden, a self-mocking and slightly melancholy fantasy that has echoes of Musset, Gérard de Nerval, of the story-tellers between the eighteenth century and the Romantics'; *Pour vous* 1928a: 8), recalling the kind of comments made for *Claudine et le poussin*, as we saw in Chapter 3.

Les Deux Timides, unsurprisingly, was frequently compared and contrasted with *Un Chapeau de paille d'Italie*. Some preferred it for its focus on a very human emotion, the shyness of the suitor and potential father-in-law indicated in the film's title (Régent 1929a: 5), a point also made by McGerr much later, who suggests that the 'true wonder of *Les Deux Timides* is not its technical brilliance but its ability to transcend its own flair and involve itself with the characters and their emotions' (McGerr 1980: 64). Structural similarities between the two films were noted, such as the importance of a key event: the wedding in the first film, the trial in the second (Épardaud 1928: 24). Épardaud suggested that *Les Deux Timides* consolidated the 'revolution' that *Un Chapeau de paille d'Italie* had introduced (Épardaud 1928: 24), confirming a welcome trend; in that respect, it was 'une gageure réussie plus qu'une grande œuvre' ('a gamble that worked rather than a great work'; Olivet 1929a: 400).

More often than not seen as inferior when compared with *Un Chapeau de paille d'Italie*, when taken in its own right, *Les Deux Timides* was criticised on two counts. First and foremost, reviewers felt that there were overlong passages: 'Il faiblit de temps à autre, je veux dire trois ou quatre fois. On rit et soudain l'aventure languit' ('It falters occasionally, just two or three times. There we are laughing, and all of a sudden the adventure slows down'; Wahl 1929b: 7); 'on ne peut reprocher aux *Deux timides* que de rester parfois un peu sur place' ('*Les Deux timides* occasionally grinds to a halt'; *Pour vous* 1928a: 8). Second, some reviewers felt that the mock battle at the end of the film was 'un peu forcé' ('overdone'), 'plus l'Harry Pollard que le Chaplin' ('more Harry Pollard than Chaplin'; Épardaud 1928: 25),[1] a view later repeated by Jean Mitry who felt that they unbalanced the film (Mitry 1960: 59) and upheld by Abel (Abel 1984: 231). With hindsight, it is easier for us to appreciate the parodic elements of the film, however, in which the 'overdone' mock battle plays an important part. Vezyroglou points out that the film can be seen as a parody of the cinema in the 1920s. It combines melodrama (at the start) with action adventure (the mock battle), and incorporates a nod towards the avant-garde as the audience sleep while the singer sings at the soirée organised by Frémissin's aunt, this being a possible reference to L'Herbier's *L'Inhumaine* (Vezyroglou 2000: 136). As we shall see below, *Un Chien andalou* can also be seen as a parody of 1920s cinema.

Reviewers may have had some doubts about the film; they had no such doubts about Batcheff, and in that respect this film, we might argue, consolidated his status as one of the leading *jeunes premiers* of the mid-1920s. Whereas before *Les Deux Timides* his starring roles had been in commercial films with, in his eyes, little artistic value, Clair's film showed him to be an accomplished comic actor, something that no other film had previously done. One newspaper review claimed that this was the funniest film he had ever seen and that Batcheff 'éclipse Charlot' ('outshines Chaplin'), expressing pleasant surprise that Batcheff had shown himself to be such a sensitive comic actor: 'Ce nouvel angle de Batcheff a surpris – son expression, son âpreté émouvante, l'atmosphère poétique qu'il créait, cachaient donc un ironiste ? Il dosa la gaucherie, l'hésitation, la stupeur ; le tout, coupé de voltes et fuites éperdues' ('Does the poetic atmosphere he normally creates hide an ironist? (In this film) he manages to combine awkwardness, hesitation and astonishment, the whole thing interlaced with him running around and running away'; Barancy 1928). Even Épardaud, who we may remember had complained about Batcheff's mannered acting in *Le Joueur d'échecs* (Épardaud 1927: 16), was fulsome in his praise: 'De l'interprétation très homogène un nom domine. Celui de Pierre Batcheff. Depuis ses débuts si remarqués dans *Claudine et le poussin* et sauf peut-être dans *L'Île d'amour*, jamais Batcheff ne nous avait donné une telle impression de spontanéité, d'intelligence scénique, de charme sentimental aussi. Sa composition du jeune avocat timide restera l'une des meilleures de l'écran' ('One name stands out: Pierre Batcheff. Since his debut in *Claudine et le poussin*, *L'Île d'amour* notwithstanding, never has Batcheff given such an impression of spontaneity, intelligent stagecraft and charm. His performance as a shy young lawyer will remain one of the best in the cinema'; Épardaud 1928: 25). This was echoed by François Mazeline, who wrote that 'chaque mouvement de l'acteur est une merveille chargée de sens psychologique et d'intelligence' ('Every gesture is a marvel laden with psychological meaning and intelligence').[2]

The other main actors are Maurice de Féraudy, Jim Gérald and Véra Flory. Actor-director Maurice de Féraudy, who plays the father in this film, was Crainquebille in Jacques Feyder's film of the same name (1923), and had starred alongside Claude France in *Lady Harrington* (1926). He was to make only one more film after *Les Deux Timides*, *Ça aussi ! . . . c'est Paris* (Antoine Mourre, 1929), alongside Gérald. Gérald, the wife-beating villain, was a familiar face in Clair's films, having appeared in *Le Voyage imaginaire* (1926) alongside Dolly Davis (Batcheff's co-star in *Claudine et le poussin*), *La Proie du vent*

(1927) and *Un Chapeau de paille d'Italie*; and a month before that film, he had a minor role in Batcheff's third major film, *Éducation de prince* in 1927. Opposite these well-established actors was Batcheff and the unknown Véra Flory playing the role of the daughter.[3] As was the case with *Claudine et le poussin*, Batcheff reprised a very similar story, as the male half of a young couple trying to get together, but kept apart by circumstances and the designs of an older generation.

ADAPTATION AND STRUCTURE

Clair reworked Labiche's farce considerably; indeed, to use one reviewer's words, he 'le métamorphosa' ('metamorphosed it'; Wahl 1929b: 7). Labiche's farce is a short single act with a single set and five characters: the shy and retiring father, the single-minded daughter, the wife-beating but dapper villain (who constantly and irritatingly files his fingernails), the shy lawyer and the maid. Clair's film introduces additional characters and constructs a clever imbroglio. The most significant change is that an event that is briefly recounted by Frémissin to Cécile – the trial where Garadoux was condemned to prison – is foregrounded in the film. Not only does the film open with it, but it is also an astounding bravura piece of filmmaking, with 'just about every unusual pictorial device extant in filmmaking: freeze frames, flashbacks, hand-held shots, reverse motion (. . .), split-screen' (McGerr 1980: 61). It was much admired at the time: 'de premier ordre' ('first-class'; Régent 1929a: 5), 'd'un effet irrésistible qui vaut l'excellente trouvaille de la cravate dans (. . .) *Un Chapeau de paille d'Italie*' ('irresistible, as good as the use of the tie in (. . .) *Un Chapeau de paille d'Italie*'; Épardaud 1928: 24–5). It is also the longest sequence, lasting approximately seventeen minutes. The second key change is that, while in the play Garadoux only meets Frémissin right at the end, providing the

Location	Duration (mins)	Theme
Trial	17	Frémissin's shyness in public
Aunt's soiree	7	Frémissin's shyness with Cécile
Countryside	12	
Thibaudier house	11	Frémissin's shyness with father
Aunt's house	5½	Frémissin's fear of Garadoux
Thibaudier house	22½	
Café	3½	Frémissin and Thibaudier bond
Trial	4	Frémissin and Thibaudier lose fear
Bedrooms	2	

Figure 6.1 *Les Deux Timides*: sequences in the film[4]

denouement, in the film he sees Frémissin from the Thibaudier house, allowing Clair to set up an additional narrative strand: Garadoux's attempts to keep Frémissin away from the house, leading to slapstick comedy, the mock battle and a second trial scene, none of which is in the play.

THE TRIAL

We shall analyse the film now in more detail, paying particular attention to Batcheff's character and his performance. The opening trial sequence is a technical tour de force. The opening melodrama of Garadoux abusing his wife turns out to be the prosecution's evocation of his misdeeds; there are only two intertitles, the first one being the demand for the maximum penalty by the prosecutor at the end of his speech. The prosecutor's speech is echoed by Frémissin's defence plea, evoking a loving and attentive Garadoux who brings flowers, places a cushion under his wife's feet, plays her the violin. Frémissin waxes increasingly lyrical and the screen splits first into two as we also see Garadoux cleaning her shoes, then into a third screen where he crimps her hair, until finally there are five images on screen with the happy couple in the centre surrounded by the previous images (cleaning shoes, crimping hair, violin playing) and an additional one where Garadoux brings her breakfast in bed.

It is at this point that a mouse disturbs proceedings, causing the chief judge to rise, as he tries to escape it, followed by others around the room. Pandemonium ensues, as people try to kill it. Frémissin is obliged to stop his peroration, and when asked to resume has completely lost his thread. We see the same images of domestic bliss as before, except that this time the actors freeze in mid-gesture signalling that Frémissin has frozen. He starts again; the images are fast-motioned until he reaches the same point where once again both he and the image freeze. The sequence winds backwards in reverse motion, there is an image of a winding spiral as Frémissin puts his hands over his eyes, and the hand-held camera roves wildly across the audience, marking Frémissin's complete loss of control. Urged on by his client and by the judges, he fumbles in his papers, falling on the note he made of the prosecutor's demand for the maximum penalty. This leads to uproar, and a second chase round the courtroom as Garadoux tries to beat up Frémissin.

It is made clear from the start of Frémissin's plea that much of what we see is from his point of view; second, the notion of performance is strongly emphasised, not just by the narrative situation – it is obviously a performance in a courtroom by a defence lawyer – but by the use of the gaze; when Frémissin is due to speak, we see the judges and the audience craning forwards in unison, the prosecutor and the judges in a low-angle shot bearing down on

Figure 6.2 *Les Deux Timides*: Frémissin evokes domestic bliss in the trial sequence
(Courtesy of the Bibliothèque Nationale, Paris)

him, while Frémissin is caught in a high-angle shot, making him seem puny by
contrast. Given the stress on performance, our attention is constantly drawn
to Batcheff's gestures; his hands flutter, his eyes and head dart wildly from side
to side, his lips purse as he tries to collect himself. The use of glasses has an
important role to play; his aunt holds a pair of glasses to watch him, stressing

Figure 6.3 *Les Deux Timides*: Frémissin fumbles with his pince-nez (Courtesy of the Bibliothèque Nationale, Paris)

the attention accorded to him not just by the audience but also by the judges at the bench, as the chief judge wears a pince-nez. Frémissin also wears a pince-nez, but it falls off his nose at key moments when he is flustered, stressing by contrast his inability to maintain his composure under the gaze of others.

The opening sequence does not just stress performance as a key theme of the film; it also establishes inadequate masculinity, in line with many male comic performers. Batcheff's performance, of course, works to underline this theme, his constant fidgeting contrasted with the gravitas of the judges. But the gags in this sequence, as later in the film, also work to this end. When the mouse emerges, people chase after it and try to kill it; similarly, when Frémissin breaks down, doing the exact opposite of what a defence lawyer is supposed to do, he is chased by Garadoux who tries to beat him. The implication is that Frémissin is not just timid, but timorously mouse-like, and the fear he has of Garadoux, absent from the play, surfaces to effect in the second half of the film.

COURTSHIP

The opening trial sequence is followed by three shorter sequences, the first two of which chart Frémissin's courtship of Cécile, where the main theme is the difficulty he has in overcoming his shyness. In the first of these, lasting about seven minutes, we see what purports to be their first encounter at a soiree organised by Frémissin's aunt (Françoise Rosay).[5] She plays an important part in urging Frémissin to declare his love to Cécile, unlike in the play, where she is just the sender of a letter. Frémissin and Cécile sit next to each other on the sofa, listening along with everyone else to the song recital. The fidgeting we observed in the trial sequence returns in a gag; Frémissin fiddles with a tassel on the sofa's throw, eventually working it loose. He tries to kick it under the sofa, but the aunt's dog retrieves it and takes it to her. The major event of this part of the sequence, however, is Frémissin's hesitant attempt to place his hand on Cécile's shoulder once they have been left in the drawing room on the sofa while the others are in another room. They are looking at a magazine together, allowing him to sit close to her. He tentatively tries to place his hand on her shoulder; she looks sideways at it, which causes him to retreat hastily. He tries again, and leaves it there when she does not react. No sooner has he surmounted this hurdle than the magazine they are looking at together opens on to a page where a couple are kissing passionately. This is doubly embarrassing for Frémissin, first because he is shy, but also because the song sung earlier was a setting of a mystical poem from Paul Verlaine's suite 'Sagesse', 'Il faut m'aimer', set to music by the organist of the Basilica Sainte-Clotilde in Paris, Charles Tournemire (1870–1939; the setting premiered in 1909). The title of the song might seem on first appearance to be echoing what is happening on screen; but it is in fact deeply inappropriate, as the voice asking for love in the title of the song is that of God. As soon as Frémissin realises the implications of what they are looking at, he quickly removes his hand, and Batcheff quickly looks over his shoulder at the people

Figure 6.4   *Les Deux Timides*: Frémissin fiddles with the tassel (Courtesy of the Bibliothèque Nationale, Paris)

gathered in the room next door, in a superb piece of acting. The use of his body in what follows is similarly subtle. His aunt takes him to one side to try to bolster his courage. We see Batcheff set his face resolutely, pull his arms down, as though summoning what little courage he has and striding manfully across towards Cécile. But in the next shot, he hesitates with the same forward movement we saw in *Le Joueur d'échecs* when he was with Boleslas; he leans forward repeatedly, lifting an arm up as though to speak, but is incapable of it. Cécile walks off, and Batcheff's shoulders droop ever so slightly, signalling a mixture of despair and resignation at his pusillanimity.

The next sequence, lasting about twelve minutes, shows Frémissin trying to pluck up courage to declare his love. Whereas in the play this occurs in a very brief soliloquy, as previously mentioned, in the film there is an extended scene where Frémissin acts out his declaration to an empty chair, Batcheff leaving the subtle gestures of the previous sequence and working towards expansive comic gesture. He imagines himself declaring his love volubly and dramatically, exactly the opposite of what he did at the soiree, ending up on his knees, just as his aunt walks in to his further and continued embarrassment. His shirt is open, motivated by the fact that he is in the privacy of his own room, but

Figure 6.5 *Les Deux Timides*: Frémissin acts out his declaration to an empty chair (Courtesy of the Bibliothèque Nationale, Paris)

recalling a familiar costume from his previous films, the stasis of the pin-up replaced and undermined in this scene by his increasingly desperate gestures, almost as if Batcheff relished the opportunity to parody his earlier roles.

He approaches the Thibaudiers' house, but leaves again, too shy to knock, this corresponding to the long soliloquy we quoted above. Cécile leaves the

Figure 6.6   *Les Deux Timides*: Frémissin's despair that he has a rival (Courtesy of the Bibliothèque Nationale, Paris)

house and they meet, walking through the village and out into the fields. The lovers' idyll is therefore resolutely pastoral – there are long shots of them standing in the middle of a large meadow, for example – and very different from the play, where they can only manage to exchange brief words for fear of others coming upon them. Clair here cleverly engages with the typically French tradition of the pastoral novel, where shepherds and shepherdesses talk amorously while tending their flocks, thereby creating a sentimental and apparently parenthetical space for the lovers that is redolent with nostalgia through its pastoral connotations. It is also a space whose tone is remote from the broad comedy and slapstick gags of much of the rest of the film. None the less, just as objects have played an important part in the affairs of the principal players in earlier sequences (glasses, a tassel, a chair and so on), here too objects interact closely with events and assume symbolic functions; and the space is not an idyllic interlude, but a moment of reckoning for Frémissin. The objects used are a bridge and the hats belonging to the two characters. Frémissin and Cécile cross a rickety bridge into an open meadow, signalling the passage into pastoral space. Frémissin leaves his boater on the handrail. In this new and privileged space, he finally screws up enough courage to kiss her, only to find out that she is pledged to another man. Batcheff's

Figure 6.7   *Les Deux Timides*: Frémissin 'crosses the bridge' (Courtesy of the Bibliothèque Nationale, Paris)

performance is as subtle as it was in the soiree. He steps back awkwardly, echoing his faltering steps or movements forward in other sequences; he bows slightly stiffly and walks away. On reaching the bridge, he exchanges the hats, but has second thoughts, and returns to her with both hats, after which they sit and kiss again. The play with the hats is full of significance. Whereas Frémissin had looked incongruous holding Cécile's hat in the meadow, underlining his sensitive masculinity, the resolute return towards Cécile with both of their hats suggests that he has indeed metaphorically 'crossed a bridge' and overcome his shyness.

The third sequence, half-way in the film (at about forty minutes) and lasting about eleven minutes, reprises the central conversation between Thibaudier and Frémissin (it corresponds to the ninth of twenty scenes in the play; see Labiche 1882: 179–82). Frémissin fiddles with his gloves, as he does in the play. But whereas in the play, the two men avoid the topic of marriage by talking about the weather and about horticulture, in the film there is silence. They do not talk to each other at all; their interactions are all gestural and non-verbal, Clair making full use of the resources of silent film and exploiting Batcheff's expressive talents. Much as was the case when he tried and failed to declare his love to Cécile at his aunt's, here too Batcheff uses the same performative gestures: the leaning forwards, the mouth open about to speak. Frémissin makes several false starts, but Thibaudier looks away embarrassed and Frémissin falters. He looks up at the clock, which returns twice more showing the passing of time (three hours). Thibaudier drops off to sleep reading his newspaper, and Frémissin jogs him in an attempt to wake him; then Frémissin drops off to sleep reading the newspaper that Thibaudier has passed over to him, and he in turn is jogged by Thibaudier. These repeated actions are characteristic of the relationship between the two 'timid souls'. When Frémissin leaves the house, he is threatened by Garadoux dressed as a masked bandit, again an addition to the play, as is the crowd of children who pester Garadoux, comically pinning a paper fish to his behind, which will flutter throughout much of the following sequence.

THE BATTLE

An intertitle telling us it is 'the next day' introduces us to the next major sequence and the second half of the film. Whereas the first half dealt with Frémissin's shyness, which he to some extent overcomes where Cécile is concerned, as we saw in the pastoral sequence, the second half deals with his legitimate fear of the 'masked bandit' who has warned him to stay away from Cécile. The second half is dominated by a single sequence, the 'mock battle', all of which is a completely new addition to the play. We see Frémissin and Garadoux preparing for battle by imagining that they are the victor in combat. Clair cleverly starts by cutting between the two men in their bedrooms, increasing the speed of the cuts between the parallel shots, and ending up with a split screen in which they accomplish the same belligerent and excessive gestures. Frémissin receives a telegram from Cécile, summoning him; but this is immediately followed by a letter from 'one of the masked men' telling him that going to the house will result in his death. Frémissin's bravado is punctured, and he has to be urged once again by his aunt to go. Having overcome his shyness when with Cécile (but not when with her father), Frémissin now has to overcome something that was not in the play: his fear.

The long mock battle sequence reflects more the fear than its overcoming, in that there are some fourteen minutes spent on Frémissin's timorous attempts to approach and enter the house, compared with only nine minutes once he enters to deal with the bandits. It is the first section of fourteen minutes that contains slapstick gags emphasising Frémissin's fear. We start with the group of children letting off firecrackers, which Frémissin takes to be gunshots, running away each time. His fear is further emphasised by parallel shots of the Thibaudiers' maid who, after being startled by the firecrackers and dropping plates on the floor, stuffs cotton into her ears so she can get on

Figure 6.8 *Les Deux Timides*: Frémissin imagines that he has conquered his rival (Courtesy of the Bibliothèque Nationale, Paris)

with things. Frémissin, on the other hand, merely keeps on running away each time. On one of the occasions when he has decided to run away, a car passing by has a puncture, and again Frémissin thinks it is a hold-up, raising his hands without looking back at the puzzled driver. When Frémissin finally screws up the courage to approach the house, beckoned by Cécile, Garadoux places a handkerchief over his face, points his cigar like a gun and scares Frémissin off, much to Cécile's consternation, because she cannot see what has happened from her bedroom window. The gag is repeated, but this time one of the guests emerges from the house spluttering on a cigar, and Frémissin believes him to be a second bandit. As Frémissin hides in the garden, the notary arrives and startles him; Frémissin tells him there are bandits and approaches the house again, only for Garadoux to repeat the gag a third time, causing both Frémissin and the notary to run away.

The turning point comes very literally when a game warden runs after the children overtaking the notary and Frémissin. They all turn and run back towards the house, where there is a further gag; the maid shakes her white duster from the kitchen window, and Frémissin, believing this to be the bandits surrendering, enters into the house, whereupon there is a furious battle. The point of all of these gags – the firecrackers, the masked men, the maid and her ear-plugs, Cécile not understanding why Frémissin is running away, the maid and her 'white flag' – is constantly to undermine Frémissin's masculinity (compared with the criminally macho Garadoux), just as he had been undermined by his relationship with his bossy aunt. He is scared by children, he misinterprets sounds and sights, and the women around him are more resourceful; essentially, he is presented to us more as a child than as a man, with even Cécile treating him like one.

During the fight in the house, he proves himself to be a man to some degree, slapping Garadoux and humiliating him in front of the assembled company by revealing his murky past – 'It was you the bandit; so you want to go back to prison' – and provoking more fighting. But in classic slapstick fashion, the situation is re-ordered by the maid, who has finally come through from the kitchen, and who puts an end to the fighting by beating everyone with her broom. Yet again, then, it is a woman who has the upper hand.

Frémissin's potential heroism is also undermined by the curious altercation that occurs between him and Thibaudier once the maid has shooed the others out of the house. They appear to quarrel, Batcheff in particular puffing himself up both physically and verbally. However, it is not very clear what is happening because there are no intertitles. The play's dialogue makes their misunderstanding much clearer:

> Frémissin, d'un ton résolu. – Pour la deuxième fois, je vous demande la main de votre fille!
> Thibaudier. – Monsieur, vous me la demandez sur un ton . . .
> Frémissin. – Le ton qui me convient, monsieur!
> Thibaudier, s'emportant. – Mais puisque je vous l'accorde, monsieur!
> Frémissin. – Vous me l'accordez sur un ton . . .
> Thibaudier. – Le ton qui me convient, monsieur!
> Frémissin. – Monsieur!!!
> Thibaudier. – Monsieur!!!
> Cécile, intervenant, à part. – Eh bien, est-ce qu'ils vont se quereller, à présent? (Haut.) Monsieur Jules, papa vous invite à dîner; voilà ce qu'il voulait vous dire. (Labiche 1882: 207)

> Frémissin (in a resolute tone of voice). For the second time, I am asking you for your daughter's hand!
> Thibaudier. Sir, I'm not sure I like your tone of voice . . .
> Frémissin. Sir, it's a tone that I'm perfectly happy with!
> Thibaudier (getting angry). But sir, I have already accorded you her hand!
> Frémissin. Sir, I'm not sure I like your tone of voice . . .
> Thibaudier. Sir, it's a tone that I'm perfectly happy with!
> Frémissin. Sir!!!

Figure 6.9 *Les Deux Timides*: the café sequence (Photo A. Masour, Collection Roche-Batcheff)

> Thibaudier. Sir!!!
>
> Cécile (intervening, a parte). They're not going to quarrel now, are they? (Aloud). Monsieur Jules, Daddy is inviting you to dinner, that's what he wanted to say to you.

Frémissin, and of course Thibaudier, make themselves look ridiculous by this misunderstanding, and by the absurdly inflated gestures that accompany it, Batcheff now building up excessive gesture, undermining the very notion of shyness and then fear conquered. This is well exemplified when Frémissin subsequently sits down on a chair to talk with Thibaudier, but the chair breaks in yet a further gag that works to deflate any authority gained by his heroic actions.

The remaining sequences are not part of the play either. The two men get drunk in a café as they wait for the trial where they are to defend themselves against Garadoux's family for damages.[6] Frémissin, full of his new-found fearlessness, slaps a customer on a neighbouring table for no particular reason, making himself look stupid, and he is made to look even more stupid as his action cascades comically and uncontrollably; Thibaudier slaps the customer, the customer slaps the café owner, and the owner slaps the boy serving at table.

The brief trial sequence at the end of the film – again an addition to Labiche's play – counterbalances the one at the start. Frémissin and his prosecuting adversary evoke the events of the mock battle in a series of split screens and freeze frames, but the trial descends into a brawl when Thibaudier, like Frémissin during the battle in the house, finally plucks up enough courage under the influence of drink to slap Garadoux. Order is restored by the brief coda, which returns to the use of split screens, this time three of them, suggesting at least partly a reference to Gance's *Napoléon vu par Abel Gance* with its revolutionary use of three split screens, as Abel suggests (Abel 1984: 232).

We would like to make three general points to conclude our analysis. The first relates to the issue of coherence. Although some critics felt that the film was unbalanced, as we reported above, we can see how it is considerably more coherent when viewed as a star vehicle for Batcheff. He works through a series of developmental stages where gesture is concerned. His gradual discovery of how to be less shy and less fearful – in short, how to become a man rather than a frightened boy – is anchored in gesture. This progresses from subtle gestures in the early sequences, stressing the difficulty of self-expression (with the exception of his flowery peroration in court, at least until the mouse disrupts proceedings), to rather more expansive comic gestures as he tries to vanquish his fear of the masked bandit, finally moving to broad slapstick in the mock battle, and the drunken brawl in the court. When seen in this light, the film is not unbalanced; the shifts through a range of generic devices and tones are less centrifugal dispersal than centripetal stages in a *Bildung*, as the frightened boy (echoed by the frightened father) learns how to overcome his dependence on female figures so as to express himself through action rather than words. The fact that he can only achieve this by accident (the 'white flag', getting drunk), and the fact that the journey of self-discovery is increasingly frenzied are what makes this a comedy, puncturing any sense of 'normal' masculinity by absurdly excessive inflation.

Second, we need to consider a slightly different issue of balance, relating to Batcheff's performance. McGerr has analysed the comic type of the character, relating him to both Keaton and Chaplin:

> Like Keaton (Frémissin) is pitted against those larger than him (. . .), bumbling and yet successful; while to Chaplin he owes his dignity, epitomised by the refined hand movements he makes in putting on his gloves and the delicacy with which he blows his nose. He does not have Keaton's physical abilities, though he is graceful and able to make a quick getaway when threatened, nor does he have Keaton's unflappable demeanor and mechanical mind. But the feeling of Keaton's inner strength and determination comes through constantly in Frémissin's character. (McGerr 1980: 66)

McGerr's analysis does not take into consideration Batcheff's performance, as the kinds of tool familiar to star studies had not yet been developed at the end of the 1980s. None the less, her analysis of a combination of Keaton and

Chaplin seems to us a reasonable point of departure. Batcheff's performance is Keatonesque in part, particularly where his gait is concerned; he tends to move stiffly, stepping or leaning forwards and when he runs towards Cécile in the meadow, his upper body is stiff, as his legs pump up and down awkwardly. But unlike Keaton, Batcheff's facial expressions – rather like Chaplin's – are particularly mobile; his facial muscles twitch, his mouth purses, his eyes swivel from side to side. The effect of all of this is a curious combination of the static and the mechanical one associates with the puppet or the automaton, combined with volatility; it is a constant and intriguing tension between the mercurial and the solemn, the excitable and the melancholic, Chaplin the sentimental and Keaton the mournful.

Finally, there is a general point to be made about parody. *Les Deux Timides* is quite clearly a parody of masculinity; but it is also a parody of cinema more generally, and a parody by Batcheff of his status not just in terms of his masculinity, but in terms of his status as a star in commercial cinema. In *Les Deux Timides* he is not just using aspects of previous performances, but also engaging with them parodically. For example, the 'distant look' familiar from the historical reconstructions is used to great effect in the trial sequence as Frémissin evokes domestic bliss; indeed, we could consider it a parody of those scenes in other films where he and his lover sit together, such as the close-up in *Éducation de prince*. Similarly, other aspects of Batcheff's performance parody his acting in previous films, such as the tête-à-tête with a lover. In this film, he sits primly, on the edge of his aunt's sofa, or forwards from Cécile when they are in the meadow. And the magazine they both look at while at his aunt's will be recalled parodically in the next film we shall consider, *Un Chien andalou*, which is in our view a logical progression on several levels from *Les Deux Timides*.

Notes

1. We believe this refers to the actor Harry 'Snub' Pollard rather than to the director Harry Pollard.
2. Clipping of a review from an unidentified source in the Collection Roche-Batcheff.
3. The high point of Flory's career, after a string of minor roles in the 1930s, appears to be as the star of her last film, *La Plus Belle Fille du monde* (Dimitri Kirsanoff, 1938), the story of a young American millionaire who falls in love with a blind girl who has a twin (both played by Flory). Kirsanoff was best known for *Ménilmontant* (1926), which, much like *Les Deux Timides*, used intertitles sparingly, telling the story through images (see Abel 1984: 395–402 for an extended analysis).
4. Timings are approximate.
5. This is briefly evoked in the play by Cécile, who recounts how Frémissin was so shy he became very clumsy at dinner, as reported in the synopsis above (Labiche

1882: 165-6). Here, Clair makes an extended scene which foregrounds Frémissin's shyness through gags, and by giving Batcheff the opportunity to use his body creatively.

6. As was the case in *Un Chapeau de paille d'Italie*, Clair uses synecdoche to denote the passage of time. In that film it was 'shots of an ashtray littered with an increasing number of cigarette butts' (McGerr 1980: 55). In *Les Deux Timides*, it is a growing pile of empty glasses.

CHAPTER 7

Parody and the avant-garde: Un Chien andalou (June 1929)

Un Chien andalou is probably the best-known film of the European avant-garde. As so many accounts of it point out, it as shocking now as it was some eighty years ago, principally due to the apparent slitting of a woman's eye in its first minutes. In this chapter we will review contemporary and later reactions to the film, the former rather more than has been the case in previous accounts, and we will then focus on Batcheff's role within the film. Our emphasis will be on an issue previously highlighted by Phillip Drummond and Richard Abel: the film is a parody not just of other film genres, but of Batcheff's films and of his role by 1929 as one of France's leading male stars.

CONTEMPORARY RECEPTION

Un Chien andalou ran for some eight months from November 1929 in the Montmartre cinema, Studio 28, after its opening at the Studio des Ursulines in June of that year. It is tempting to think that audiences for *Un Chien andalou* would have been the Parisian intelligentsia, a view we might well be conditioned to accept, given the status of the film as an avant-garde classic in the later years of the twentieth century. In practice, as the eight-month run suggests, the film did well, attracting a broad cross-section of the cinema-going public, as Alexandre Arnoux describes:

> J'observais, l'autre jour, un dimanche et en matinée, la salle du Studio 28. Pas d'esthètes, pas de connaisseurs, de bons spectateurs honnêtes venus au cinéma pour se divertir, quelques jeunes gens un peu mieux informés. Dès les premiers mètres, le public sursaute, s'irrite, cherche vainement à comprendre, déclare que ça le dégoûte, qu'on ne photographie pas des horreurs pareilles, que cela n'a ni sens, ni queue, ni tête. Mais ses yeux ne quittent pas l'écran, suivent passionnément le déroulement de la pellicule; il siffle l'image actuelle et attend fébrilement la suivante. (Arnoux 1929)

> (I was looking round the auditorium of Studio 28 one Sunday matinee. No aesthetes, no connoisseurs, just decent folk who had come to the cinema to be entertained, and a few younger better-informed ones. No sooner had the film started than the audience winced, fidgeted, tried vainly to understand,

voiced their disgust, that you just don't photograph such horrors, that it doesn't make any sense at all. But their eyes were glued to the screen, they couldn't tear themselves away, they whistled and hissed at the image they could see on screen while waiting frantically for the next one to follow.)

There is a fundamental tension in audience responses between attraction and repulsion; there is attraction to the surface images, combined with repulsion where the possibly deeper implications of those images are operating. We can see these two views in a series of reader columns in *Mon ciné*, which started during the film's run at Studio 28. A reader in February 1930 admires the technical qualities of the film, but complains about the lack of sense inspired by 'théories inexistantes' ('nonexistent theories'; a reference to Freudianism) and the thought processes of the mentally unstable, concluding that this is just the sort of thing you might expect from the avant-garde (*Mon ciné* 1930b: 2). This view is repeated four months later by another reader, who considers that the film represents the 'amusements de jeune gens d'avant-garde parfaitement équilibrés au point de vue mental, mais qui éprouvent une bizarre élégance à passer pour fous' ('the way young people belonging to the avant-garde amuse themselves; they are perfectly sane but for some obscure reason want to appear mad'; *Mon ciné* 1930d: 14); and a final intervention the following week supports the view that the photographic technique is good, but that the film can be seen as 'un amusement de collégiens cinégraphistes qui plus tard emploieront sans doute mieux leur temps' ('the amusement of schoolboys with cinegraphic pretensions who will no doubt later use their time more wisely'; *Mon ciné* 1930e: 2).[1]

The critics replicated this dual reaction, displacing it into related issues. Whereas audiences might simply have reacted adversely to what they felt was gratuitous violence, critics rationalised that violence as an example of the exotic and quintessentially Hispanic. Auriol wrote of 'la férocité de l'ironie espagnole' ('the ferocity of Spanish irony'; Auriol 1929), and another reviewer of the 'exagérations d'un cerveau latin, rongé par la méthode de Freud' ('exaggerations of the Latin mind, weakened by Freudianism'; Olivet 1929b: 990). Arnoux exchanged one set of clichés for another when he wrote that the film showed the 'real' Spain, not 'ce pays ridicule (. . .) de castagnettes et de toreros, mais (. . .) la véritable. Il unit naturellement le réalisme le plus grossièrement raffiné au mysticisme et au goût d'un sublime âcre et véhément; il vit dans la familiarité de l'hallucination ('the country (. . .) of castanets and toreros, but the real Spain. The film combines refined realism with mysticism and a taste for the caustically passionate sublime and the hallucinatory'; Arnoux 1929). *Pour vous*'s reviewer was only too well aware of the dangers of stereotype: 'Je regrette de savoir que M. Buñuel est espagnol. Car cela m'évoque fatalement l'Espagne et tous les clichés dont j'ai retenu les images (. . .) J'ai peur de parler d'une violence brutale' ('I regret knowing that Mr Buñuel is Spanish, because this immediately calls up Spain and all its clichés, so my imagination muddies my critical faculties (. . .) and I worry that I'll end up talking about brutal violence'; Lenauer 1929: 4). Finally, even Brunius, the fellow-traveller, talked of how Buñuel had 'ce qui peut nous séduire dans le caractère espagnol' ('the seductiveness of the Spanish character'), manifested in the film by 'une violence sans espoir' ('violence without hope'; Brunius 1929a: 68).[2]

It is important to place the film in its industrial and intellectual contexts. Where the first is concerned, *Un Chien andalou* came at a time when sound was beginning to be introduced. While at one level it clearly shows a mastery of silent film techniques, it can also be seen as a transitional film. One reviewer places the film, together with Man Ray's *Les Mystères du Château de Dé*, in the context of the hiatus between silent and sound film, arguing that these avant-garde films compensate for the dearth of commercial films as producers prepared for sound cinema. He, like many other reviewers, argues that the film's success is largely down to its humour, which he links to Chaplin's: 'Un humour absolument personnel, âpre, fort, imbibe chaque image (. . .) Un humour qui bouscule à tout instant l'équilibre du monde, libre, cruel et audacieux (. . .) celui de Chaplin (. . .) Et quelle réalisation impeccable. Quelle technique simple et sobre!' ('Each image is full of an absolutely personal humour, fierce and strong (. . .) A humour upsets the status quo, free, cruel, bold (. . .) Chaplin's humour'; Gorel 1929: 855). This feeling of a return to the poetic, as the same reviewer argues, while waiting for the industry to organise itself and align with the new technologies, might well explain why many critics enthused about the film, much to Buñuel's amazement.

The other important aspect of context is the intellectual one, on which we will spend a little more time. Critics, as can be seen in one of the above comments, regularly rationalised the difficulty of interpreting the film by claiming that the film was related to the newly fashionable Freudian theories. Arnoux, for example, whom we have already quoted at length, advised his readers that the film was 'matière à la mode, matière freudienne. Le refoulement (. . .), la perversion sexuelle, la libido, le transfert, les complexes coulent à pleins bords' ('fashionably Freudian. Repression, perversion, libido, transfer (. . .) complexes spill over throughout'; Arnoux 1929). *Cinémonde*'s review starts thus: 'Freud ! Que de crimes on commet en ton nom' ('Freud! What crimes are committed in your name'; Olivet 1929b: 900). Another reviewer, whose review was entitled 'Fakirs . . . fumistes' ('fraudsters and jokesters'), expressed surprise at the favourable reactions of many journalists, suggesting that they, like everyone else, did not understand the film, but pretended to do so out of snobbery: 'Seuls certains snobs s'enthousiasment de telles œuvres; ils n'y comprennent pas grand-chose eux non plus; (. . .) et puis, il peuvent toujours faire intervenir le grand nom de Freud au milieu de leurs divagations; ils n'en demandent pas plus. Si le philosophe Viennois pouvait les entendre, qu'est-ce qu'il leur passerait' ('Only snobs enthuse about such films; they don't really understand them; (. . .) and then they can always invoke Freud's name to back up their ramblings. If only the Viennese philosopher could hear them, what he wouldn't do to them'; Saubes 1929).

As a corrective to these views, it is worth quoting extensively a piece by the cinema buff Paul Ramain[3] the year after these exchanges. Ramain, as Richard Abel points out, 'passed himself off as a doctor of psychology, although he apparently had no formal training' (Abel 1988: 364), and we can see how in the following extract he stakes a claim to what is essentially a rather spurious medical authority. His review attempts to establish the film as artifice, as a conscious simulation of states of insanity:

> Ce film est un essai d'illustration psychanalytique, une association assez suivie des phantasmes engendrés par la lecture toujours mal comprise, toujours mal assimilée, de la théorie du refoulement et de la libido mise à la mode par Sigmund Freud. Ainsi les critiques qui discutent l'œuvre de Buñuel sur cette base ont raison quant au fond et ont tort quant à la forme (. . .) *Un Chien andalou* n'est donc pas un rêve. C'est presque une confession. C'est une œuvre consciente d'images vivantes extraites d'un état subconscient d'images refoulées. Là, autant que dans sa technique, réside le grand intérêt dudit film, ainsi que son extraordinaire puissance, et sa ténébrante perversité qui agit sur vous, même blasés . . . (. . .) J'ai vu d'admirables dessins faits par des aliénés obsédés (. . .) qui sont de la même veine visuelle que la moitié des images du fameux et enfantin *Chien andalou* (. . .) Sans (. . .) Freud, le film de Buñuel n'eut *jamais* vu le jour sous la forme actuelle : il serait resté la suite d'images, non-coordonnées entre elles, que certains aliénés exécutent avec un réel sens artistique et persuasif. C'est pourquoi Buñuel raisonne et fit une œuvre somme toute intelligente, bien que primitive et non raffinée : explosion d'un tempérament mal bridé et sincère dans l'erreur et la perversion *en partie* voulue. (Ramain 1930: 7; his emphases)

(The film is an illustration of psychoanalysis, a coherent association of fantasies generated by a mistaken and poorly understood view of Freud's fashionable theories of repression and libido. Critics who talk about Buñuel's film from this point of view are therefore correct in terms of content but are mistaken in terms of form (. . .) *Un Chien andalou* is not a dream, it's almost a confession. It is a consciously composed set of living images extracted from a subconscious state of repressed images. The film is interesting for this reason as much as for its technique, and it is this which accounts for its extraordinary power, and its dark perversity which affects you no matter how blasé you are . . . (. . .) I have seen admirable drawings by the mentally ill (. . .) which are in the same vein as many of the images we find in the famous and facile

Un Chien andalou (. . .) Without (. . .) Freud, Buñuel's film would *never* have seen the light of day in this form; it would have remained a set of uncoordinated images such as those sometimes produced by the insane who have artistic leanings. Buñuel has operated rationally and made a film that is intelligent, even if it is primitive and unrefined; it is the explosion of an unbridled temperament, sincere in its misapprehensions, and in its *partly* deliberate perversion.)

It is important to note that Ramain is not taking Buñuel to task for fraudulence; he stresses the 'sincerity' of Buñuel's project. Whereas other critics had merely latched on to Freud as a marker of modernity, Ramain is conscious of the way in which Buñuel uses 'Freudianism' as artistic material consciously fashioned into an aesthetic object. He was writing this only a few months before the publication in November 1930 of a canonical surrealist text, *L'Immaculée Conception* (Breton and Éluard 1930). The first section of this collection of texts was imbued with Freudian concepts found in the second of the *Three Essays on the Theory of Sexuality*; and the central section, 'Possessions', consisted of texts that mimicked different states of madness (debility, mania, paralysis, delirium, schizophrenia), extending earlier surrealist preoccupations with states of madness, as we discussed in Chapter 3. (We shall return to this text in our discussion of hysteria in the next chapter.)

As was the case with Breton and Éluard's collection, in *Un Chien andalou*, Freud is base matter to be playfully rearticulated as poetic gold. Robert Short reminds us that the surrealists may well have been inspired by Freud, but that they did not necessarily subscribe to Freudianism and its ideological underpinnings, stating that the film 'is a play not only *of* the Freudian paradigm but *with* it' (Short 2002: 98). This is why, as Ramain hinted in the extract quoted above, any attempt to normalise the kaleidoscopic flow of images into a linear narrative, focused on a singular subjectivity – whether the character played by Batcheff (his 'dream' or his 'fantasy'), or some kind of metatextual and abstract subjectivity – was missing the point. Oddly, an article by Jean Goudal in 1925 had already pointed to the way in which 'the cinema functioned not as a *representation* but as a *construction*, an approximation of the *form* of unconscious desire' (Abel 1988: 338; his emphasis), suggesting that it was 'une *hallucination consciente*' ('a conscious hallucination'; Goudal 1976: 308/Goudal 1978: 51; his emphasis). But this view was not to be taken up until the 1960s, as we shall see below.

Buñuel himself was startled by the favourable audience reactions: 'I was stupefied [sic], confused, by the avalanche of enthusiasm which its showing awakened. I actually believed it was a joke' (cited in Aranda 1975: 58). This is no doubt one of the reasons why he wrote a brief preface for the shooting script of the film which appeared in the surrealist journal *La Révolution surréaliste* alongside the equally aggressive second manifesto of surrealism by André Breton. One of the most famous passages from Breton's text concerns an act of brutal aggression, and we can compare it with the preface to the shooting script:

> L'acte surréaliste le plus simple consiste, revolvers au poing, à descendre dans la rue et à tirer au hasard, tant qu'on peut, dans la foule. Qui n'a pas eu, au moins une fois, envie d'en finir de la sorte avec le petit système d'avilissement et de crétinisation en vigueur a sa place toute marquée dans cette foule, ventre à hauteur de canon. (Breton 1929: 2)

> (The simplest Surrealist act consists of dashing down into the street, pistol in hand, and firing blindly, as fast as you can pull the trigger, into the crowd. Anyone who, at least once in his life, has not dreamed of thus putting an end to the petty system of debasement and cretinisation in effect has a well-defined place in that crowd, with his belly at barrel level.) (Breton 1972: 158)

> La publication de ce scénario dans *La Révolution surréaliste* (. . .) exprime, sans aucun genre de réserve, ma complète adhésion à la pensée et à l'activité surréalistes. *Un chien andalou* n'existerait pas si le surréalisme n'existait pas. *Un film à succès*, voilà ce que pensent la majorité des personnes qui l'ont vu. Mais que puis-je contre les fervents de toute nouveauté, même si cette nouveauté outrage leurs convictions les plus profondes, contre une presse vendue ou insincère, contre cette foule imbécile qui a trouvé *beau* ou *poétique* ce qui, au fond, n'est qu'un désespéré, un passionné appel au meurtre. (Buñuel 1929a: 34)

> (This scenario (. . .) expresses without reservation of any kind my complete adherence to the thought and activity of the surrealists. *Un Chien andalou* would not have existed if surrealism had not existed. *A successful film* is what the majority of people who saw it thought. But what can I do about people who are crazy for anything new even when the novelty outrages their innermost convictions, or a venal or insincere press, or about that pack of imbeciles who found *beauty* or *poetry* in what is, essentially, nothing less than a desperate, passionate appeal to murder.)[4]

LATER ACADEMIC COMMENTARY

Academic commentators, encouraged no doubt by Buñuel's statement in 1947 that 'the only method of investigation of the symbols would be, perhaps, psychoanalysis' (Buñuel 1978: 153), began applying psychoanalytical frameworks as early as 1949 (see Piazza 1949, Mondragon 1949).[5] These remained largely unknown, as Renaud later pointed out in his own psychoanalytical reading (Renaud 1963: 149), and it is only with Durgnat's book on Buñuel in 1968 that an academic psychoanalytical reading gained a wide audience. Durgnat, like

Mondragon and Renaud before him (both of whom he quotes), assumed that a psychoanalytical interpretation of *Un Chien andalou* should tell an allegorical master narrative, filling the gap left by the evident fractures of the film. The fact that the psychoanalytical interpretations by Mondragon, Renaud and Durgnat are all slightly different did not appear to be a problem for Durgnat, who points out that 'in the indiscriminate, global terms of the unconscious, each formulation is an aspect of another, each applies to a different sphere of experience, a fundamental pattern of repression, rage and panic' (Durgnat 1968: 38). What the three readings have in common is that they all recount the sexual development of a single hypothetical protagonist. The shortest of these is Mondragon's, which we reproduce here (the account contains inaccuracies):

> Il était une fois un petit enfant qui avait été conçu [plan correspondant: rasoir frotte sur du cuir]; lorsqu'il fut à terme [pleine lune], il naquit [cf. la membrane de l'œil coupé]. Puis il grandit, fit ses premiers pas [ce que Buñuel illustrerait par le personnage en bicyclette ayant autour du cou une bavette]; mais sa démarche est encore incertaine, il tombe et a besoin de sa mère pour se relever. S'il aime sa mère, il se chérit lui-même, il cherche dans son propre corps les sources de son plaisir [cf. les mains perforées où grouillent les fourmis] et trouve parmi ses compagnons un camarade à qui donner son affection [c'est-à-dire l'être androgyne filmé dans la rue]. Puis il se tourne vers la femme-mère et veut la saisir à différentes reprises. Toujours barré par son sur-moi, il traîne derrière lui tout un passé [des citrouilles ou les traditions ancestrales; des frères des écoles chrétiennes ou les contraintes de la morale catholique; un piano, ou des harmonies immuables, enfin des ânes ou la stupidité]. Il a tendance à faire des régressions infantiles lorsqu'il se souvient des ses livres et de ses cahiers de classe; il se révolte contre lui-même et tente de tuer ce moi qui le condamne à demeurer enfant. Personne ne l'aide [les personnages dans le parc restent immobiles, insensibles au cadavre emporté]. Un jour, une femme vient à lui: il ne sait pas l'accueillir avec simplicité, se moque d'elle [rouge à lèvres]. Comme un autre garçon l'appelle, vexée, elle court se jeter dans ses bras. (cited in Renaud 1963: 149–50)

(Once upon a time there was a small child who was conceived (corresponding shot: the razor stropped on leather); when the pregnancy was reaching its end (full moon), he was born (c.f. the slit eye). Then he grew up, learnt how to walk (which Buñuel illustrates with the character on a bicycle wearing a bib); but his steps are unsteady, he falls and needs his mother to get up again. Although he loves his mother, he also loves himself, seeking pleasure from his own body (c.f. the hands with holes where ants are swarming) and finds amongst his companions someone whom he can love (i.e. the androgyne filmed in the road). Then he turns to the Mother, trying to grab her. Stopped by his super-ego, he drags his past behind him (gourds or ancestral traditions;

monks or the constraints of Catholic morality; a piano, or immutable har-
monies, and finally donkeys or stupidity). He reverts to infantile regressions
when he remembers his schoolbooks; he rebels against himself and attempts
to kill the ego which condemns him to remain a child. Nobody helps him (the
characters in the park do not move, indifferent to the body being taken away).
One day, a woman comes to see him: he does not know how to handle her,
and makes fun of her (the lipstick). Another man calls her; annoyed, she
throws herself into his arms.)

The problem with this kind of approach was highlighted by the next major
type of critical approach, the semiotic, although not before the surrealist
scholar John Matthews had pointed out how the film was a critique of 'van-
guard trends', 'an attack upon systematisation in film commentary' and comprising 'deliberately humorous effects' (Matthews 1971: 85, 87).[6] Phillip
Drummond pointed out how the 'whole film has still to be rescued from the
ravages of a primitive psychoanalysis bent on the unearthing of a straightforward psychosexual allegory at the "core" of *Un Chien andalou*' (Drummond
1977: 91). Stephen Kovács tried to take a broader view, accepting that at one
level the film was a psychosexual allegory, but not trying to force every detail
into it as previous commentators had done; moreover, he stressed other key
aspects of the film, such as its humour, and even more so the tactility of the
images which Buñuel uses to evoke an instinctual and non-rational response
(Kovács 1980: 196–210).

Under the impact of critical theory arising in the wake of May 1968, semiotic criticism, inherited from Metz in his mid-1960s structuralist phase and
based on a disinterested and sceptical analysis of the object, resisted judgement or the ascription of meaning, particularly a meaning generated by the
surrealist movement itself, confining its analysis to aspects of disruption,
similar in that respect to the views of Jean Goudal reported above.
Drummond's painstaking formalist description of *Un Chien andalou*, which
appeared in *Screen* in 1977, is the best example of this approach.

During the early 1970s, Metz moved away from semiotic and structuralist
approaches to a Lacanian-inspired psychoanalytical approach which was considerably more rigorous than the early psychoanalytical views. Whereas
Mondragon, for example, had posited a unified subject as the origin of
meaning (*Un Chien andalou* being the dream of a unified subject, or the the-
matised development of that subject), Metz's approach examined film as a
vehicle for the positioning of the spectator, attempting to answer not 'what
does this film mean?', but 'in what position does this film place the spectator?'
Among the various critics Drummond patiently and ruthlessly dismantled in
1977 was Linda Williams in her study of *Un Chien andalou*'s prologue, which
had appeared in *Screen* the previous year (Williams 1976). Williams developed

her approach in a major work in 1981, inaugurating a new trend in surrealist film criticism, inspired by the psychoanalytic Metz of the mid-1970s and Jean-Louis Baudry. Durgnat, keen to use Buñuel's own suggestion that psycho-analysis might be the only productive way to analyse *Un Chien andalou*, had used psychoanalysis uncritically, applying it to tell a 'story' which the film is bent on undermining. Williams's approach was to conceive of the film's disruptions not as something to be resolved, but as the whole point of the film. As she said, 'unconscious desire, if it is to be present in film in the way in which it is present in dreams, cannot also be "represented" there as a subject: it must be perceived, as the unconscious desires of dreams are perceived, through the transgressions of a more familiar discourse' (Williams 1981: 28).

This approach corresponded to the more general late 1970s view of the film as formal and parodic play with cinematic conventions, already broached by Matthews in 1971. Allen Thiher, for example, viewed the film as 'an antigame that, by the systematic way it proposes to destroy the rules of earlier cinematic genres, transforms itself into a superior form of play' (Thiher 1979: 25),[7] also pointing out, more clearly than Ramain, that part of that play was 'ludic subversion' of psychoanalytic discourse itself (Thiher 1979: 36). Michel Marie, at about the same time, commented that the film's intertitles 'constitute in parodic form a theoretical reflection on the function of intertitles in the silent cinema' (Collet *et al.* 1976: 171; cited in Abel 1988: 481). And Drummond suggested in passing that 'it is not unreasonable to detect a parody in *Un Chien andalou* of (Batcheff's) previous conventional romantic roles' (Drummond 1977: 78–9).

Unsurprisingly, perhaps, given that Star Studies only developed as a field of study during the 1980s, neither of the two broad views we have just outlined – that the film is a psychosexual Freudian allegory, or conversely that it is a parody of filmic conventions – takes account of Batcheff's role as star. It is arguably odd that Batcheff's star persona has not been used to smooth over the structural and narrative discontinuities of the film. Drummond mentions *La Sirène des tropiques* as the most likely parodic intertext, and indicates very briefly how the star might form the focus of an investigation: 'Such a connection installs *Un Chien andalou* within the realm of parody by isolating the "star", underpinned by authorial continuity, as the main axis for its intertextuality with previous cinema' (Drummond 1977: 79). The suggestion of 'authorial continuity' indicates how Drummond might well have felt that Batcheff's image, combined with his friendship with Buñuel during *La Sirène des tropiques*, would act as a glue for the disparate fragments and unstable characters of the film; his later article on the film does not take up this challenge, however, merely restating the main theses of the 1977 article (see Drummond 2004). Richard Abel built on Drummond's sense that Batcheff's role may well represent a parody of his previous roles by picking up on more than just *La Sirène des tropiques*: 'His various selves may seem parodic forms of his earlier screen roles – the self-sacrificing heroes of *Joueur d'échecs* (1927) and *Napoléon* (1927) and the sentimental heroes of *La Sirène des tropiques* (1928) and *Les Deux Timides* (1929)'[8] (Abel 1984: 483).

PARODY OF PREVIOUS FILMS

Our view is that an exploration of how Batcheff's image is inflected by this film is crucial to its understanding; but, equally, we reject any notion of 'continuity'. On the contrary, in the same way that commentators during the late 1970s pointed to the necessary dismemberment of the film, so too we shall focus on a necessary discontinuity in the use of Batcheff as star, both in the way in which we can interpret his function in the film, and also in the general trajectory of his career. Shifting the emphasis on to Batcheff will also, crucially, replace the film into the contexts of its reception in 1929. Much ink has been spilled on the respective contributions of Buñuel and Dalí to the film; but they were, in comparison to Batcheff, complete unknowns in 1929 where the general public was concerned. No commentators – with one exception – have suggested that Batcheff himself may have played an important part in the film, extending beyond just acting a role. The exception is Michael Richardson, who, while admitting that the film is very much a collaboration between Buñuel and Dalí, adds: 'One feels that Pierre Batcheff's contribution must also have been of some significance' (Richardson 2006: 28); but he does not pursue the issue further. We have already discussed Batcheff's contribution from a biographical perspective in Chapter 1. In what follows, we will address in more detail the issue of parody: parody of previous films and, in the following chapter, parody of the notion of the star in the 1920s.

Drummond was the first to explore possible echoes of other films, pointing out the physical resemblance between Batcheff and Buster Keaton, as others had before him, as we saw in Chapter 2. In his view, the sequence in *Un Chien andalou* where Batcheff hauls the two pianos across the room could be seen, particularly given Buñuel's interest in Keaton (he had reviewed *College* in 1927; see Buñuel 1927), 'as an attempt to re-stage the kind of gag typified by Keaton's own attempt to haul a piano into his new and equally unstable home in *One Week* [1920]' (Drummond 1977: 79).[9]

In the same year, Thiher was concerned to show how the film 'parodies some standard mimetic devices of the times' (Thiher 1979: 31),[10] and suggests that the film refers to *Feu Mathias Pascal* on more than one occasion. The first of these occasions is the scene where Mareuil has been staring at the reproduction of Vermeer's *Lacemaker*, then looks up abruptly and goes to the window:

The woman's rising and looking down in surprise is a parody of the type of cutting used in L'Herbier's *Feu Mathias Pascal* when the young heroine looks down into the street from her window and is frightened by the appearance of the sinister medium, Caporale. The high-angle shot, linking the inner world with the outer world (as in the Vermeer paintings that the Buñuel heroine is looking at) is usually motivated by some form of revelation that the filmmaker wishes to dramatize. But Buñuel uses shooting angle and cutting so that they turn against themselves, serving only to underscore the absurd revelation of a cyclist who gratuitously falls on his head. (Thiher 1979: 29–30)

One might argue that such a technique is generic to a large number of films. Thiher's second example from *Feu Mathias Pascal* is rather more specific in that it deals with the use of the double, and the way in which it parodies the 'subjective mimesis' (Thiher 1979: 31) attempted by the so-called Impressionists during the 1920s (the better-known of whom are Dulac, Epstein and L'Herbier).[11] He is referring to the sequence we explored in Chapter 3, where Mathias/Mosjoukine splits into two personalities, the discreet and the aggressive, and comparing it with the moment in *Un Chien andalou* when the Man/Batcheff splits into two characters, one of whom kills the other with guns blazing in both hands.[12]

Batcheff played a role in *Feu Mathias Pascal* which was significant precisely for its links to hysteria and epilepsy used as a front for a duplicitous character; it was therefore a role that also emphasised the split personality of the main character played by Mosjoukine. None the less, the echoes of previous films in *Un Chien andalou* are much more obviously, as both Drummond and Abel suggested, those of the films in which Batcheff played more significant roles. In the absence of copies of all Batcheff's films, we cannot do a thorough review of likely parodic references to his earlier films in *Un Chien andalou*. However, as several of the comments in previous chapters have indicated, there are standard situations in which Batcheff's characters find themselves, which are more than just the generic roles of self-sacrificing and sentimental heroes listed by Abel.

Given Batcheff's typical role as a lover, it is hardly surprising that the basic narrative situation of *Un Chien andalou* is his pursuit of Simonne Mareuil. Of the seventeen films preceding *Un Chien andalou*, his role involves the amorous pursuit of a woman in nine (*Claudine et le poussin, Princesse Lulu, Éducation de prince, Le Joueur d'échecs, La Sirène des tropiques, L'Île d'amour, Vivre, Le Perroquet vert, Les Deux Timides*). Interestingly, his character steals money or its equivalent in three of the remaining eight films, all from early on in his career (*Autour d'un berceau, Le Double Amour, Feu Mathias Pascal*). *Un Chien andalou* trades on Batcheff's amorous hero persona, but explodes the conventions of such romantic roles by making his desire excessive and over-determined. In *Le*

Joueur d'échecs, as we saw in Chapter 4, there is a long sequence where he paints Sophie, the situation requiring him to stare intently at her. In *Un Chien andalou* he also stares obsessively at the woman, but desire is writ large and excessively on Batcheff's face, the most obvious example being when he caresses what we take to be Mareuil's bare breasts and buttocks. His character also incorporates the criminal element associated with stealing in the early films, as he appears to steal the hair under Mareuil's arm.

More specific than these generic situations is the trope we have previously mentioned of the passive effeminate hero. In many of his films, Batcheff ends up lying in bed or on a sofa, ill or wounded or desperate, more often than not tended by a woman. This is such a persistent trope that it is clearly no coincidence when it reappears liminally in *Un Chien andalou*, Mareuil tending him in the street when he has fallen off his bike, and a few shots later watching over the bed where the clothes associated with him are laid out. His desperation as a gambler leads his mother to comfort him as he lies in her arms in their apartment in *Le Double Amour*. Similarly, in *Le Secret d'une mère*, Marcel Vincent defends Denise from an importunate suitor, and is hurt in the resulting fight; his adoptive mother tends him as he lies in bed. Batcheff's characters are tended by their lovers as well as their mothers. His desperation as a young lover leads Claudine to cradle him protectively in her arms in *Claudine et le poussin* (Figure 3.3). In *Destinée*, Roland is wounded during the Battle of Lodi, and Floria tends him at his hospital bedside. Similarly, in *L'Île d'amour*, he is injured by a car driven by the rich uncle of the woman he loves, when he is trying to save a young boy from being run over; he ends up in hospital, where Xénia visits him and looks after him (Figure 5.11). In *La Sirène des tropiques*, André Berval is attacked by the villain and his henchmen in the remote countryside, and is tended by Papitou as he lies concussed (Figure 5.7). In two of the films released close to *Un Chien andalou*, Batcheff is under the influence of drugs. In *Vivre* the consumptive Baron attracts the attention of the doctor's wife, and eventually commits suicide through an overdose of cocaine; while in *Monte-Cristo* Albert also succumbs to the effect of drugs, this time hashish, watched over by the Orientalised Count. This trope of passivity, touched with effeminacy and hedonism, can also be seen in a more valiant mode with Batcheff's General Hoche in *Napoléon*, where he graciously and self-effacingly gives up Josephine to Napoleon. In *Un Chien andalou*, then, we find clear references to a passive, effeminate and frequently bed-ridden character, who is looked after by the woman, whom he frequently loses to another man.

There are more minor isolated references to previous films. In both *Claudine et le poussin* and in *L'Île d'amour* a car accident plays a significant role. In the first, it is Claudine and her family who crash outside the Puygiron family home; while in second, it is, as we noted above, Bicchi who is knocked over.

Given that in this second film the car accident motivates the love affair, it is not unreasonable to see the death of the androgyne followed by Batcheff's pursuit of Mareuil as a reference to that film, which had been released only eighteen months before. We have already noted that Mareuil's intense scrutiny of Vermeer's *Lacemaker* is a strong echo of the scene in *Les Deux Timides,* when Batcheff's shy character and the woman he finds it difficult to declare his love to are leafing through a magazine and end up looking embarrassingly at a picture of two lovers kissing passionately. This point in no way detracts from the well-explored links between the Vermeer and Dalí's iconography of the period (see, for example, Short 2002: 76–7), or indeed other ways of considering the function of the image;[13] rather, it adds another layer to the polysemic images of the film. Finally, the scene in which Batcheff shoots his double, who shakes his head sadly and falls, inexplicably not in the room but in a park, his hands scraping down a naked woman's back, is a direct reference to *Le Joueur d'échecs.* In a key scene of that film, the lovers plight their troth in the gardens of the castle, surrounded by statues; in the close-up of their faces, Batcheff has the same dreamily distant look of the double just before the double is shot, and his fall in the park against a real woman looking like a statue refers back to the statues surrounding the lovers in *Le Joueur d'échecs.*

Given Batcheff's characters' relationships with generally strong women who mother him or who direct him, and given his generally passive presence in his films, here undermined by excessive expressions of desire, audience views of Batcheff's parodic persona in *Un Chien andalou* would undoubtedly have been affected by the presence of Simonne Mareuil. To our knowledge, no commentators have explored this aspect of the film, beyond the occasional very brief biographical mention in passing.[14] We shall therefore explore Mareuil's persona before returning to more theoretical considerations of parody.

SIMONNE MAREUIL

Simonne Mareuil (born in 1903) had begun her film career in 1921 with a walk-on part in Henri Desfontaines's *Chichinette et Cie*, appearing in minor roles in some eighteen films before *Un Chien andalou*, usually, according to an early interview, as a chambermaid (Henry 1926: 22). The better-known ones in the early part of her career were *Jocelyn* (Léon Poirier, 1923; see Abel 1984: 102–3, 259) and *Paris* (René Hervil, 1924; see Abel 1984: 125). By 1925, she had more substantial roles; in *Chouchou poids-plume* (Gaston Ravel, 1925), she was described favourably by an enthusiastic reviewer prone to questionable similes as 'le petit moineau parisien, toute de charme, de gaminerie, de grâce juvénile: deux grands yeux étonnés, une petite bouche gonflée comme un fruit des tropiques mûri à l'aurore' ('a little Paris sparrow, all girlish charm and full of youthful grace: two big saucer eyes, a small plump mouth like some ripe tropical fruit at dawn'; Querlin 1925: 20). By the following year she was signalled as an up-and-coming star with a two-page spread in *Cinéa-Ciné pour tous* (Henry 1926: 21–2), and in 1927 she had her first lead role in *Genêt d'Espagne* (Gérard Ortvin), followed by *Peau de pêche* (Jean-Benoît Lévy and Marie Epstein) in March 1929, a few months before the release of *Un Chien andalou*. In this film, a young boy gradually falls in love with his older cousin, played by Mareuil (see Abel 1984: 137). While *Un Chien andalou* had its long eight-month run, audiences would also have seen her in her next film, *Ces Dames aux chapeaux verts* (André Berthomieu), which was released in October 1929. Mareuil plays a young Parisian who stays with provincial cousins; she manages to arrange the marriage of one of them, while at the same time getting her own man. She made eight more films, mostly in the 1930s, but generally in small roles,[15] before committing suicide in 1954.

Mareuil's star persona in the late 1920s was very much that of a comic star; Henry pointed out in his 1926 article that French cinema 'qui jusqu'ici ne comptait guère qu'une jeune première de comédie en la personne de Dolly Davis,[16] en possède maintenant une deuxième avec Simonne Mareuil' ('which up until now only seemed to have one *jeune première* in the comic mould in the person of Dolly Davis, now has a second one with Simonne Mareuil'; Henry 1926: 22). *Peau de pêche* and *Ces Dames aux chapeaux verts* gave her image a certain wholesomeness, as can be seen in the following extract from an article in *Pour vous*, which helps us situate the way in which audiences might well have viewed Mareuil at the time of *Un Chien andalou*:

> Comme il y a loin du *Chien andalou* à *Peau de pêche*! (. . .) Simonne Mareuil a su réussir dans les genres les plus opposés. Nous l'avons vue, dans *Peau de pêche*, jeune campagnarde plantureuse, fille des champs perchée sur une haute charrette de foin, une fourche sur l'épaule, un brin d'herbe entre les dents . . . Nous l'avons vue courir dans les blés coupés, jouer à cache-cache derrière les gerbes, tourner éperdument autour d'un arbre pour que le garçon du village ne parvienne pas à l'attraper. Dans *Ces dames aux chapeaux verts*, elle est devenue la petite Parisienne scandalisant les braves gens du village, se moquant des vieilles demoiselles de la sous-préfecture dont les guimpes montent jusqu'au menton, du professeur de collège (. . .) amoureux et timide, riant de tout, enfin . . . Et c'est dans ce village dont elle s'est tant moquée qu'elle trouvera l'amour. (Régent 1929b: 4)

> (What a difference there is between *Un Chien andalou* and *Peau de pêche*! (. . .) Simonne Mareuil has been successful in very different genres. In *Peau de pêche* she was a buxom country girl, running wild in the meadows and perched high on hay carts, a hayfork over her shoulder, and chewing on a stalk of grass . . . We saw her running across the mown meadows, playing hide and seek behind

the sheaves, chased round and round a tree by a boy from the village. In *Ces Dames aux chapeaux verts*, she was the little Parisian shocking the good people from the village, poking fun at the old ladies' high-necked blouses, poking fun at the shy and lovelorn (. . .) teacher, laughing at everything . . . And it's in this village that she made so much fun of that she will find love.)

Mareuil's 'wholesome' image affected the way she was seen by reviewers in *Un Chien andalou*; we might well assume the same applies to contemporary audiences. For one, she was 'très simple et naturelle et sa santé ronde est bien reposante' ('very simple and natural, and her hale and hearty curves are quite soothing'; Lenauer 1929: 4); another wrote that she fulfilled her role 'avec gentillesse' ('sweetly'; Auriol 1929).

We can now see how her persona worked alongside Batcheff's. Her comic connotations echoed the parodic-comic performance of Batcheff, as well as emphasising rather more than we might be used to thinking the more general comic aspects of the film. This was a point already made by Drummond: 'Over and against moralistic readings of the "symbolism" of *Un Chien andalou*, the traces of Keaton, and of Batcheff's self-parody, would locate *Un Chien andalou* more firmly within a comic nexus than that other moralising tradition would encourage or permit' (Drummond 1977: 79–80); and Thiher also pointed out how the film is redolent of the black humour celebrated by André Breton in the mid-1930s (Thiher 1979: 27–8; taken up by Short 2002: 99). Exploring Mareuil's image confirms and deepens the comic aspect of the film. But, more crucially, Mareuil's well-developed 'wholesome' image – all fresh air and fun – acts as a foil for Batcheff. His own image was mainly that of the dreamily distant sentimental lover; having her opposite him highlights the radical departure from this persona, as an aggressively drooling testosterone-laden male pawing at Mareuil's breasts and buttocks, combined with an excessively effeminate and childish male with a penchant for cross-dressing. In that respect, it is as if his persona has been split apart into two radically opposing poles. It is the nature of that split that we will explore in the next chapter, relating it to the central image of the slit eye.

Notes

1. The concept of *cinégraphie* has a complex history, admirably explained by Abel. Although it had its roots in the critical discourse of Émile Vuillermoz and Marcel L'Herbier during the Great War, it was revived as a concept by Louis Delluc and Léon Moussinac in particular during the early 1920s, although different writers had different views as to what it meant. See Abel 1988: 107–8, articles by L'Herbier and Vuillermoz (Abel 1988: 148–58), Abel 1988: 206–13, and an article by Moussinac (Abel 1988: 280–3). In the extract quoted here, it is clearly being used in a very broad and loose sense.

2. See also Aranda 1975: 66–7 for an explanation of the Spanishness of the film's violence.

3. Ramain was a cinema enthusiast who had set up a cine-club in Montpellier in 1924 (see Ramain 1928), where he praised avant-garde cinema in moderation. He had written a piece on cinema and the dream in *Cinéa-Ciné pour tous* in 1925, where he suggested that 'all the expressive and visual processes of the cinema are found in dream' (Ramain 1925: 8). Laurent Guido has explored the work of this writer in some detail (Guido 2002).

4. Dalí similarly wrote in the weekly Spanish magazine *Mirador*, which started in 1929: '*Un Chien andalou* has had unprecedented success in Paris; we confess that all this arouses our indignation (. . .) The public had been soiled by the reviews and disclosures of the avant-garde which itself applauds anything that appears to be new or bizarre. This public did not understand the moral basis of the film that steered directly against it with total violence and cruelty' (Dalí: 1929: 6). The parallel between the second manifesto and the shooting script was drawn by Buñuel himself; see Buñuel 1982: 152 (part of the text has been dropped in the English translation; Buñuel 1984: 125).

5. Part of this section has been previously published as Powrie 1998.

6. Matthews, relying heavily on the shooting script, shows how Buñuel and Dalí 'included several disparaging allusions to the conventions of the silent movie drama, ridiculing its pantomime of passion and stylised gesture' (Matthews 1971: 86). But he is also very conscious of the ways in which the film raises 'intellectualist' expectations only to disrupt them: 'Dramatic interest is generated as readily as the impulse to psychoanalyze is stimulated. Yet every time humor intervenes, to dissipate effects it appeared at first the director's wish to create. Everything conspires to disorient the audience and undermine confidence in their ability to handle the material this movie assembles' (Matthews 1971: 89).

7. A view supported by Paul Sandro a decade later, who writes that the film's success 'stems from the fact that it takes into account the conventions of cinema's dominant discourse and systematically disrupts them by turning them against their classical ends' (Sandro 1987: 15).

8. Abel's date corresponds to the year of general release; we have systematically used the date of the premiere in this book, which for *Les Deux Timides* is December 1928.

9. Drummond was picking up on comments made by Randall Conrad in 1974 (see Drummond 1977: 79, note 37). He repeats this point word for word in Drummond 2004: 105 (where the release date for *One Week* is wrongly given as 1922).

10. Thiher's article was previously published in 1977; see Bibliography.

11. Dulac wrote that Impressionist cinema was characterised by 'the psychological film' which placed a 'character in a particular situation (. . .) in order to penetrate into the secret domain of his inner life' (cited in Abel 1984: 280).

12. This point is reprised by Short 2002: 85.

13. Fotiade links the image to the slitting of the eye in the 'prologue' (Fotiade 2004: 27); Drummond to the dress of the cyclist (Drummond 1977: 110); Liebman to the teeth of the donkeys (*dent*ellière (lacemaker)/dents (teeth); Liebman 1986: 153). Other views are less functional. Sandro relates it to the Freudian notion of narcissism (Sandro 1987: 46), Williams to the Lacanian notion of lack (Williams 1981: 208–9). While all of these interpretations are acceptable given their particular frames of reference, none of them addresses the key issue of previous filmic references. Dalí, as is well known, was obsessed by this painting (see Finkelstein 1998: 55, 433, note 1).

14. For example: 'Simone Mareuil was a professional actress of modest notoriety who appeared in twenty or so mainstream French films between the wars. She was to commit a spectacular suicide in 1954 by setting fire to herself and running in flames through the woods' (Short 2002: 65). Note that Mareuil's Christian name tends to be spelt with one 'n' by most writers. In the film press of the period, it is also spelt 'Simonne', which is the form found on her birth certificate, her original name being Marie Louise Simonne Vacher. We have adopted the official spelling 'Simonne'.

15. With the exception of the starring role in another film by Jean-Benoît Lévy and Marie Epstein, *Cœur de Paris* (1931).

16. Who, we may remember, was Batcheff's partner in *Claudine et le poussin*.

CHAPTER 8

Un Chien andalou: *Parodying Stardom*

In this chapter we will begin by exploring the functionality of the slit eye, arguing that it establishes a principle of fracture. We will then explore the ways in which that fracture is related to hysteria, leading to an analysis of the disarticulation of Batcheff's star image in terms of the ethnicity of his roles and the costumes he wears. This will return us to issues of femininity, which we will analyse by focusing on masochism. Finally, we will use an image that is often mentioned but little talked about, that of the death's-head moth, to show how anamorphosis, a key preoccupation of Dalí and Lacan, can be a productive way of conceiving of Batcheff's function in the film.

THE SLIT EYE

Un Chien andalou clearly emphasises vision in a number of ways. Most obviously, there is the slit eye of the Prologue.[1] But there are other eyes: the gouged-out eyes of the donkeys, the intense gazes of the actors, as they stare at each other, or at objects such as the death's-head moth. Then there are objects that recall the slit eye of the Prologue, such as the round shapes morphing into each other: the hole in Batcheff's palm; the underarm of a woman; a sea urchin; the head of the androgyne viewed from above. And later, there are the breasts and buttocks we assume to be Mareuil's, echoed in Batcheff's round eyes and pursed lips as he kneads them lewdly. At another level, the film emphasises the fragility of vision, interrogating the veracity of what we see in the world around us by its play with conflicting spaces, and mobile characters who are never quite what they seem.[2]

The split eye itself is part of a broader context. It has been argued that it is rooted in a specifically Spanish sensibility (see Morris 1972: 115–18); but we can equally well see it as part of the interest in such images on the part of the surrealists who wished to undermine rationality and 'clear' vision (Powrie 1992).[3] At yet another level, we can see the slit eye as a symptom of a particularly sceptical and suspicious view of vision on the part of twentieth-century French culture as a whole (Jay 1994). This broader historical context has not prevented a wide variety of context-free interpretations arising, some of which we have alluded to in Chapter 7.

Drummond reviewed a number of these in 1977. The slit eye could be a sexual metaphor for birth, or for masturbation, or for castration. It could also be a metaphor of reception for opening the eyes of the spectator. It could be a formal metaphor drawing attention to aspects of the film's structure, or to formal techniques such as framing and montage (Drummond 1977: 91–2). Williams and Sandro, as Lacanians, see it as a metaphor for the threat of loss of unity (Williams 1981: 85–6; Sandro 1987: 26), a view gestured at even by the more sceptical Drummond, who, in a rare moment of interpretation, suggests that the Prologue 'marks the neurosis of a narrative excited precisely by its loss of origins' (Drummond 1977: 104).

The Prologue may well be a metaphor, but it is a false metaphor, as Williams has shown.[4] Its purpose is precisely to force us to ascribe meaning, much like the prologue to a book, where the author tries to persuade the reader to adopt a particular view of what will follow. This is what Drummond might mean when he points out that it does not anticipate events that follow, because there is no direct causative link between the Prologue and the rest, but that it does at one level 'satisfy the rites of narrative exposition' (Drummond 1977: 103); and Williams has also shown how the Prologue drives meaning production for the rest of the film. Meaning is less important, however, than the affective reaction to what we see on screen, the recoiling of the body from inexplicable and unmotivated violence. This serves as a purposeful disorientation of the rational and intellectual faculties, in keeping with the aims of surrealism, as Matthews had already argued in 1971.[5] We are therefore less inclined to see this as a metaphor for what each individual spectator has lost when entering what Lacan would call the Symbolic, the world of language and symbol. We are more inclined to Drummond's view that the slit eye establishes a general principle of anxious loss, echoed by the constant fragmentation, doubling and dismemberment that follow the Prologue. As Sandro points out, body parts are a 'pattern that echoes the initial slicing of the eye and recalls *en abyme* the film's own dismemberment as a body of meanings' (Sandro 1987: 48). Such views have been well rehearsed by Drummond, Williams and Sandro, and reiterated more recently by Short. None, however, attempts to link such formal and figural processes to the image of the star.

DISMEMBERMENT OF THE STAR: SEEING BEHIND THE SURFACE

The comments made above on the film can be equally applied to Batcheff as star. What is dismembered and fragmented in a fairly obvious way is Batcheff's image. We need to remind ourselves that the reason many spectators would have gone to see this film by a couple of unknown Spaniards loosely associated (and then only once the film had been released) with one of many

avant-garde groups (although admittedly the most prominent at the time) was the star. What might have seemed to audiences and critics alike a fairly stable image prior to 1928 was reoriented – one might say wrenched – towards the comic, as we can see in the following reviews:

> Vous n'ignorez plus, depuis *Les Deux timides*, l'aisance étonnante de Pierre Batcheff. Dans *Un Chien andalou*, Pierre Batcheff nous montre que son jeu s'est encore enrichi; ses gestes plus sûrs, ses expressions encore plus subtiles et son comique d'une délicatesse qui rappelle parfois Buster Keaton (. . .) On a trop longtemps mal employé un acteur très doué en le forçant de se servir uniquement d'un visage plaisant. Maintenant (. . .) il nous a prouvé pour la deuxième fois où est sa véritable force. (Lenauer 1929: 4)

> (You must have noticed what an accomplished actor Pierre Batcheff is since *Les Deux Timides*. In *Un Chien andalou*, his acting has come on in leaps and bounds; his gestures are more assured, his expressions even more subtle, and his comedy as skilful as Buster Keaton's (. . .) He has too often been forced into roles that trade on his good looks. Now he has shown us for the second time where his strengths lie.)

> Pierre Batcheff, autrefois astreint à des rôles idiots, déjà révélé par René Clair dans *Les Deux timides*, fait preuve ici d'une sensibilité et d'une intelligence qu'il est impardonnable d'avoir dissimulées si longtemps. (Brunius 1929a: 68)

> (Pierre Batcheff, previously obliged to play silly roles, and already revealed by René Clair in *Les Deux Timides*, demonstrates in this film a sensitivity and an intelligence which it is unforgivable to have kept hidden from us before now.)

While these two reviews stress the shift from 'silly' romantic roles to the comic, other reviewers stressed something less compartmentalised generically, as, for example, the following appraisal. It focuses on mobility contrasted with the rigidity of stereotype in terms that we have seen appearing time and time again in reviews throughout this book: 'Nous lui appliquions volontiers l'épithète: charmant, sensible . . . *Le Chien andalou* [sic] nous a révélé un artiste d'une souplesse, d'une intelligence, d'une mobilité surprenante. Et quel sens du tragique! Puissant, oui' ('We have tended to use the words charming and sensitive to describe Pierre Batcheff . . . *Un Chien andalou* has revealed an artist who shows a surprising level of fluidity, of intelligence, of mobility. And what a sense of the tragic! Very powerful'; Normand 1929).

   Indeed, this sense that *Un Chien andalou* fragmented the previously stable image of the star led some reviewers to attempt to reconfigure a homogeneous image. In this extract from Arnoux's lengthy review, we can see that, obliged to confront the evidence of fragmentation and multiplication of the film's character, he tries to counteract this by appealing to a sense of unity

embedded in the star's performative skills. This unitary 'selfness' is combined, paradoxically, with a form of 'selflessness':[6]

> Pierre Batcheff, à qui nous devons déjà tant de créations romanesques ou comiques, s'est dévoué à l'œuvre avec un talent et une intelligence qui forcent l'admiration. Pas une fausse note, pas une attitude gauche, pas un trait forcé. Son rôle, où il se dédouble et se détriple même, exigeait un grand effet de composition. Très varié, comme le commandaient ses personnages, il a réussi à ne pas les dissocier, à leur garder leur unité fondamentale, à ne pas nous offrir une série de sketches (. . .) Un homme simplement habile, consciencieux et froid ne nous eût pas imposé ce héros fragmentaire, feuilleté, trouble, seuls la conviction profonde et le don absolu de soi pouvaient ne pas trahir les intentions compliquées de l'auteur. (Arnoux 1929)

> (Pierre Batcheff, the star of so many romantic and comic films, has committed himself to this film with admirable talent and intelligence. There is nothing false, nothing forced. His role, where he splits into two and even into three, required skilful performance. While varying his characters, he has managed not to dissociate them; he has maintained their fundamental unity, rather than giving us a series of sketches (. . .) If he had just been skilful, conscientious and cold, he would never have been able to create this fragmentary, layered and troubled hero. Only deep conviction and an absolute selflessness could translate the director's complicated intentions.)

Arnoux uses the term 'selflessness' ('don de soi') as a moral imperative, according to which Batcheff is supposed to have sacrificed his individuality, complying with whatever Buñuel may have required of him.[7] We would like to push this sense somewhat further and see it in structural terms as the attempt to evacuate any sense of unitary identity. In that respect, Arnoux's attempt to maintain a precarious equilibrium between 'self' and 'selflessness' is a productive line of enquiry, which will take us into the discussion of masochism later in this chapter.

This is because the film's narrative structure, based on repetition, mimics the tensions inherent in Batcheff's position as star. As Sandro wrote in the first (1978) version of his article on the film: 'The desires of the characters are constantly frustrated (. . .) they are condemned to repeat variations of the same scenario' (Sandro cited in Abel 1988: 484). This encapsulates Batcheff's dilemma as a reluctant star of the popular cinema. He was condemned to repeat the same scenario of the romantic lead from one film to the next, his desire to be a writer-director constantly frustrated; and in so doing, he was obliged to give up his identity in the service of a stereotype. The dismemberment that pervades *Un Chien andalou* is therefore a means to disarticulate and undermine that stereotype in the search for a different identity or set of identities, to see behind the surface of the star persona. In that respect the slit eye is a useful metaphor for this dismemberment of the stereotype, for the seeing-behind-the-surface.

It is also part of way in which the seeing-behind-the-surface is achieved; it is an affective shock sensitising the audience to such operations of deconstruction, the achievement of what Buñuel called a 'cathartic state' (Aranda 1975: 67). Audiences are both attracted and repelled, just as Batcheff himself both accepts the stereotypes that comprise his image, and deconstructs them, in an explosive moment combining both the static and the mobile. It was what Breton called 'convulsive beauty' (Breton 1988: 753) in *Nadja*, published in May 1928. As Hal Foster has shown, convulsive beauty is fundamentally anxious; and anxiety is a 'device of repetition triggered by danger in order to mitigate a traumatic situation of perceived loss' (Foster 1993: 194). Whereas previous commentators have tended to express this 'loss' as a generic loss for the spectator of some metapsychic 'origin', we would prefer to see the loss as that of Batcheff-as-actor faced with the invasive public persona(s) of Batcheff-as-star.[8] In this respect, the 'madness' we identified as part of one of his very first roles – Scipion the epileptic-hysteric in *Feu Mathias Pascal* — runs as an undercurrent through all of his roles, but most of all when it is exteriorised in the man of *Un Chien andalou*.

HYSTERIA, ETHNICITY, COSTUME

Un Chien andalou 'acts out' hysteria, making it visible through aesthetically elaborated images in much the same way that Breton and Éluard's 'Possessions' simulated or 'acted out' different types of mental disorder. Dalí wrote a text for *L'Immaculée Conception* to be inserted into the volume (published November 1930 and cited in full in Breton 1988: 1632), and it is therefore part of a wider landscape of surrealist interest in madness, affecting all aesthetic forms. It is true that hysteria is not one of the five simulated disorders in that volume; none the less, the principle of simulation, and the interest in mental illness as a poetic and ontological driver remain for *Un Chien andalou*. Dalí talks of the advantage of 'faire apparaître d'imprévues et toutes nouvelles formes poétiques' ('provoking unforeseen and novel poetic forms'; Breton 1988: 1632), as well as pointing to the more ontological considerations of the reconciliation of rationality and desire ('l'adaptation de la connaissance aux désirs' ('the reconciliation of knowledge and desire'; Breton 1988: 1632). Hysteria, as we saw in Chapter 3, was fundamental for the surrealists in this period. David Lomas points out how surrealism cannot be divorced from an 'exotic *fin-de-siècle* cocktail of discourses on automatism, hysteria and hypnosis' combining 'induced somnambulism, dissociated secondary selves, alternating and multiple personalities' (Lomas 2000: 70). In *Un Chien andalou*, we find Batcheff split into three versions of himself (the cyclist, the lustful pursuer of Mareuil and the version that tells off the lustful pursuer). Hysteria was seen in this period as a female disorder, which raises the issue of gender identities as well. In what follows, we wish to explore the splitting of Batcheff's image through issues of ethnicity and costume, so as to move towards broader issues of gender identity. Our contention will be that the slit eye inaugurates hysterical convulsions of identity exteriorising the femininity inherent in Batcheff's image.

We spent some time on the perceived 'Spanishness' of the film in Chapter 7, because it suggests a curious displacement. One aspect of this displacement is to legitimise the film's violence by relating it to a national stereotype, the excessively passionate South, object of Orientalist fascination for well over a century in French culture. Spain was one of the Romantics' 'Others', a country of strong emotions, danger, picturesque customs and folklore: in other words, the contrary of prevalent bourgeois values. To travel to Spain if one was an aristocrat doing the Grand Tour in the nineteenth century, or to read about Spain in accounts of the Grand Tour, was to escape, to live life more 'authentically';[9] we can surmise that this notion of authenticity might well have remained in cinematic renderings of Spain or Spanish characteristics, and would have overlapped neatly with the surrealist fascination for Rimbaud who gave up poetry to go gun-running in Abyssinia.

But Batcheff was also and above all associated with Russia, both by his name, and even more so by his films for the White Russians who had set up Films Albatros.[10] In this sense, his image in *Un Chien andalou* is suddenly disarticulated, stretched in the geography of the mind between a Deep South of Orientalist violence and passion on one side, and on the other a Far North and East of Slavic dreaminess and distance. The sweaty proximity of dangerous desire rubs shoulders with cool, detached remoteness. The head and the genitals are conflated, as the moment when Batcheff places Mareuil's armpit hair over his absent mouth, which can be read as displaced pubic hair, might well suggest to us.[11] That remoteness was signalled in his performances by the distant look, the gaze towards a far horizon, a gaze made all the more remote for being inscrutably interior, a private motherland of the melancholic spirit. The sheer lust exhibited in Batcheff's gaze in *Un Chien andalou* clearly works to undermine the dreamy aloofness of the 'head', articulating an ecstatic and desiring proximity to what surrounds him.

Batcheff's cool detachment in many of his previous films was supported by costume. In dramas set in the present, he tends to wear formal suits, often tails; and in the historical reconstructions, he wears high-collared costumes. Both these variants of formal wear suggest constraint; this is at its most obvious in *Le Joueur d'échecs*, because of the contrast between Pierre

Blanchar's very active Boleslas and Batcheff's much more placid and sedate Oblonoff. The suit is the most characteristic male attire in the modern period. The clothes theorist John Flügel sees in the sartorial simplicity exemplified by the suit what he calls the Great Masculine Renunciation, whereby men gave up beauty for usefulness as a result of egalitarianism (the French Revolution had proclaimed that all men were equal) and the development of the work culture in the nineteenth century, which required simple clothes (Flügel 1930: 111–12). The suit, as the most characteristic element of male clothing, signifies 'devotion to the principles of duty, of renunciation, and of self-control' (Flügel 1930: 113),[12] as well as conformism to the principle of social cohesion. Flügel cites Gerald Heard, another 1920s clothes theorist, in some revealing comments about the function of the male coat (Heard 1924):

> Man's coat, that 'strange compromise between the gravitational and the anatomic' (. . .) with its hanging sleeves, its dragging on the armpit and the elbows, is so ill-suited to movement, except of the slowest and most solemn kind, that, by the restrictions imposed, it must — both psychologically and physiologically — reduce the efficiency of the male. (Flügel 1930: 233)

John Harvey goes one step further with regard to the suit, speculating that the black suit in modern European culture combines power and death, 'intensity' and 'effacement'; it suggests 'abandonedness and depth of need', and 'a power claimed over women and the feminine' (Harvey 1995: 257), echoing Flügel who writes of the self-effacement of 'quasi-neurotic asceticism', as he calls men's dress more generally (Flügel 1930: 213). Batcheff was, of course, not the only male star to wear suits and coats; but the combination of the detached look, and narratives where he is frequently placed in situations of disempowerment, shows how costume supports a 'Slavic' image whose key characteristics are renunciation, effacement and 'reduced efficiency' (rather than the more macho 'power claimed over women'). We shall consider the connection with the feminine below, but here wish to explore the interface between formal and informal clothing, before looking at the ways in which *Un Chien andalou* plays with audience expectations.

Batcheff's 'Slavic' image is mitigated in certain films by his role as the young, passionate lover associated with the South. In these circumstances, his costume changes, and we find him dressed in open-necked shirts, his clothes a metaphor for the unbuttoning of the buttoned-up 'Slavic' image. This does not necessarily mean, however, that this 'Southern' image is part of a binary with the 'Slavic' image. This is because the open-necked shirt functions as a sign of the pin-up, the passive ephebic boy of Solomon-Godeau, or the equally static Sad Young Man of Dyer. The narratives also function to contain

Batcheff, to reduce, almost literally, the room for manœuvre to which the unbuttoning of his image might have led.

In *La Sirène des tropiques*, for example, as we showed in Chapter 5, Josephine Baker is more 'other' than he is, normalising his outsider status; she is more mobile than he is; and the narrative structures his tropical interlude as just that, a moment of ludic play, where in any case he is more often the observer (of village festivities, of nefarious activities) and is literally immobilised by the villains and by Papitou (Baker) who insists on nursing him, and takes away his agency in the crucial duel at the end of the film.

In *L'Île d'amour*, any closeness to instincts baser than those associated with the 'head' are neutralised by having Xénia watch over him as he is immobilised in a hospital bed, and by ensuring that part of the narrative deals with educating him. He is thus literally led away from 'Italian' passion towards the kind of sophistication required to make him a worthy consort for the American heiress.

In *Monte-Cristo*, finally, a film that fans of Batcheff would have been able to see at the same time as *Un Chien andalou*, any letting down of the hair suggested by Albert de Morcerf's visit to the island, with an open-necked shirt to match, is similarly neutralised. He is drugged in the boat by the sailors, and drugged again by the Count; in both cases he is immobilised, made helpless under the gaze of more powerful men.

Attention is drawn to costume in a very obvious way in *Un Chien andalou* through the figure of the cyclist, one of three personas played by Batcheff in the film (we shall call this character version 1). His narratively inexplicable 'frills' (as they tend to be called by most commentators)[13] overlay his suit and tie, and return when Mareuil places them on the bed and (we assume) tries to visualise the absent body underneath them. The whole character returns dressed as he was in the cycling scene when he lies on the bed in the room to which Mareuil escapes from his more lustful double (version 2). And the clothes will return right at the end when Mareuil and the new sporty character pick them up on the beach, only to cast them away. Batcheff version 2 is dressed in a suit but without a tie; while the third version of Batcheff, who tells off version 1 for wanting to retain his 'frilly' clothes, is dressed in a less formal small-check suit with a tie, echoing his costume in *Les Deux Timides* (but oddly with a wing collar). We therefore have a range of costumes, all of which have the suit as their basis, but none of which is full formal wear (i.e. a black suit with a tie). The cyclist's costume is clearly intended to suggest feminisation; as Drummond points out when discussing the image of Vermeer's *Lacemaker* and its relationship to the cyclist, there is an obvious echo in the mantelet (Drummond 1977: 110), and most commentators state or imply that the purpose of the costume is to suggest feminisation.[14]

Costume in *Un Chien andalou* therefore works to undermine Batcheff's image in two related ways. First, his suits remind us of those that he might have worn in other films, but none of them is quite the same; there is no tie, or when there is a tie, it is informal, but worn with a formal wing collar. Second, what we might have considered to be 'interiorised' in Batcheff's star image is exteriorised in the costume of the cyclist. The ephebic characters of his previous films were placed into feminised and passive positions as disempowered objects of the gaze; the cyclist's 'frills' exteriorise this feature of Batcheff's image. It is this feminisation that we shall pursue in the next section.

THE GAZE OF THE WOMAN AND MASOCHISM

We saw above how Batcheff's image from his very first films incorporates hysteria, suggesting multiple personalities. We have been suggesting that this immanent hysteria functions as a driver for the splitting of Batcheff's persona across ethnicities and gender in *Un Chien andalou*. Buñuel and Dalí's film does not simply parody Batcheff's previous films and the image created by them; it makes manifest the contradictions and tensions in the figure of the *jeune premier* more generally, as passive object of the audience's gaze. It is almost as if Batcheff plays along with this disempowerment, making acting a statement of masochistic acceptance of the inevitability of reification. To put it more simply: the star has no identity, but is the absent centre of a circle constituted by his roles.[15] While it remains open to conjecture as to whether this statement might apply to all stars, we are proposing that the particular configurations of Batcheff's image – disempowered object of the gaze, combined with detachment from the role at hand – make this statement valid for him. Our exploration of costume has shown how his male attire is undermined in *Un Chien andalou*. We now wish to turn to what we might call the feminisation of space, time and the gaze in the film.

Considerable work has been done on gender configurations in the film. Drummond argues that the woman, despite or perhaps because of the aggressive slitting of her eye, is placed in a position of power structurally, as the figure of Buñuel as 'author' is evacuated from the remainder of the film: 'It is the face of the woman which suppresses, redefines and refigures the male presence and activity within the film' (Drummond 1977: 102). Williams shows how the 'frills' we explored in the previous section suggest a collapse of the gender binary: 'The feminine frills the woman lays out on the bed (. . .) are fetishistic figures of the cyclist himself that wishfully present him as a sexually undifferentiated being, as both male *and* female' (Williams 1981: 84; Williams's emphasis). Williams also points out how the androgyne echoes the cyclist as 'a dominantly feminine version of the contradictory gender traits of the dominantly masculine cyclist' (Williams 1981: 85). More recently, Gilberto Pérez, adopting Drummond's view that the woman 'takes over' from Buñuel as 'author', argues that the woman 'represents the spectator' (Pérez 2004: 402–3).

The work done by these commentators suggests how the film disturbs the gender binary, and to some extent constructs a viewing space that is as feminine as it might be masculine, but which is certainly dominated by the feminine. To the extent that many spectators would have been inclined in the first instance to identify themselves with the major star, Batcheff, we can argue convincingly – on the basis of costume and point of view – that Batcheff is as feminine as he is masculine in this film. The key image in this respect is Batcheff as hysteric, his eyes rolled up in one of the typical attitudes of the hysteric, with blood drooling from his open mouth. Not only does it recall hysteria; it also recalls the slit eye of Mareuil and the gouged-out eyes of the donkeys, reified and abjected matter, in a moment of masochism. We should remember that the hysterical face suggests self-harm, and comes immediately after Batcheff version 2 has pursued Mareuil and we have seen him express his lust; the shooting script uses the words 'lascives' ('lascivious') and 'luxure' ('lust'; Buñuel 1929a: 35 for the French; Buñuel 1929b: 130 for the English) to describe Batcheff's gestures and expressions. The script also describes the hysterical face as having 'une terrible expression d'angoisse, presque mortelle' (Buñuel 1929a: 35) ('a terrible expression of almost mortal anguish'; Buñuel 1929b: 130). The intention is clearly to suggest the combined ecstasy and guilt of desire, etched into flesh masochistically, a parody of the distant look so frequently adopted by Batcheff in his films and redolent of the 'head', the cool detachment of the 'Slav', combined with the hysterical ecstasies associated with orgasm or St Theresa-like mystical excess that Lacan was to associate later with inexpressible female *jouissance*.

Masochism has been extensively explored by Freud, Theodor Reik and Gilles Deleuze, and was taken up by film theorists such as Kaja Silverman and Gaylyn Studlar during the 1980s and 1990s as a paradigm for spectatorship. Their work confirms the 'femininity' of masochism. Silverman, quoting Reik, for example, evokes the 'selflessness' we discussed above in relation to Batcheff in terms of femininity: 'The male masochist (. . .) leaves his social identity completely behind – actually abandons his "self" — and passes over into the enemy terrain of femininity' (Silverman 1992: 190). She points out that Deleuze's 'utopian' account of masochism 'is a pact between mother and son to write the father out of his dominant position within both culture and masochism, and to install the mother in his place' (Silverman 1992: 211), and, crucially, constituting 'a feminine yet heterosexual male subject' (Silverman 1992: 212). Jacqueline Cosnier suggests that feminine masochism is associated with maintaining the primary relation (Cosnier 1985). In that respect it is caught in a paradox: that of a desire for union which collapses difference, but at the same time a desire for separation which intensifies difference. The centrifugal and the centripetal coexist in a single convulsive event. It is not a case of either/or, but both, as we can see with the costumes of Batcheff-as-cyclist, where both feminine and masculine coexist uncomfortably in the context of a fall, an accident: mobility followed by immobility.

We have previously argued that masochism was intimately bound up with the surrealist project of achieving the Hegelian aim of the Second Manifesto, that of resolving opposites:

> The surrealist text, particularly the automatic text which depends upon the notion of automatism as a privileged form of access to the surreal, must gesture towards its own abolition in the surreal (. . .) The surrealist text gestures towards the surreal, indeed the surreal is brought to light by the text, but remains just beyond it, in idealist transcendence. The text itself can do no more than gesture towards the point where all opposites, including the opposites which constitute the surreal image itself, the verbal and the visual, will vanish in one apocalyptic transcendent moment. That transcendent moment also abolishes gender distinctions. (Powrie 2000: 50)

So far, we have shown how Batcheff's star image is fractured, hysterical, feminised, articulating the evacuation of subjectivity. In the next section we will explore how the ruin of the subject can be linked to a key notion for Dalí and Lacan, that of anamorphosis.

ANAMORPHOSIS

Objects are not what they seem in *Un Chien andalou*. As we have already noted in Chapter 2, there is a particularly rich sequence of dissolves, much commented on, focusing on round-shaped objects (ants emerging from the hole in the hand, a woman's armpit, a sea urchin, the head of the androgyne). We pointed out that this sequence could be seen as part of a more general interest on Dalí's part in anamorphic objects. There is another anamorphic object in the film: the moth, a close-up of which reveals the death's-head on its body, the point of view being that of Mareuil who stares intently at it, as she does at many shifting objects in the film. The moth has led to less commentary than the series just mentioned, most commentators assuming that it is a straightforward symbol of death.[16]

Gwynne Edwards thinks that 'the death's head becomes the young man himself dressed in his frills' (Edwards 1982: 54). Although this is wrong (in this scene it is Batcheff version 2, rather than version 1), the error was proba-

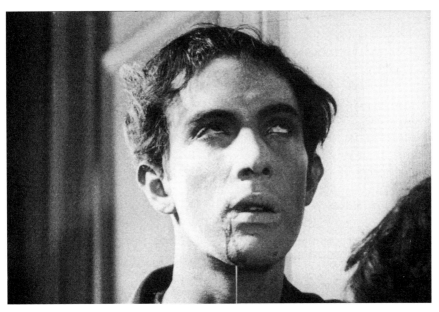

Figure 8.1   Batcheff as hysteric in *Un Chien andalou* (Courtesy of the Bibliothèque du Film, Paris)

bly made by adhering closely to the shooting script, which says: 'paraît brusquement l'homme des mantelets qui porte vivement la main à la bouche' (Buñuel 1929a: 37) ('The man who was wearing the ruffles comes suddenly into view [. . .] bringing his hand swiftly to his mouth'; Buñuel 1929b: 133). Error aside, the relationship between Batcheff version 2 and the moth is made very clear in the script:

> On voit de nouveau le mur, au milieu duquel il y a une petite tache noire.
> Cette petite tache, vue de plus près, est un papillon de la mort.
> Le papillon en *G.P.*
> La tête de mort des ailes du papillon couvre tout l'écran.
> En *P.I.* paraît brusquement l'homme des mantelets. (Buñuel 1929a: 37)[17]

> (The wall is seen once again; in the middle of it there is a small black spot.
> Seen much closer, this small spot appears to be a death's-head moth.
> Close-up of the moth.
> The death's head on the moth's wings fills the whole screen.
> The man who was wearing ruffles comes suddenly into view in a medium
> shot.) (Buñuel 1929b: 133)

Although the man in this shot is emphatically not the same as the cyclist, none the less Batcheff version 2 is assimilated to the death's-head moth, and it is reasonable to assume that the two are linked in some way (by which we mean both that it is the likely intention of the filmmakers, and that it is a likely inference of the spectators).

Oddly, few commentators have related the moth to anamorphosis, a key notion for Dalí,[18] which he began investigating at this time. Lomas points out how Dalí, in all probability referring to Holbein's famous painting, *The Ambassadors* (1533), thought that anamorphosis was related to death: 'The most successful anamorphoses are those which represent death concretely by a skull' (cited in Lomas 2000: 161); and Lomas points out that Dalí first connected anamorphosis to his famous soft forms in September 1929 with a juxtaposition of images in the journal run by Georges Bataille, *Documents*.[19] If we accept that one of the purposes of *Un Chien andalou* is to place the spectator in a position where rationality has less purchase over the images on screen, then the use of anamorphosis as a theoretical tool is key. This is because for Lacan, whose reflections on anamorphosis rely heavily on Holbein's painting, anamorphosis places the subject in crisis.

Lacan draws a contrastive parallel between the stable Cartesian subject and the Lacanian subject on the one hand, and geometric or central perspective and inverted anamorphic perspective on the other. Combining this with the ostensible theme of *The Ambassadors*, *vanitas*, Lacan is able to say of the anamorphosis that 'il nous reflète notre propre néant, dans la figure de la tête de mort' (Lacan 1973: 86; 'it reflects our own nothingness, in the figure of the death's head'; Lacan 1994: 92). The anamorphosis comments on the central or geometric perspective without which its dissident and distorted form could not exist, while at the same time annihilating metaphorically the I/eye (the unified subject equivalent to the central perspective) that actualises the anamorphosis. Anamorphosis leads not just to loss, but also to a loss of bearings for the spectator. If we return to the round-shaped series of dissolves, we can see how they might constitute an anamorphic object, something gestured at in the series but always just out of sight, just as Holbein's anamorphosis can only be decoded once one has decided to walk away from it and look at it furtively, from the corner of one's eye and from the corner of the room in which the painting is hung. The object we cannot quite see in the series of dissolves is neither a stigmata, nor an armpit, nor a sea urchin, nor a woman's head. In each case, however, we obscurely understand that whatever it is must involve something round and linked with hair or objects resembling hair. This obscure object of desire is the woman's eye (round and bordered with lashes) earlier destroyed, but which, as we have pointed out, remains liminally and powerfully as her point of view. It is both there and not there, seen and not seen, a destroyed eye, but a viewing eye all the same. The question then becomes one of location: where exactly is this object?

Lacan relates anamorphosis to baroque forms:

> Le retour baroque à tous les jeux de la forme, à tous ces procédés, dont l'anamorphose, est un effort pour restaurer le sens véritable de la recherche artistique – les artistes se servent de la découverte des propriétés des lignes, pour faire resurgir quelque chose qui soit justement là où on ne sait plus donner de la tête – à proprement parler, nulle part. (Lacan 1986: 162)

> (The Baroque return to the play of forms, to all manner of devices, including anamorphosis, is an effort to restore the true meaning of artistic inquiry: artists use the discovery of the property of lines to make something emerge that is precisely there where one has lost one's bearings or, strictly speaking, nowhere.) (Lacan 1992: 136)

The sense of loss is compounded by Lacan's suggestion that the anamorphosis in *The Ambassadors* could be seen as a (per)version of the phallus, and therefore a vanishing of the (masculine-identified) subject (although, typical of Lacan, there is a slippage between the phallus as a symbol and the penis as a biological fact): 'Comment se fait-il que personne n'ait jamais songé à y évoquer (. . .) l'effet d'une érection ? Imaginez un tatouage tracé sur l'organe ad hoc à l'état de repos, et prenant dans un autre état sa forme, si j'ose dire, développée' (Lacan 1973: 82; 'How is it that nobody has ever thought of connecting this with the effect of an erection? Imagine a tattoo traced on the sexual organ *ad hoc* in the state of repose and assuming its, if I may say so, developed form in another state'; Lacan 1994: 87–8). He suggests that the distortion represented by the anamorphosis is 'symbolique de la fonction du manque – de l'apparition du fantôme phallique' (Lacan 1973: 82; 'symbolic of the function of lack, of the appearance of the phallic ghost'; Lacan 1994: 88).

Two issues emerge from this discussion of Lacan's view of anamorphosis. First, the hidden-ness of the object is coterminous with the ruin of the subject. Subject (as rational point of view) and object (of the rational subject's point of view) are both there and not-there in a collapse of space-time; there remains only disrupted affect, a crisis of embodiment, a body thrown back on itself and bereft of rational frameworks in which to locate itself. This is all the more the case when we consider, second, that the multiple distortions (of objects-in-flux, objects indicating loss of boundaries without a terra firma; and of subjects-in-flux, evacuated points of view) are due to the irruption of desire. Commenting on Lacan's view of Holbein, Hanjo Berressem suggests that 'visual distortions (. . .) serve as a (visual) metaphor of psychic distortions; the effects of the interference of the libido within the perceptual apparatus' (Berressem 1996: 270).

The anamorphs – Holbein's death's-head, Buñuel's death's-head moth – are representatives of the libido which distorts, unimportant in themselves but important in their function. They are our point of identification, the 'nowhere' from which the 'somewhere' is constituted, the letter-box we look through into the signifying system of the film. Lacan uses the term 'trompe-l'œil' to describe the relationship between the painter and the spectator of the painting, although we could just as well replace the painter by the film director in the following: 'Le rapport (. . .) du peintre et de l'amateur, est un jeu, un jeu de trompe-l'œil' (Lacan 1973: 95; 'The relation (. . .) between the painter and the spectator, is a play, a play of trompe-l'œil'; Lacan 1994: 103). The anamorphs are lures, trompe-l'œils whose function is to capture our attention, quite literally to bring us to attend to the narrative. They are ghostly bodies which force us to take up a position in relation to the film, much as the anamorph is what attracts us to place ourselves physically in front of Holbein's *The Ambassadors*. We are unlikely to care much what the painting is about.[20] We simply want to see the anamorphosis out of an almost physical curiosity.[21] What attracts us is the placing of our body so that we can see from that 'nowhere', from that utopian space or place ('utopia' signifying the 'no-place'). The place where 'we' are is like the blind spot, the point where the optical nerve is fixed, and so the point which cannot see itself seeing, to recall the formula which Lacan uses as the springboard for this discussion of the gaze (Lacan 1973: 76/Lacan 1994: 80).

Hence the importance of the image of the slit eye, which functions like an anamorphosis to the extent that we know that it is supposed to represent the eye of the woman; but we can equally well see that it is not really a woman's eye that is being slit. It is no coincidence, we would contend, that immediately after the death's-head moth we see Batcheff wipe away his mouth and magically 'steal' Mareuil's underarm hair. Batcheff has no mouth, and we know from our discussion above that the underarm hair forms part of the series of dissolves that themselves gesture back to the slit eye. Batcheff's gesture therefore – the 'oops' gesture of someone who regrets what he might have said – suggests the loss of speech (mouth) and the loss of vision (the slit eye gestured at in the armpit hair). These functions (words emanating from a mouth; the gaze emanating from the eyes) are replaced by what the hair is supposed to indicate: yet another hole nestling invisibly beneath what has been construed as female pubic hair. Mareuil can leave Batcheff, because the work of the film has been completed where he is concerned. He has almost literally incorporated the feminine; his mouth is the invisibilised vagina which silences him forever as far as the film is concerned. We have arrived at much the same conclusion as Williams, although with some disagreement over detail. Williams implies that because Batcheff does not have a mouth, we cannot assume the transfer of the vagina on to his face (Williams 1981: 97). Our view is that, when placed into the context of the anamorphic series, it does not much matter whether the mouth is sealed or open, as what we see suggests in a fairly obvious way that Batcheff's face has somehow magically become feminine, even if the biological specificities of femininity are less than clear. It is therefore not so much that he has no gender or virility, but that he combines both. He can now disappear from the narrative because he has died and risen again as both man and woman.

The fact that the vagina cannot be seen, as Williams reminds us, is none the less important. A contrast is established between the wholesomeness of Mareuil, who goes on to establish what seems like a less fraught relationship with the sporty young man on the beach, and the frenzied relationship she has with Batcheff, 'under the sign of death', as several commentators put it. The contract the spectator has with Batcheff in this film is one of emptiness; the origin, the 'origin of the world', as Courbet might have it (the vagina, hidden in Courbet's painting under a particularly thick cover of pubic hair),[22] is an always already lost origin. Batcheff can only gesture towards centrifugal shards of identity, mirror splinterings whose function is to indicate a non-existent origin rather than its centrifugal explosion. The wholeness and 'wholesomeness' of Mareuil is forever impossible.

Our exploration of the film using psychoanalytic concepts brings out an irremediable hollowness at the heart of the commercial star, as represented by Batcheff, a scooping out of substance, his trajectory creating layer upon layer of destitution, until what is left seems no more than a parody. Hysteria and masochism are embedded in his roles from the beginning of his career; *Un Chien andalou*, we have argued, merely makes them more manifest through parody. He comes across in the film as an uneasy amalgam of testosterone-laden Valentinian tango-pirate, combined with a swooningly ecstatic Saint Theresa. The musical accompaniment to the film underlines this amalgam; he is both hyper-male with the tango, the music of lust and passion, and hyper-female with the lush Romanticism of the *Liebestod*, generally taken to represent Isolde's ecstatic fantasy of a live Tristan as she stares at his dead body. Hysteria and masochism feminise his persona; the shifts in gender, echoed by anamorphic objects in the film, complete the process of evacuation. Both objects and subjects are in crisis. The circle that they try to create, both in their circulation and in their circularity, does not have a centre. It is, like the slit eye, emptied of humour, an orbit without a sun.

The surrealist star, as exemplified by Batcheff, is without identity; he is merely a gesture, an empty skin, a blind twinkle.

Notes

1. While Drummond writes 'prologue', calling attention not only to its narrative status but also, by virtue of the inverted commas, to his scepticism that it

functions in any clear or recognisable way narratively, most other commentators on this film have tended to call the opening section the 'Prologue' (with an upper-case P); we see no reason to do otherwise.

2. Robert Aron had already pointed out this aspect of disorientation in 1929, although dismissing it as mere play, like so many others we have already quoted; see Aron 1929, translated as Aron 1988.

3. This article shows how the split eye image can be found consistently in the work of surrealist poets at the end of the 1920s. See also Eager 1961 and Siegel 1961a/1961b for a discussion of the eye in painting.

4. 'Though formally modeled on the typical metaphor, (it) actually functions as a deconstruction of the anticipated metaphoric process in which the denotative content of the eye-cutting refuses to be absorbed immediately into a connotative expression' (Williams 1981: 72).

5. See also Abel 1988: 205–6.

6. Arnoux was one of several reviewers savaged by Brunius in his account of critical reception, saying that Arnoux 'aime ça sans savoir pourquoi, et croit cependant comprendre; il en profite pour mêler quelques considérations ethnographiques aux lieux communs d'un bon sens qui prend feu' ('likes the film without really knowing why, and yet thinks he understands it; he takes the opportunity to jumble a few ethnographic considerations with a riot of clichés'; Brunius 1929b: 78).

7. There is some evidence of this from Buñuel's brief account of the making of the film in his autobiography: '"Regarde par la fenêtre comme si tu entendais du Wagner. Plus pathétique encore." Mais il ne savait pas ce qu'il regardait, ce qu'il voyait' (Buñuel 1982: 126) ('"Stare out of the window and look as if you're listening to Wagner," I remember telling Batcheff. "No, no – not like that. Sadder. Much sadder." Batcheff never even knew what he was supposed to be looking at'; Buñuel 1984: 104).

8. It should not be thought that we are trying to establish a simple binary between 'being' and 'appearance' here; these are two different forms of appearing, two different types of performative gesture involving the persona. To use Barry King's useful distinction, acting is 'impersonating', while being a star is 'personifying' (King 1985).

9. See Powrie *et al.* 2007: 1–2 for a brief historical account of Spanishness in French culture.

10. To the extent that only a few months later, *Mon ciné* responded to a reader's impassioned 'Pierre Batcheff, je vous adore' ('Pierre Batcheff, I adore you!') by replying: 'Hélas ! Vous allez devoir entrer dans un couvent, Batcheff est marié. Il a épousé une charmante jeune femme russe qui tenait un emploi dans une administration cinématographique' ('I'm afraid you're going to have to enter a convent, Batcheff is married to a charming young Russian woman who was working in cinema administration'; *Mon ciné* 1930c: 2). Batcheff was not yet married, and Denise Tual was not Russian; it would seem that Batcheff's 'Russianness' was somehow contagious.

11. This is at least the inference made by several commentators (Durgnat 1968: 34; Williams 1981: 97; Short 2002: 86), the latter two relating it to Magritte's painting of a woman's face in the form of a torso, *Le Viol* (*Rape*, 1934), so that the pubic hair is where the mouth should be.

12. Flügel is careful to point out the relativism of such connotations, 'there being no essential connection between, say, a black coat and tight, stiff collar and the due sense of responsibility and duty for which these garments stand' (Flügel 1930: 197).

13. For example, Durgnat, who also uses the word 'prissy' to suggest feminisation: 'He has a prissy expression, and wears frilly white trimmings on his head, back and hips' (Durgnat 1968: 24). Durgnat also talks about 'the feminine atmosphere of his frills' (Durgnat 1968: 24). See also Williams 1981: 76 and Short 2002: 76 for the use of the word 'frills'. Drummond calls it a 'maid's costume' (Drummond 1977: 65), which is making assumptions that are not borne out by the evidence. Buñuel uses the term 'mantelets' in the shooting script (Buñuel 1929a: 34), which is exactly what the garment on his shoulders is: 'A kind of short, loose, sleeveless cape, cloak, or mantle covering the shoulders' (*Oxford English Dictionary*).

14. For example, Higginbotham writes that Batcheff 'wears over his suit articles of clothing denoting effeminacy' (Higginbotham 1979: 37).

15. Indeed, it is no coincidence, we might argue, that the word role is connected etymologically to the idea of rolling, or wheels.

16. 'The sign of death' (Durgnat 1968: 35); 'an ominous sign' (Higginbotham 1979: 38); 'death permeates the world of eros' (Thiher 1979: 33); 'a conventional symbol of death' (Williams 1981: 95); 'the sign of death' (Short 2002: 86). This is because the moth has always been connected with death. *Acherontia atropos* is named after Atropos, one of the three Greek goddesses of fate, whose role was to choose the way an individual died, and traditionally ended each mortal's life by cutting life's thread with her shears.

17. Buñuel makes a curious mistake in his positioning of the death's-head; it is found on the moth's thorax, not its wings.

18. Drummond mentions it in passing in the context of a brief discussion of 'anatomical' surrealism (Drummond 1977: 118).

19. Lomas reproduces the images, which are of 'Saint Anthony of Padua with the Infant Jesus', by an unknown artist, and two paintings by Dalí, 'Bathers' and 'Female Nude' (Lomas 2000: 162).

20. Although, given that we are considering the way the subject is split, it is interesting to note that the painting is in all probability, and unsurprisingly, an oblique reference to a division, that of Henry VIII's divorce from Catherine of Aragon, which was to lead to the divorce between Henry and Rome. See Foster and Tudor-Craig 1986.

21. As can be ascertained by watching visitors in the National Gallery, London, tricked by the anamorphosis into a physical activity which they are unlikely to resort to in front of other paintings. They take little account of the rest of the

painting, which is in fact a complex political allegory. The anamorphosis may lead us to attend to the painting, but our attention is deflected.

22. See Gustave Courbet, *L'Origine du monde* (1866), Musée d'Orsay, Paris. It is curious, to say the least, in the context of this discussion that Lacan was the last private owner of this painting.

CHAPTER 9

Looking back

We are at a disadvantage in this chapter in that many of the films following *Un Chien andalou* are either not extant or extant only in part, giving us a partial view of Batcheff's work in this period. They are not extant partly, we suspect, because they are, according to contemporary accounts, uninspiring films. We have none the less presented an analysis of them based on archive material, because they serve to confirm, as we shall see, many of the elements of Batcheff's star image. We present a more sustained analysis of Batcheff's final film, *Baroud*, whose two language versions are extant.

Why were Batcheff's last films so unsuccessful? A first reason is that they looked backwards rather than forwards, one might argue, replaying aspects of his image at a time when he himself had moved radically away from it with *Les Deux Timides* and *Un Chien andalou*. Where there are slight variations on that image, it would seem that audiences did not react favourably, as we shall see below. A second reason is the transition to sound, which affected Batcheff in two ways. His star image was built on distance and enigma, the mysterious other; introducing his voice into this configuration was damaging at a time when the *jeune premier* more generally was changing to the wholesome, sporty type that we described in Chapter 2. This may well explain why he chose to star in a late silent film, *Illusions* (all the others in this chapter being sound films). This was all the more the case when we consider the timbre of his voice. In those films we have been able to see, in common with many actors at that time, he fails to project his voice, this being at least partly due to his more general turn towards a more realist style of acting based on understated gesture. Unfortunately, the sound technology of the time did not allow for understated vocality.

A final reason for the relative lack of success of these films is directly linked to the arrival of sound; many of them were released in multiple versions, as was the habit in the period 1929–34 (see Billard 1995: 46–52). As one writer put it, anxious to point out the poor quality of such films: 'La nécessité où se trouvent les producteurs de réaliser coûte que coûte des versions multiples pour exporter leur pellicule les poussent à négliger (. . .) la qualité artistique' ('The need for producers to release multiple versions so as to export their films is leading them to sacrifice the artistic quality'; Desclaux 1930: 7). The first of these films, with the rather unfortunate title of *Illusions*,[1] was not a multiple-version film, but was poorly received none the less.

ILLUSIONS (JANUARY 1930)

Shooting for this film started in September 1929, and was completed by mid-October. It was the last silent film shot in the studios of the rue Francœur, leading to die-hard statements by some reviewers: 'Que les fervents du cinéma muet se réjouissent: le film muet n'est pas encore tout à fait mort!' ('Fans of silent cinema can rejoice: the silent film is not yet quite dead!'; Doré 1929b: 606). It was a first film for Lucien Mayrargue, described in one review as a playwright (Régent 1930a: 6), although he had participated in the making of *Le Perroquet vert* in 1928. He went on to direct another film, again starring Mary Serta (with Albert Préjean), later in the 1930s, *Neuf de trèfle* (1937). The reviews were amongst the poorest for any of Batcheff's films. The main complaint by reviewers was that the film was too long and boring: 'action languissante' ('slow-moving'; Anri 1930); 'histoire ennuyeuse' ('boring story'; Mairgance 1930); 'si son film durait une demi-heure, ce serait charmant d'un bout à l'autre' ('if his film had lasted half an hour, it would have been charming'; Régent 1930a: 6); 'Mayrargue a donné trop d'ampleur à un sujet qui n'en comportait pas' ('Mayrargue has given the story-line a scale it did not warrant'; Vincent-Bréchignac 1930: 5). Valentine/Mary Serta plays hard to get, and we see an overlong series of meetings between her and Batcheff's Henry as he woos her: in the Bois de Boulogne, at a drinks party, in a shop, at the races, at a society dinner where he slyly changes name tags to sit next to her. Not only are there too many of such scenes, but the chemistry between the actors is absent. Even more tedious is a long sequence with Valentine visiting her mother in the country. Narratively, Valentine needs to be away from Paris so that Henry can be tempted by Odette; but we see Valentine walking in the fields, in a farmyard, playing cards with her mother, turning a narrative necessity into an unmotivated bucolic interlude. This leads to a problem of tone, exacerbated by two sequences with diametrically opposed effects, but both over-emphatic. In one of the wooing sequences, in Valentine's apartment, Henry tries to kiss her repeatedly, and every time she rings the bell for her maid, preventing him from doing so. This comic routine goes on, like so many other sequences in the film, just a little too long to be convincing, and jars with an equally drawn out and equally over-emphatic sequence when Valentine staggers melodramatically out of Henry's apartment, having overheard him and Odette in a passionate embrace.

In the circumstances, it is not surprising that Batcheff himself came out of it badly. While one reviewer described him in ways we are familiar with, as 'élégant' ('elegant'; Chataignier 1930), the many wooing scenes allowing frequent changes of clothes, several others complained about his performance and its excessive cheekiness, almost as if Batcheff had not quite managed to shake himself free of the comic performances of *Les Deux Timides* and *Un Chien andalou*: 'Batcheff joue trop avec son menton et ses épaules, et son air gouailleur le quitte trop rarement' ('Batcheff uses his chin and shoulders far too much, and his cheeky look is too much in evidence'; Anri 1930); 'Batcheff (. . .) joue surtout avec son sourire gouailleur, ses épaules et ses bras raides comme des cannes, joue souvent très mal (. . .) son allure un peu mécanique' ('Batcheff (. . .) plays on his cheeky smile, his shoulders and arms held stiffly by his side, often performs badly (. . .) and mechanically'; Mairgance 1930). *Pour vous*'s reviewer, normally supportive of Batcheff, summed it up: 'Batcheff a presque toujours été mieux' ('Batcheff has almost always been better than this'; Régent 1930a: 6).

Part of the problem lies in his performance, which is unusually active for him. He swings his body about, his arms often flailing wildly; in one sequence, where it is clear that he has won Valentine, they are on a beach, and he rushes into the water, rolling about in the surf and doing handstands. His performance is closer to the comic routines of *Les Deux Timides*, and it is possible that audiences reacted badly to the shift away from the melancholic and distant lover. A second problem for a star known for his youthfulness was the denouement. He plays the unfaithful lover of the letters, but turns out to be a happily married husband when the passer-by (Gaston Jacquet) eventually finds the old couple. There may well have been a feeling that this went counter to his star image; not only is he happily married, but he is also no longer the *jeune premier* at the end of the film. He is an old man, with white hair and beard, glasses and a dressing gown, a feature commented on by one review, which takes up the general theme of illusion when commenting on stills from the shoot:

> Mary Serta et Pierre Batcheff (. . .) paraissent d'abord, sur la pellicule, dans tout l'éclat de leurs vingt ans. Puis, brusquement (. . .) voici qu'ils se montrent affublés de rides et de cheveux blancs (. . .) Voici d'ailleurs deux photos de travail qui montrent d'un côté Batcheff et Mary Serta en pleine jeunesse et, de l'autre, les mêmes artistes considérablement vieillis. (*Mon ciné* 1930a: 7)

> (Mary Serta and Pierre Batcheff first appear on screen in the full bloom of their twenty years. Then, suddenly, they are wrinkled and white-haired. Here are two photos taken on the set showing Batcheff and Mary Serta in their youth on one side, and the other the same actors considerably older.)

The film is disappointing, but there are interesting touches none the less. The couple's first kiss takes place in a taxi, and we see their faces backlit and framed in the rearview mirror, complementing almost expressionistic lighting effects in the opera, with stark backlighting isolating them from the theatrical space. There are also a couple of effects audiences would have seen in the Impressionist cinema of Epstein or Dulac. When Henry kisses Odette, he turns away the photograph of Valentine, which is immediately superimposed by Valentine's tearful face. A similar effect with water occurs later in the film, when Valentine stops on a bridge, evidently contemplating suicide, and the ripples of the Seine are superimposed once more with her face as tears trickle down, echoing the surface of the river. But these touches, interesting though they are, merely confirm the oddly fractured tone of the film.

Six months later, Batcheff starred in his first talkie, a remake of an early silent, which was shot in two language versions.

Le Roi de Paris (August 1930)

This was a remake of the film of the same title starring Jean Dax eight years earlier (Charles Maudru and Maurice de Marsan, 1922), based on a 1898 novel by the popular nineteenth-century novelist Georges Ohnet (1848–1918), whose work had been adapted in over twenty films since 1910. It was Leo Mittler's first talkie; he also directed the German version, released in the same year, *Der König von Paris* (which did not star Batcheff). Like the previous film, this one was a failure, as the following reviews indicate:

> Ce n'est pas brillant . . . (. . .) Les caractères des personnages ne sont pas solidement posés, ils semblent, devant nous, n'avoir aucune vie: trop de personnages importants, aussi, mais aucun essentiel . . . (Régent 1930b: 5)

> (It isn't brilliant . . . (. . .) The characters are not fleshed out, they seem lifeless: too many important characters, as well, but none of them essential . . .)

> L'intrigue est tellement conventionnelle et banale, que l'habilité de la réalisation disparaît derrière tant de platitude. (Villette 1930: 5)

> (The plot is so conventional and banal that the interesting elements of the direction sink beneath the platitudes.)

The readers' column of *Mon ciné* is instructive in this respect: 'Une vaste rigolade', says one ('a big joke'; *Mon ciné* 1931a: 14), reporting that the audience shouted it down, a reaction corroborated by another reader a few weeks later, who stated that the film 'a provoqué des protestations innombrables' ('led to countless protests'; *Mon ciné* 1931c: 2). Two weeks later, another reader reports soberly that '*Le Roi de Paris* n'est pas un bon film' ('*Le Roi de Paris* is not a good film'; *Mon ciné* 1931b: 2), a response repeated six months later in a facetious but damning comment: '*Le Roi de Paris* ne s'est pas révélé le roi des films' ('*The King of Paris* turns out not to be the king of films'; *Mon ciné* 1931d: 14).

Batcheff's next film was more successful, at least where he was concerned.

Les Amours de minuit (January 1931)/*Mitternachtsliebe* (September 1931)

Multiple-version films came in different guises. These were more often than not films made in several languages in the same studio, usually French and German, as was the case with *Le Roi de Paris*. Then there were foreign-language versions of American films, made in a different studio, in Europe, after the original film, as was the case with *Le Rebelle*, which we will consider below, made in the Paramount studios in Joinville. *Les Amours de minuit* is unusual; it was the first time an originally French film had been made in another language.[2] The seasoned Italian silent-film director, Augusto Genina (his first film was made in 1912), had moved to France to make *Quartier Latin* with Gina Manès (1929), followed by a star vehicle for Louise Brooks, *Prix de beauté (Miss Europe)* (1930), scripted by René Clair and Georg Wilhelm Pabst. *Paris-Béguin* (1931) was one of Jean Gabin's early films, and the film Genina made just before *Les Amours de minuit* was *La Femme en homme* (1931), starring Françoise Rosay. Genina was therefore working with 'A-list' actors, and *Les Amours de minuit* might reasonably have been expected to do well, not least because it was also the first talkie to be made at the Billancourt Studios after an extensive refit (see Régent 1930c: 14).

The reception of the film was mixed, however. Marcel Carné praised it for its dreamlike atmosphere: 'Beaux éclairages nocturnes de toute la partie "chemin de fer" à laquelle le son donne une force presque hallucinante' ('Beautiful night lighting in the train section to which the sound gives an almost hallucinatory impact'; Carné 1931: 14), and *Le Courrier cinématographique* thought the narrative 'fluide, sans heurts, sans bavures, bien lié, bien équilibré' ('flowing, smooth, without botches, coherent, well-balanced'; *Courrier cinématographique* 1931: 25). But it was unfavourably compared with *Der blaue Engel* (Josef von Sternberg, 1930), released in Paris only six months before. The poet Philippe Soupault, amongst others, expressed indignation at what he considered to be inept plagiarism, Danièle Parola suffering the brunt of his wrath: 'Il y a une scène qui se passe dans le cabaret du Paradis qui est servilement copiée sur celle qui se passe dans le cabaret de *L'Ange bleu*. Le costume de la vedette est identique. Malheureusement Mlle Parola n'a pas l'espèce de génie de Marlene Dietrich ni sa voix "prenante"' ('There's a scene in the Paradise cabaret slavishly copied from the cabaret scene in *The Blue Angel*. The

Figure 9.1   *Les Amours de minuit*: strangers on a train (Collection Roche-Batcheff)

star's costume is exactly the same. Unfortunately, Miss Parola doesn't have Marlene Dietrich's particular genius, nor her "captivating" voice'; Soupault 1979: 216).

A second complaint was that what little mystery might have been gener-ated by the unexplained relationships or events surrounding Batcheff's char-acter was dispelled by the revelation at the end of the film that the character was a bank thief, thereby reducing the poetic to the crassly materialistic: 'De l'histoire, un seul élément curieux, l'énigme de ce jeune homme. Pourquoi montre-t-il qu'il possède une grosse somme à Bouchard qu'il rencontre dans un train? D'où vient-il ? Où va-t-il ? Dommage qu'à la fin, nous apprenions que ce garçon est un voleur' ('There's only one element of curiosity in this story: the enigma of this young man. Why does he show Bouchard the large sum of money when he meets him on the train? Where does he come from? Where is he going? Shame that at the end we learn that he is a thief'; Wahl 1931: 5). Another reviewer, who praises the film in general for its 'qualité exceptionnelle' ('exceptional quality'), makes a similar point: 'La faiblesse de la fin (. . .) ne gâche pas trop une bande qui émeut par son mystère humain' ('The weak ending doesn't spoil too much a film whose human mystery is moving'; *Ami du peuple* 1931).[3]

Critics may have had reservations about the plot; most were very complimentary about Batcheff. *Mon ciné* thought he acquitted himself well in what was a difficult role (Villette 1931a: 5), a point also made by Wahl who emphasised Batcheff's 'jeu simple' ('straightforward performance'; Wahl 1931: 5). Others stressed his 'finesse et (. . .) émotion' ('sensitivity and (. . .) emotion'; Dassonville 1931), or depth and intensity: 'Batcheff demeure l'un des seuls jeunes premiers français qui sachent composer un rôle et le vivre intensément' ('Batcheff is one of the few French *jeunes premiers* who knows how to put together a role and live it intensely'; *Ami du peuple* 1931). Carné thought Batcheff 'fiévreux et tourmenté à souhait' ('perfectly feverish and tormented'; Carné 1931: 14). Soupault may have disliked the derivative nature of the film, but he was fulsome in his praise for Batcheff, emphasising, like Wahl, Batcheff's naturalistic performance:

> Ce qui donne à ce film sa véritable valeur, c'est l'interprétation, du moins l'interprétation masculine. Le rôle de Marcel est remarquablement interprété par M. Pierre Batcheff, celui du criminel par M. Jacques Varenne. Voilà deux acteurs, et particulièrement le premier nommé, qui ont compris ce qu'était le cinéma. La sobriété de leur jeu, leur naturel, leur simplicité prouvent que dans un film les moindres intentions peuvent être indiquées sans gesticuler en vain. (Soupault 1979: 215–16)

> (The film's real value lies in the performance of its male stars. Marcel's role is remarkably performed by Mr Pierre Batcheff, the criminal by Mr Jacques Varenne. These two actors, and especially the former, have understood what cinema is. Their performance – restrained, natural, simple – proves that intentions can be conveyed without undue exaggeration.)

From what we have been able to view of the film, Batcheff's performance is indeed understated, as well as a return to the kind of form and the slightly shady characters of some of his earlier films. Batcheff repeated his role in the German version, made in Berlin in April 1931, and released later that year in Berlin.

Le Rebelle (August 1931)

Although *Les Amours de minuit* was a relative success, *Le Rebelle* was a return to the poor form of the first two films following *Un Chien andalou*. It was based on a play entitled *A Tabornok* (*The General*) by the Hungarian novelist and playwright Lajos Zilahy (1891–1974). It was made in multiple versions across the globe. The first was the US version, entitled *The Virtuous Sin*, released in November 1930, directed by George Cukor and Louis J. Gasnier, and starring Kenneth MacKenna in the Batcheff role. This was followed a year later by

Figure 9.2   *Les Amours de minuit*: Pierre Batcheff and Danièle Parola (Collection Roche-Batcheff)

three foreign-language versions, including the French version that concerns us here, all made in Paramount's Joinville studios: Dimitri Buchowetzki's German version, entitled *Die Nacht der Entscheidung*, released in September 1931 and starring Peter Voss; and a Swedish version by Gustaf Bergman (November 1931), starring Paul van der Osten. As one reviewer of the French version commented in relation to the international nature of just the French

Figure 9.3 *Le Rebelle*: Pierre Batcheff as the self-absorbed scientist with a characteristic stoop, and Suzy Vernon (Collection Roche-Batcheff)

version, 'version française d'un film parlant américain *The Virtuous Sin*, tournée aux Studios Paramount de Joinville, par un réalisateur espagnol, *Le Rebelle*, dont l'action se déroule en Russie (. . .) est ce que l'on peut appeler un film international' ('French version of an American talkie, *The Virtuous Sin* was made at Paramount's Joinville Studios, by a Spanish director, and it is located in Russia (. . .), so a truly international film'; *Hebdo-Film* 1931: 14). The film was seen by many as conventional and uninspiring, the characters mere ciphers; Batcheff's partner for this film, Suzy Vernon (who had played Madame Récamier in Gance's *Napoléon*), 'fait l'impossible pour sauver un rôle impossible', said one reviewer ('does her best to save an impossible role'; Villette 1931b: 5).

Batcheff's role was the reverse of the role he played in *Vivre*. In that film, he was the consumptive lover, and the husband was the scientist who neglected his wife; in this film, he plays a scientist too absorbed in his work to pay much attention to his wife. Like *Illusions*, then, there is a mismatch with his previous roles (even if, like some of his previous films, he plays a Russian in a Russian context). That, when added to the contrast between the intellectual buried in his work and his sudden and excessive 'revolt' on sentimental grounds, led to charges of inconsistency: 'Malgré son talent, (il) nous fait difficilement supporter le côté inconsistant de Boris' ('Despite his talents, (he) doesn't manage to carry off Boris's inconsistencies'; Villette 1931b: 5). More generally, however, reviewers tended to accentuate the intensity of conflicting emotions, in terms that remind us of the excessive performance of *Un Chien andalou*:

> Tour à tour las, désaxé, vaincu par l'amour, inquiet de son destin, traversé de révoltes, (. . .) Pierre Batcheff rend pitoyable sa détresse à force de talent et d'intelligence. Son masque mobile et fin, qu'éclairent des yeux fiévreux et suppliants, reflète toutes les incertitudes de son âme ballottée. (*Ciné-Miroir* 1931: 307)

> (By turns weary, unbalanced, vanquished by love, anxious for his future, shot through by defiance, (. . .) Pierre Batcheff makes us pity his distress through his talent and his intelligence. His fine mobile features, lit up by feverishly pleading eyes, reflect the uncertainties that buffet him.)

> Il traduit avec un naturel profond les sentiments qui le bouleversent et il parcourt toutes les étapes de son douloureux calvaire avec une intensité d'expression qui rend son personnage infiniment sympathique et touchant. (*Progrès du Nord* 1931)

> (He conveys in the most natural way the emotions that tear him apart and he goes through all the stages of his painful ordeal with an expressive intensity that makes his character incredibly sympathetic and touching.)

Batcheff's role conforms to the stereotype of the weak and effeminate intellectual. *Pour vous*'s reviewer describes him as an 'adolescent palot et chétif, avec de grands yeux, un grand front, de faibles mains timides' ('a pale and puny adolescent, wide-eyed, broad-browed, with weak and shy hands'; Sauvage 1931: 12), and a regional newspaper talks of his 'taille frêle et souffreteuse' ('frail and sickly figure'; *Petit Niçois* 1931). Although in one sense this conformed to his image – the combination of effeminacy with intellect – the element of recklessness and pusillanimity was a new one. Although his characters in some of his previous films may have been weak, this was due less to intimations of cowardice than of some kind of tragic flaw, such as an addiction to gambling.

Many regional newspapers, however, seemed not to notice this new element, and recycled well-established aspects of Batcheff's star image in their appraisals, such as elegance and sensitivity: 'Sensible et douloureux' ('sensitive and pained'; *Moniteur du Puy-de-Dôme* 1932); 'jeu naturellement élégant et sobre' ('a naturally elegant and low-key performance'; *Nîmes Journal* 1932). A final quotation illustrates how these latter aspects combine with the element of distance we have identified as a crucial component of his persona: 'Racé, svelte, élégant, avec un regard profond et presque lointain, tel est Pierre Batcheff, qui

Figure 9.4　*Le Rebelle*: Batcheff as the effeminate hero (Collection Roche-Batcheff)

semble toujours poursuivre un rêve ou un regret' ('Distinguished, slender, elegant, with a deep and almost distant gaze, such is Pierre Batcheff, who always seems to be chasing a dream or a regret'; *Progrès du Nord* 1931). The dreaminess and vacant gaze return in Batcheff's final film, *Baroud*, seasoned with elements of Valentino-like exoticism.

BAROUD (ENGLISH VERSION SEPTEMBER 1932/FRENCH VERSION NOVEMBER 1932)

Rex Ingram, the director of *Baroud*, was a well-established Hollywood figure. He had launched two 'Latin lovers': Rudolph Valentino in *The Four Horsemen of the Apocalypse* in 1921, and then Ramon Novarro, whose first major success was *Scaramouche* (1923),[4] followed by *The Arab* (1924), again with Ingram. His films were often (fourteen out of twenty-seven) located in exotic or European countries, with several of his later works filmed in the Mediterranean or North Africa, locations made somewhat easier geographically by his purchase of the derelict Victorine studios in Nice in 1925.[5] Ingram spent four weeks in Morocco, visiting Tangiers, Rabat, and the strongholds of the chief El Glaoui in Telouet in the Atlas Mountains, and Marrakech (see O'Leary 1993: 194–7), steeping himself in local colour, this leading to a much-admired documentary-like record of life at the time. Indeed, he had had strong connections with North Africa since the mid-1920s when he had made *The Arab* in Tunisia, and may even have converted to the Muslim faith (see O'Leary 1993: 129, 139, 197); during the 1930s, after *Baroud*, he spent much time 'wandering in North Africa' (O'Leary 1993: 199).[6] He had tried unsuccessfully to engage Batcheff in 1926, as we recalled in Chapter 1.

Baroud was his first talkie and his last film, and was a throwback to those earlier successes with Valentino and Novarro; indeed, the sequence in the Oasis-Bar, where we see Batcheff smoking and moodily watching Arlette and André dance, is a direct reference to Valentino's first appearance in *The Four Horsemen of the Apocalypse*. Already in the mid-1920s, however, 'the so-called "sheik craze" was waning' (Ellenberger 1999: 37), and the regressive feel of the film was undoubtedly one of the reasons it did not do very well. O'Leary reports that at its British premiere on 28 September 1932, 'before the final credits reached the screen the projectionist had drawn the curtains, a rather humiliating gesture towards its maker' (O'Leary 1993: 187). Although the documentary aspect led to considerable praise, most reviewers were less impressed by the narrative. One newspaper thought the film a masterpiece largely due to its use of non-professional actors, a very unusual practice for the time: 'Sans doute les deux rôles principaux sont-ils remplis par des artistes que nous connaissons; mais tous les autres interprètes, depuis le Caïd Si Alah jusqu'au dernier spahi sont recrutés parmi les gens que cette magistrale production a utilisés comme ils devaient l'être' ('It's true that the main roles are played by well-known actors; but all the other actors, from the Caïd Si Alah right down to the last Spahis [Cavalry regiments of the French army recruited mainly from the indigenous populations of the North African French colonies] are recruited from the people that this masterful production has used as they should be used'; d'Ast 1932). Another was fascinated by the way in which the film 'nous transporte vraiment en Afrique' ('really transports us to Africa; Méré 1932), as was another by Ingram's avoidance of American-style 'faux exotisme' ('false exoticism'; Lagrange 1932). And *Cinémonde* praised the film's 'vie intense, et sa couleur locale, son pittoresque, son exotisme rendu familier' ('intense life, its local colour, its picturesque qualities, its exoticism made familiar'; *Cinémonde* 1932: 919). A British reviewer was similarly smitten by the film's documentary beauty, noting the 'skilfully composed scenes of Moroccan landscapes and white-walled towns in which the quality of the sunlight is so vivid that the shadows are translucent' (G. A. Atkinson cited in O'Leary 1993: 189). The American view of *Love in Morocco*, as it was called in the USA, did not differ, singling out various elements for praise:

It is . . . definitely charming in its recreation of the Moroccan atmosphere and the dark beauty of its people as idealized by Mr. Ingram's canvas. The pastel skies, the mountains and the desert country, the narrow winding alleys of Marrakesh, the flat white houses and the Moorish civilization make a fascinating background. The picture is flooded with picturesque types, Spahis, African serving women, beggars, dancing girls, bandits from the desert and sinister Europeans. (*New York Times* 1933)

Compared with the documentary realism and the beauty of the photography in real locations, however, the narrative had no chance. *Le Figaro*'s reviewer focused on that disparity: 'La beauté des paysages supplée à la faiblesse de l'intrigue (. . .) *Baroud*, qui eût sombré dans le ridicule, réalisé en de médiocres décors, se soutient par ses extérieurs, une mise en scène à grand spectacle et la rare qualité de ses photographies' ('The beauty of the landscapes makes up for the weakness of the plot (. . .) *Baroud*, which would have lapsed into the ridiculous if it had been made in mediocre decors, holds up thanks to its exteriors, a spectacular mise en scene and the rare quality of its photography'; Laury 1932). *L'Écho*'s reviewer summed this up in a lapidary statement: 'Un film brillant, bruyant, mouvementé, aussi vivant qu'un documentaire – sur le scénario le plus puérilement conventionnel' ('A brilliant film, noisy, eventful, as vivid as a documentary – but based on the most childishly conventional script'; Gordeaux 1932). The dialogue was judged to be 'plat, pauvre' ('dull and poor'; Méré 1932), the same reviewer regretting that it was not a silent film.

Indeed, the general sense one takes from many of the reviews is that Ingram's day was past, that the cinema had moved on, but that he was ill at ease with it. As Méré wrote: 'Nous ne sommes plus en 1920. Nous sommes en droit d'exiger beaucoup plus du cinéma, depuis qu'il a appris à parler' ('We are no longer in 1920. We have a right to expect much more of the cinema since it has been talking'; Méré 1932). *Pour vous* made a similar point, dismissing what was now felt to be Ingram's regressive naiveté: 'On y retrouve ce goût des grands tableaux pittoresques, ce romanesque facile, cette habileté et cette naïveté qui avaient déjà fait (son) succès (. . .) Et pourtant, ce n'est plus la même chose: M. Rex Ingram n'a pas changé; mais nous, nous avons changé' ('We rediscover his taste for broad picturesque tableaux, the breezy stories, the skill and the naiveté that were the hallmark of his success (. . .) But it's no longer the same: Rex Ingram hasn't changed, but we on the other hand have changed'; Frank 1932: 8).

As had been the case with *Les Amours de minuit*, a film that looked back at *Der blaue Engel*, Batcheff none the less came out of this film – which looked back to the North African-based films of Valentino and Novarro – surprisingly well, although clearly his recent death may well have led to greater praise than might have been warranted had he been alive. While one reviewer thought that he had 'joué avec plus de sincérité et de conviction dans sa trop courte carrière' ('acted with more sincerity and conviction in his too brief career'; Lagrange 1932), others thought that he was one of the high points, at least in comparison with the other main roles: 'L'interprétation, si nous exceptons Pierre Batcheff, Roger Gaillard et la figuration (s'est) montrée faiblarde' ('the acting, with the exception of Pierre Batcheff, Roger Gaillard and the extras, is poor'; *Européen* 1932). It is true that most of the major actors are laughably stilted, partly because they are not French native speakers; but then Rex Ingram himself, in the English version, is just as stilted, and our view is that Batcheff is the only actor who comes across with any conviction in either version.

Batcheff has three key scenes: the Oasis-Bar scene, to which we have already referred; and two scenes that take place in the barracks, the first underlining the camaraderie between Hamed and André, the second the conflict between friendship and duty for Hamed when he learns that André has tried to seduce his sister. These scenes raise in acute form the questions to which we have returned constantly in this book: the gaze that turns Batcheff into an object, the tensions between his 'orientalism' – defined in this film, as we shall see, as 'savagery' – and the forces that work against it, such as his sophistication, his Frenchness and the 'vacancy' of his look as he attempts to escape reification.

In Chapter 2 we explored the parallels between Batcheff and Valentino. The Latin Lover was, we might argue, a logical step for a *jeune premier* associated with childlike effeminacy of the *Claudine et le poussin* type. The Latin Lover had a more dangerous erotic promise for women spectators, and may well in France, as he did in the USA, represent a significant shift in female emancipation, his 'darkly foreign' nature acting as a magnet for 'women and their restless desires' (Studlar 1996: 151), 'exciting sexual promise' being combined with 'dangerous foreign bestiality' (Studlar 1996: 178). This aspect of Batcheff's character is emphasised in the Oasis-Bar scene early on in the film. Batcheff is first reified as an erotic object. We see him in medium long shot sitting with one leg resting on the other, leaning forwards slightly, draped in his ornately embroidered burnous, smoking languidly; the camera travels up from his leather boots to take in the full figure. This turns out to be the point of view of an elderly European woman, evidently a tourist, who adjusts her spectacles as she looks at him, underlining the fetishistic nature of Batcheff-as-spectacle. She draws further attention to him as spectacle, when she points out 'all that beautiful costume, and all those medals', suggesting to her companion that Hamed could act as their guide. He informs her that Hamed is the son of the pasha, to which she exclaims: 'You mean to tell me he's a real sheik!'[7]

It is not just the use of the word 'sheik' that references Valentino. The bulk of the sequence is taken up with a discussion between Hamed and the European singer Arlette, to whom he is attracted. They discuss the moral code which obliges a brother to kill the offender if his sister has been sexually compromised by a non-Maghrebi. Arlette's response is slightly different in the two versions, but the gist is the same. She calls Hamed 'sauvage et mignon' in the French version, ('savage and charming'). The English version insists rather more on the 'savage':

> Arlette – I adore being in Morocco. You're a lot of savages.
> Hamed – Perhaps we are more civilised than you are.
> Arlette – And yet, if you caught a man with your sister, you'd kill him.
> Hamed – Ah, that's different.
> Arlette – There, I knew you were a savage.

Later in the film, we discover that Arlette has written 'à mon beau sauvage' ('to my beautiful savage' in the English version) on the photograph she has given to Hamed. In *The Sheik*, Rudolph Valentino is frequently called a 'savage' by the leading lady, Lady Diana Mayo (Agnes Ayres), although later in the film she learns that he is not North African at all, but Anglo-Spanish, thus to some extent neutralising the alien violence inherent in the character.

That, of course, is part of the point. Oriental 'savagery' must be contained by European 'charm' and sophistication for both Valentino and Batcheff. Hamed may be a 'savage', savagery here being defined as violence associated with sexuality, but this is mitigated by his upper-class status in Moroccan society (echoing the aristocrats he plays in historical reconstructions, as well as in many of his dramas). It is also mitigated in this narrative by the relationship with André. They both have the same rank in the Spahis, they share the same room in barracks, they share secrets, and they engage in the usual homosocial bonding where women are objects of conquest or of misogynistic gazing, such as the scene celebrating the Spahis' return where the two of them wordlessly comment on the overly buxom nature of one of the women dancers. The French version, indeed, engages very directly with homoeroticism, as they roll about on the same bed in their barracks room, André tickling Hamed's foot with a brush. This is absent from the English version where Rex Ingram plays the role of André; interestingly, the two characters seem much less close in the English version, something that the camera underlines, as its position tends to privilege Ingram rather more than Batcheff in a number of scenes. None the less, the two are clearly intended to be close; Hamed even lends André his distinctive burnous so that he can seduce a woman who, unbeknownst to him of course, is Hamed's sister. It is

Figure 9.5   *Baroud*: Hamed draws his knife and prepares to kill André (Photo R. Tomatis, Collection Roche-Batcheff)

important for dramatic tension that they should be close, so that Islamic law can separate them, at least momentarily, as Hamed draws his knife and prepares to kill André (see Figure 9.5); but their closeness also minimises Hamed's otherness.

Their closeness also paradoxically helps to distinguish between them at the end of the film. They may both have attempted to cross ethnic boundaries, but it is likely that only André will be lucky in love; Hamed does not get his girl. In this he is very different to Valentino, and *Baroud* concords with the vacant and masochistic persona with which we are familiar from so many of Batcheff's previous films. André is paired with a virginal child-woman; Hamed, on the other hand, is paired with the world-weary Dietrich lookalike, the rather more mature woman for whom Hamed is only a passing interest. Hamed/Batcheff is too 'other' for him to be paired with Arlette; the distant gaze, the look off, is therefore crucial (see Figure 9.6). When we see him as an erotic object of the gaze in the Oasis-Bar, he looks off, in classic pin-up mode. But he also looks off when his flash of anger at André has subsided, and he realises that he cannot kill his friend. Although this remains unsaid, he has not

Figure 9.6 *Baroud*: Batcheff's look off (Collection Roche-Batcheff)

fulfilled the tenets of Islamic law and remains ineluctably in between cultures, abandoned to himself, adrift.

The most poignant expression of this no-man's-land in which Hamed/ Batcheff is abandoned, is Arlette's song. In both versions, the song is sung in French; we have provided our attempt at a translation below, trying to convey its melancholy. We see Batcheff, drooping forwards and smoking

Figure 9.7   *Baroud*: the melancholic 'savage' (Collection Roche-Batcheff)

melancholically, when we hear the lines: 'It's just that you're down/When your days are full of sadness', and then again for the lines 'When you lose your liking/For the woman who can't stop talking'. In other words, the song underlines loss and sadness, in a typical Batcheffian moment of melancholic destitution.

Song lyrics	Translation
Quand tu perds l'empreinte	When on loveless days
De nos folles étreintes,	The marks of our passionate embrace
Par des jours sans amour,	Fade away,
T'en fais donc pas, c'est le cafard.	Don't worry, it's just that you're down.
Quand sous le soleil	When the burning sun
Tout ton sang perd son vermeil,	Pales the ruby of your blood,
Le dégoût gardera tout,	And only disgust seems to have any colour,
T'en fais donc pas, c'est le cafard.	Don't worry, it's just that you're down.
Quand tu connais des jours de peine,	When your days are full of sadness,
Marchant vers le grand désert,	As you walk towards the open desert,
Crois pas que t'as perdu ta veine,	Don't think that your luck's out,
T'es mordu par le sale cafard.	It's just that you're down, really down.
Quand tu perds le goût	When you lose your liking
De la femme qui parle de tout,	For the woman who can't stop talking,
Quand la vie semble finie,	When life seems about to end,
T'en fais donc pas, c'est le cafard.	Don't worry, it's just that you're down.

Notes

1. As one reviewer pointed out: 'Il est toujours dangereux de donner à une œuvre un titre appelant trop facilement le sarcasme, lorsqu'elle ne répond pas à ce qu'on attend d'elle (. . .) D'*Illusions* à la désillusion, il n'y avait qu'un pas à franchir' ('It's always dangerous to give a film a title that can be used against it sarcastically when it is not as good as expected (. . .) There is only one short step from *Illusions* to disillusion'; Mairgance 1930).
2. Reported in *Pour vous* 1931: 2.
3. We have not been able to verify this judgement, as the last reel in the Cinémathèque Française is missing.
4. Valentino also starred in Ingram's *The Conquering Power* (1921). Novarro had appeared in three films by Ingram before his breakthrough in *Scaramouche*: *The Prisoner of Zenda* (1922), under the name Ramon Samaniegos; *Trifling Women* (1922); and *Where the Pavement Ends* (1923).
5. *Broken Fetters* (1916) in Hong Kong; *The Chalice of Sorrow* (1916) in Mexico; *The Reward of the Faithless* (1917) in Russia; *The Pulse of Life* (1917) in Italy; *The Flower of Doom* (1917), although set in the USA, is located in Chinatown; *Under Crimson Skies* (1919) in Central America; *The Four Horsemen of the Apocalypse* (1921) in a Europe ravaged by war; *The Conquering Power* (1921), a version of a Balzac novel, *Eugénie Grandet*; *The Prisoner of Zenda* (1922) in the fictional European country of Ruritania; *Trifling Women* (1922) in Paris; *Scaramouche* (1923) in revolutionary France; *The Arab*

(1924) in North Africa, a film intended to rival Valentino's *The Sheik* (1921); *Mare Nostrum* (1926) in the Mediterranean; *The Garden of Allah* (1927) in North Africa once more.

6. O'Leary makes some errors in his brief sketch of Batcheff: 'This young man of Russian origin had a most beautiful face and was very cultured, an excellent jeune premier of the thirties. He had begun his career with George Pitoeff in Geneva but from 1921 had played in films by Gance, L'Herbier, Bernard, Cavalcanti, Clair, and in Bunuel and Dali's *Chien Andalou*. His tragic suicide in April 1932 just after *Baroud* was a loss to the French cinema. He was a brother-in-law of Jacques Doniol-Valcroze, film critic and founder of *Les Cahiers du Cinema*' (O'Leary 1993: 189; we have respected O'Leary's spelling without accents). The 'Notes and Amendments' (p. [iv]) rectify the error of the 'thirties'. However, Batcheff's film career began in 1923 not 1921; he never acted in a film by Cavalcanti; and he was not the brother-in-law of Doniol-Valcroze. This last confusion stems from the fact that Jean-George Auriol married Batcheff's sister, Sonia, in 1932, just after Batcheff's death.

7. We are using the dialogue from the English version. There are, as one might expect, differences between the two language versions, but they are less significant than some of the differences in the camerawork, as we shall see.

CHAPTER 10

Conclusion: uncanny bodies

> J'ai l'impression que vous aurez beaucoup de mal à faire un livre sur lui, ne l'ayant pas connu, parce que c'est un personnage tellement divers, avec des facettes à la fois comique, dramatique, emballé, déprimé . . . avec ça, qui sont finalement pas des très bons films. (Interview with Denise Tual, 1996)

> (I think you'll find it difficult to do a book on him, because you didn't know him, because he is such a multi-faceted character, comic, dramatic, enthusiastic, depressed . . . and with films which in the end weren't that good.)

> À jouer au fantôme, on le devient. (Caillois 1935: 5)

> (If you play the Phantom, you will become a Phantom.)

There is a sense in which the last films Batcheff made were an unwelcome return to the star persona that he had worked hard to shift with *Les Deux Timides* and *Un Chien andalou*. In that respect, his persona came back to haunt him. This notion of haunting is fundamental to surrealist aesthetics at the end of the 1920s, and clearly articulated in *Nadja* in 1928, as we mentioned earlier in this volume, with Breton's claim that his rhetorical question, 'who am I?', should be rephrased as 'whom do I haunt?' It is also fundamental to one of the more provocative studies of surrealism of the 1990s, Hal Foster's *Compulsive Beauty*, which argues strongly for a reading of surrealism as an engagement with the uncanny. Foster studies 'an anamorphic array of practices and texts in the belief that the return of the repressed not only structures the central œuvres of surrealism but also surfaces in its marginal sites,' and hopes that his analysis will be of use for surrealist film, amongst other practices he does not investigate (Foster 1993: xix). We wish to take up the challenge, at least in part, in our concluding remarks.

Two broad points made by Foster are of relevance for our purposes. The first of these is the argument that surrealist objects can be viewed as the 'failed refinding of a lost object' (Foster 1993: xix). For our purposes, we posit that Batcheff functions for the spectator as a 'lost object'. Then we will consider Foster's productive contrast between two key surrealist figures, that of the automaton and the mannequin, and their link with Hans Bellmer's dolls, arguing that they are the structuring devices for the performative simulacrum (what we call 'vacancy'), and its transformation into 'evacuation', a partly imposed, partly self-imposed disarticulation of the star body.

First, however, we need to deal with a doubt that may have arisen in the reader's mind with our use of Foster's analyses based on the uncanny. We are aware of Ramona Fotiade's concern with Foster's use of the uncanny as a hermeneutic device. She argues that Breton would not have been aware of Freud's essay during the 1920s, as it was only translated in 1933, and that in any case the surrealists rejected the 'therapeutic finality' of psychoanalysis (Fotiade 2007: 19). This is a reasonable objection, given that we have laid considerable store by an archivally based study, where cinema discourses are underpinned by other cultural discourses of the period. Foster himself is well aware of the objection articulated by Fotiade. He argues convincingly, however, that the key issue in Freud's essay, that of the death drive, was already apparent in surrealist discourse by 1929 (Foster 1993: 13–16), and that Breton was not interested in the Freudian version of the death drive: 'Breton first conflates the Freudian drives and then reverses them in value' (Foster 1993: 15). As he points out, the surrealists used psychoanalytical theories as part of a toolkit whose purpose had a very different finality; they used 'the uncanniness of the return of the repressed, the compulsion to repeat, the immanence of death for disruptive purposes' (Foster 1993: 17). Our project, however, recognises the uncanny as only one provisional tool amongst others we have used in this volume to articulate the paradoxes and enigmas of Batcheff-as-star.

THE LOST OBJECT

Foster analyses Breton's wooden spoon as a Lacanian *objet petit a*, 'the object from which the subject must separate in order to become a subject – the object that must be "lost" in order for the subject to be "found"', and suggests that 'the found object of objective chance is a lost object that, never recovered, is forever sought, forever repeated' (Foster 1993: 42). Although clearly Batcheff is not quite like the object found apparently by chance, but rather an object actively sought, we would suggest that his function is similar. This is first because, like the found object he is the locus of desire, revealing erotic latencies in the spectator. In this function he is no different, we might say, from any star. Where he begins to resemble the found object rather more is in his mysterious otherness, the sign of a being-other, of a being-elsewhere, cryptic and dislocated. Batcheff has always already vacated the location in which he acts; he is, as we claimed earlier in this book, an absent presence, liminally there but fundamentally elsewhere, figured by his deathly immobility and his deflected gaze, the looking away or off. In that sense he can never be graspable or recoverable.

So what is in the 'there', the location which makes him 'not-here' and unavailable in his fullness? He is a fetish, tightly sheathed in figure-hugging black tails or tuxedos, or draped lasciviously in open-necked silk shirts, coyly revealing his neck and upper chest. The key figure for this in *Un Chien andalou*, that repository of symptoms, is the wiping away of his mouth, as Mareuil, like the spectator, attempts to pin him down with her gaze. Batcheff's man, as earlier in the film, begins to become a woman, as her underarm hair – that can be read, as we pointed out in Chapter 8, as pubic hair – covers his mouth. The figure signals a double and disarticulated fetish; the penile body hidden beneath the costume is the 'missing' penis of the female, so that Batcheff, like any fetishised body, is rendered passive. This is then overlaid magically with a vagina; but this vagina has disappeared, leaving only what hides it, the hair, in what is a literal effacement and defacement of the male. Batcheff is doubly 'femaled', his maleness forever lost in what is, in the central section of the film, a poignant elegy to ruined masculinity.

Batcheff is also absent because what we see is the past, a dislocation that is temporal as well as spatial. The temporal and the spatial come together in his otherness, his 'Russianness', connoting the alien culture and the fixed reference point of 1917, even if he did not mix with the White Russians.[1] Batcheff is a displaced person. That displacement, we might wish to argue, is a complex mix. It is the result of 1917, a social and historical alienation, a being-displaced; but it is also an enactment, or performance of displacement, a self-alienation (from himself and others). This emerges in comments on his voice; some say he has a Russian accent, others not. Evidence from *Baroud*, the only sound film we have been able to consult in its entirety, suggests not. It is, of course, entirely possible that spectators imagined a Russian accent where none existed, because this concurred with the otherness of his star persona. But it is not inconceivable that he played on his alienness, performing the border, acting out the cusp. Either way, Batcheff's in-betweenness is always on display, his identity convulsed like the Bretonian definition of beauty: exploding and fixed in the same moment, as we shall discuss below.

As spectators of stars we seek the renewed pleasure of past images, which is by definition lost. We attempt to recapture the identifications experienced as vicarious pleasure in the star body. In that sense, like desire itself, the attempt to capture the star body in its fullness can never succeed, because it is configured as a past experience. The present image of the star body on screen will always be 'read' as a fluid recombination of past images, uncannily haunting the present image precisely because they are from the past. The only way to refresh the image is to convulse it, which is what *Un Chien andalou* tries to do. To be able to do so, it must use recognisable images, but reposition them within an unrecognisable context or narrative. Roger Vailland wrote perceptively on a central paradox of *Un Chien andalou*: the film cannot easily be reduced to the kind of literary synopsis current in the film press, and yet its elements are all drawn from reality, unlike the technologically based artifice of 'pure cinema' (Vailland 1929). In other words, the images are recognisable, but their context is not, thus doubly othering what we see. The images of Batcheff, as Abel rightly pointed out, are those we recognise from his previous films, returning uncannily to haunt the present image; but in addition, those images are distorted and further othered by their unrecognisable narrative context, where, crucially, time is made infinitely pliable, past and present too disarticulated for temporality to function as an anchor for the 'real'. The 'loosening' of time allows the uncanny to slip through in multiple doublings, sliding doors on to impossible landscapes (the first-floor room that suddenly opens on to a windswept beach).

Batcheff's star persona is essentially double, in the strongest sense of the word 'essential'; there are no spatial or temporal contingencies to constrain that uncanny doubling, something that the real rather than metaphorical doubling in his last dual-version films serves to reinforce. A first conclusion then, following Abel, is that this helps us to understand the doubling of his character in *Un Chien andalou*, itself predicated on the doubling of the characters in his previous films. The two selves of *Un Chien andalou* are patterned on two of his main roles, that of the young lover and that of the rebel-criminal. And that doubling underscores while excessively magnifying his star persona, which combines normality and a rejection of that normality.

A second conclusion is that the doubling generates the feeling of the uncanny, that which is both familiar and yet also strange. The double, or *Doppelgänger*, is a key feature of the uncanny, which Freud relates to the fear of death; once a narcissistic projection of the ego in the form of spirits or the soul, and 'an assurance of immortality' to use Freud's words in his essay on 'The Uncanny', the double becomes, as he puts it, 'the uncanny harbinger of death' (Freud 1955: 235). He also relates it to the capacity for self-observation, later defined by him as the super-ego. Audiences of *Un Chien andalou* would have recognised the familiar, made strange by excess: the rolled-up ecstatic eyes and the gouged-out eyes of the final shot are versions of the amorous gaze of the noble young lover; the frenetic pursuits are an excessive version of his normal although slightly stiff-armed gait, informed in *Un Chien andalou*, as they had been to some extent in *Les Deux Timides*, by the performances of comic actors such as Chaplin, Keaton and Sennett, for whom, particularly Keaton, Batcheff had very publicly professed his admiration, as we saw in Chapter 2.

The uncanny for Freud was a resurgence of animistic mental activity, something which he himself would not necessarily have valorised, unlike the surrealists. Hence the paradox of Batcheff, as exemplified in *Un Chien andalou*. The film is a return to primitive modes of feeling, combining elements of reality and unreality, in an attempt to achieve surreality, just as his persona more generally articulates the same sensibility, with the same kind of consequences it had for Artaud: a feeling of living on the edge, of not inhabiting the body, of being someone else, of being a mere performance of masculinity. Batcheff, we are suggesting, is typical of a crisis in the male body which we see in other art-forms, but not typically in the other *jeunes premiers* of the period. This is no doubt because, unlike Batcheff, they did not mix with the avant-garde of the time, and therefore do not appear to have reflected on themselves in quite the way that Batcheff did. They were merely pin-ups, all surface; Batcheff is a pin-up wracked underneath by doubt, conflict and inexpressibility.

THE AUTOMATON, THE MANNEQUIN AND THE DOLL

We would like to suggest, following Foster's second major point, that Batcheff as pin-up is related to the uncanniness of the mannequin (as are the automaton and the doll).[2] Foster links the mannequin to the Romantic ruin so as to explain how they tend to work together in surrealist practice: 'As the Bretonian pairing of the mannequin and the ruin implies, the mechanical-commodified and the outmoded are dialectically related: the mechanical-commodified produces the outmoded through displacement, and the outmoded in turn defines the mechanical-commodified as central' (Foster 1993: 126). Batcheff, as we saw in Chapter 2, is both outmoded as Romantic *jeune premier*, and by the same token, commodified as star and as replicable *jeune premier*. The 'vacancy' we have defined as his distinguishing feature renders him even more like a mannequin, we might argue, than his fellow *jeunes premiers*, with the possible exception of Catelain. Even Batcheff's turn to comedy in *Les Deux Timides* and *Un Chien andalou*, although arguably a break with the outmoded, is none the less, like any counter-cinema, dependent on what preceded it for us to understand it fully. Moreover, his Keatonesque performance with stiff walk and stiff arms, in both of those films, merely reinforces the mannequin-like effect of his persona. His appearance in a historical reconstruction predicated on a chess-playing automaton figure in *Le Joueur d'échecs* might in this respect be seen as more than a purely superficial coincidence, even if Batcheff is on the margins of the narrative as an outmoded ineffectual lover – underlined by his ridiculous wig – overtaken and abandoned by the exigencies of history.

One issue we have not addressed directly in this analysis is the extent to which the 'vacancy' we have tried to define in Batcheff's star persona is reactive ('I don't like the films I star in') or proactive ('I reject the films I star in').

In other words, is the distant look of the martyred Sad Young Man an escape or a statement? While clearly it could be both, we would emphasise the latter, not least because, like any star Batcheff, could choose which films he wished to star in. We have seen in previous chapters how many of the 'lover' narratives are underpinned by equivocal situations such as incest, undermining the straightforwardly clean Romantic persona and inclining it more to the morbidity of the fin-de-siècle. As Bellmer said in a wonderfully apt statement, 'the body is like a sentence that invites us to rearrange it' (cited in Foster 1993: 103). And like Bellmer's dolls, we would suggest that Batcheff rearranged his persona through a variety of narratives, chosen by him, to perpetuate two terms that Foster usefully links: aura and anxiety. Like Bellmer's dolls, Batcheff consciously disarticulated his persona, 'evacuating' it, leaving behind the uncanny shell, the automaton-mannequin with the vacant gaze, a residue, as we called it in Chapter 2.

That residue is both feminine, as we pointed out in Chapter 2, and convulsive. Foster explains how the surrealists projected aura and anxiety on to the figures we have been exploring so as to create the convulsion allowing access to the surreal:

> The surrealists (. . .) project this ambivalence on social ciphers such as the automaton-machine and the mannequin-commodity as so many figures of desire and death, as well as on outmoded images, which, through a relation to the things of childhood, also appear as both redemptive and demonic. In all these ways, aura and anxiety are combined in surrealism, with the energy of the first often used to detonate a temporal shock, a convulsive history (. . .) and the ambivalence of the second often used to provoke a symbolic ambiguity, a convulsive identity. (Foster 1993: 200)

He also points out how the figures we have been referring to are generally feminine in surrealism (Foster 1993: 134), as is the figure determining the notion of beauty for Breton, with which we would like to conclude.

'EXPLOSANTE-FIXE'

In this book we have constantly returned to the doublings and splittings that inform Batcheff's star persona: fatalist and enterprising; sensitive and savage; French and Russian; masculine and feminine; distant eyes and cheeky smile. These crisscross and form the texture of Batcheff's performance. We have suggested that Batcheff, who frequented the surrealists more than he did his fellow actors, knew perfectly well what Breton meant by the definition of surrealism as the combination of two distant realities, and we hope to have proved that he put that definition into practice in his performance style. In this

final section, we want to insist that the doublings and splittings we have identified are not organised in binary configurations, as the preceding list undoubtedly suggests. They are a fluid network, best described in the same terms as
one of Batcheff's first roles, in *Feu Mathias Pascal*: hysterical convulsions.
Those convulsions underpin all of his roles, we have claimed, although they
are much more evident in *Un Chien andalou*, as a contemporary reviewer,
Robert Aron, intimated:

> C'est aux frontières de notre corps, là où nos amours s'extravasent et où le
> monde nous assiège, que Buñuel, carré sur ses hanches, fondé sur sa chair
> intérieure, cherche à porter le vertige. Tout ce sur quoi son corps bute ou
> s'arrête, tout ce qui le limite, chair étrangère, distance, temps, se disloque au
> cours de son film. Le temps recule : un personnage menace du revolver
> l'image de son passé ; l'espace s'abolit pour un mourant, dont l'agonie extra-
> rapide commence dans les murs d'une chambre pour se terminer sous les
> arbres. Des chairs se revêtent ou se cachent, se déshabillent ou se rhabillent,
> se couvrent de poils ou d'insectes, selon que le désir les presse, ou que la mort
> les menace. Et pour défier jusqu'au désir, ce sensuel que la chair oppresse
> impose un masque d'impuissant, bavant, yeux révulsés et douloureux, à
> l'amoureux qui caresse des seins et des fesses nues. (Aron 1929: 42)

> (It is on the borders of our body, there where our desires pour forth and
> where the world assaults us, that Buñuel (. . .) seeks to bring to bear the ver-
> tiginous. Everything on which the body rests or halts, everything which limits
> that strange body – distance, time – is dislocated in the course of his film.
> Time retreats; a character threatens his own past image with a revolver; space
> is obliterated for a dying man so that the slow motion agony begins within the
> walls of a room and ends under the trees. Bodies dress or conceal themselves,
> undress or dress again, covering themselves with hair or insects, according to
> the desire that impels them or the death that threatens. And in order to defy
> even desire, the body suppresses its sensuality by prescribing a slobbering,
> impotent mask with sorrowful upturned eyes for the lover who caresses naked
> breasts and buttocks; Aron 1988: 433)

The dizzying dislocations of time, space and bodies are tropes of convulsion. We referred in Chapter 3 to the first sentences of *Nadja*, where Breton's
question on his identity is rephrased as a haunting, and part of our purpose
has been to show how Batcheff is 'haunted' by his roles. Here, we end with the
last sentence of *Nadja*: 'La beauté sera CONVULSIVE ou ne sera pas'
('Beauty will be CONVULSIVE or not at all'; Breton 1988: 753, his emphasis). The idea was taken up by Breton a few years later in an article entitled 'La
Beauté sera convulsive', published in *Minotaure* (May 1934). This eventually
became the first chapter of *L'Amour fou* (1937), where the statement
is reprised at the end of the article/chapter: 'La beauté convulsive sera

érotique-voilée, explosante-fixe, magique-circonstancielle, ou ne sera pas' ('Beauty will be erotic-veiled, exploding-fixed, magic-circumstantial, or not at all'; Breton 1992: 687), the middle epithet, 'explosante-fixe' being illustrated by a Man Ray photograph of a faceless woman dancing with her skirt caught swirling around her (Breton 1992: 683).

We want to suggest that the 'explosante-fixe' is emblematic of Batcheff's persona and trajectory. It encapsulates the femininity of the *jeune premier*, as well the paralysis and passivity of cliché, the 'arrested motion of a body become an image' (Foster 1993: 27). And it is an exemplary illustration of what Elizabeth Bronfen calls the 'knotted subject', 'the snarled knot of memory traces, which as a wandering foreign body haunts the psyche' (Bronfen 1998: xiii), and which she considers to be less a symptom of repressed femininity than a mark of deep cultural shifts manifesting the vulnerability of the symbolic, of identity and, of course, of the body itself.

Breton's 'explosante-fixe' also indicates the struggle by Batcheff to shake free of fixity, to explode the constraints in a convulsive frenzy of activity, to turn the inanimate mannequin, the lifeless automaton, into its ill-defined agonist, ultimately the writer-director that Batcheff longed to be. What Breton's position leads to is both an explosive tension and a disarticulation. That disarticulation, we hope to have shown, is writ large on to Batcheff's body. His body is, to reprise Bellmer's statement, with all the ambiguities it might suggest of imprisonment and punishment, a rearranged sentence; Batcheff represents not just a transition in cinematic terms, but the articulation of a transitional masculinity, caught between a reactive post-(WW1)war idealism, expressed most clearly in the sanitised ephebe, and a newer pre-(WW2)war masculinity, that of the proletarian man of action. That this could only be achieved in a convulsive moment of comic violence tells us much about the period, and also much about the nature of masculinity more generally.

Notes

1. Denise Tual told us in interview that 'il n'aimait pas du tout revoir les Russes réfugiés, il détestait ça (. . .) J'avais beaucoup d'amis russes de l'aristocratie . . . il ne voulait pas les voir' (He didn't like to mix with the Russian refugees, he hated it (. . .) I had a lot of aristocratic Russian friends . . . he didn't want to see them'; interview 1996).
2. 'The surrealists (were obsessed) by the strange (non)human character of the mannequin, the automaton, the wax figure, the doll – all avatars of the uncanny' (Foster 1993: 126).

Appendices

1. SUMMARY BIOGRAPHY

1907–24

22 or 23 June 1907:	Benjamin Batcheff born in Harbin, Manchuria.
Summer 1914:	Family stays in Switzerland when war breaks out, first in Lausanne, then in Geneva.
1919-21:	Collège Calvin, Geneva. Acts as an extra with Pitoëff's theatre company.
June 1921:	Family moves to Paris at 88, rue de la Convention, 15th *arrondissement*.
1922:	Acts in the Théâtre de la Comédie Mondaine.
22 December 1922:	Apollo in *La Nuit des muses*, Théâtre de la Potinière.
1923:	Works as a set-painter and film extra.
Summer 1923:	*Claudine et le poussin* shot.
March 1924:	*Claudine et le poussin* released.
Summer 1924:	*Princesse Lulu* shot.

1925

January:	*Autour d'un berceau* shot. Some time this year Batcheff moves into 8, rue Jean Lantier, 1st *arrondissement*.
February:	*Feu Mathias Pascal* shot.
March-April:	*Le Double Amour* shot.
April:	Batcheff's first magazine cover (*Mon ciné*).
May:	*Autour d'un berceau* released.
May-November:	*Destinée* shot.
June:	Batcheff's first major newspaper article (*Quotidien du Midi*).

August: *Princesse Lulu* released.
November: *Le Double Amour* released.

1926

January-February: *Le Secret d'une mère* shot.
February: *Feu Mathias Pascal* released.
March: *Destinée* released.
March-October: *Le Joueur d'échecs* shot. Batcheff meets Denise Tual.
July: *Le Secret d'une mère* released. 'Bal des victimes' scene
                         of *Napoléon* shot.
Summer: Batcheff meets Rex Ingram in Nice.
November: Acts in play *La Comédie du bonheur* (November-
                         May). Substitutes briefly for Jaque Catelain in *Le
                         Diable au cœur*.
December: *Éducation de prince* shot.

1927

January: *Le Joueur d'échecs* released.
January-March: *Éducation de prince* shot.
March-May: *Le Bonheur du jour* shot.
July-October: *L'Île d'Amour* shot.
July-November: *La Sirène des tropiques* shot; Batcheff meets Buñuel.
                         Batcheff moves into Denise's flat at 11, rue
                         Sédillot, 7th *arrondissement* in the autumn. He works
                         on the film script for *La Faim*.
November: *Napoléon* released. *Éducation de prince* released.
December: *La Sirène des tropiques* released. Cover of *Ciné-
                         Miroir*.

1928

February-April: *Le Perroquet vert* shot. *Le Bonheur du jour* released.
March: First star interview in *Ciné-Miroir*.
April-June: *Vivre* shot.
July: *Vivre* released.
July-October: *Les Deux Timides* shot. Batcheff and Denise move
                         to 57, avenue de Ségur, 7th *arrondissement* in the
                         summer.
October: *Le Perroquet vert* released.

November-December:	*Monte-Cristo* shot. Batcheff works on the film script for *L'Homme invisible*.
December:	Cover of *Cinémagazine*.

1929

January-May:	*Monte-Cristo* shot.
January:	Batcheff contracted for *Le Collier de la reine* alongside Pola Negri.
March:	*Les Deux Timides* released.
March-April:	*Un Chien andalou* shot.
April:	Batcheff pulls out of *Le Collier de la reine*.
6 June:	Cover of *Mon ciné*. *Un Chien andalou* opens.
September-November:	*Illusions* shot.
October:	Cover of *Pour vous*.
October-November	*Monte-Cristo* released.
Winter:	Batcheff and Denise move to 3, square de Robiac, 7th *arrondissement*. Batcheff meets Jacques Prévert.

1930

February-May:	*Le Roi de Paris* shot in Berlin and Paris.
1 April:	Batcheff and Denise attend the premiere of *Der blaue Engel* in Berlin.
August:	Contracted for *L'Ensorcellement de Séville*. Batcheff and Denise get married 8 May, in Paris, 7th *arrondissement*. *Le Roi de Paris* released.
October-November:	*Les Amours de minuit* shot in Billancourt. Batcheff announces *Émile-Émile* in the film press. Cover of *Le Courrier cinématographique* 11 October. Drops out of *L'Ensorcellement de Séville*.
Winter:	The 'lacoudem' holiday in Chamonix and Cherbourg. Natan rejects *Émile-Émile*.

1931

January:	*Les Amours de minuit* released.
February-July:	*Le Rebelle* shot.
April:	Batcheff and Denise in Berlin to shoot *Mitternachtsliebe*.

June: *Vingt-quatre heures de la vie d'une femme* announced,
                               but Batcheff pulls out very quickly.
August-December: *Baroud* shot in Nice and Morocco.

1932

January-March: Batcheff works on the filmscript for *Pour ses beaux
                               yeux*.
12 April: Batcheff commits suicide.
September: *Baroud* released. *Pour ses beaux yeux* released under
                               title *Amour . . . Amour . . . .*

2. INTERVIEWS AND STAR PORTRAITS (CHRONOLOGICAL ORDER)

- Millet, J.-K. Raymond (1928), 'Nos Jeunes Premiers: Pierre Batcheff', *Ciné-Miroir*, 156, 30 March, p. 215.
- *Ciné-Miroir* (1928), 'Du Studio à la ville: Pierre Batcheff nous écrit', *Ciné-Miroir*, 162, 11 May, p. 315.
- Lenoir, Jacqueline (1928), 'Brune ou blonde ? ...', *Ciné-Miroir*, 169, 29 June, p. 419.
- Lenoir, Jacqueline (1928), 'Leur Violon d'Ingres: Pierre Batcheff', *Ciné-Miroir*, 176, 17 August, p. 534.
- Lenoir, Jacqueline (1928), 'Nous avons aussi ... Pierre Batcheff', *Cinématographie française*, 526, 30 November, p. 17.
- Frank, Nino (1928), 'Un Russe naturalisé français par sa carrière: Pierre Batcheff', *Pour vous*, 6, 27 December, pp. 8-9.
- Doré, Claude (1929), 'Nos Enquêtes: l'influence du partenaire', *Ciné-Miroir*, 207, 22 March, p. 183.
- Kolb, Jean (1929), 'Parlez-nous du public: Pierre Batcheff nous dit', *Mon ciné*, 383, 20 June, p. 12.
- Bernard-Derosne, Sabine (1929), 'Les Grandes Vedettes de l'écran: Pierre Batcheff', *Minerva*, 205, 14 July, p. 16.
- Ciné-Miroir (1930), 'Du studio à la ville: le sourire de Pierre Batcheff', *Ciné-Miroir*, 271, 13 June, p. 380.
- Saurel, Louis (1930), 'Un Entretien avec Pierre Batcheff, l'un des protagonistes du Roi de Paris', *Mon ciné*, 441, 31 July, p. 4.
- de Mirbel, Jean (1930), 'Quelques instants avec Pierre Batcheff', *Cinémagazine*, 9, October, p. 53.
- Doré, Claude (1930), 'Pierre Batcheff devient metteur en scène', *Ciné-Miroir*, 288, 10 October, p. 647.

- Sannier, Mireille (1930), 'De l'Autre Côté des sunlights: Pierre Batcheff va faire de la mise en scène', *Cinémonde*, 104, 16 October, p. 665.
- Verdier, Michel (1930), 'Dans nos studios: la réalisation d'*Amours de Minuit'*, *Ciné-Miroir*, 293, 14 November, p. 726.
- *Spectateur* (1931), 'Pierre Batcheff', *Le Spectateur*, 12 April, in Batcheff file, Bibliothèque Nationale, Collection Rondel, 8°Rk17740.
- Saurel, Louis (1931), 'Pierre Batcheff', *Paris-Midi*, 9 August, in Batcheff file, Bibliothèque Nationale, Collection Rondel, 8°Rk17740.
- Mital, Bernard (1931), 'Une Heure chez Pierre Batcheff', *Mon ciné*, 503, 8 October, p. 6.

3. FILMSCRIPT FROM KNUT HAMSUN'S *SULT* (*HUNGER*, 1890)

Eleven manuscript sheets each with the address '11, rue Sédillot, PARIS VIIe, SEGUR 94-92'.

Sheet 1

LA FAIM
Tiré du roman de Knut Hamsen

Au grand matin la brume recouvre la ville. Au port des gens attendent, tournés vers la mer, un canot qui approche, accoste. – On débarque. –

Sur le quai les derniers adieux s'échangent. – On embarque. – Les voyageurs descendus du canot, valises en main, affairés, se heurtent aux parents, amis, restés sur le quai à suivre d'un dernier regard le canot qui déjà file sur la mer.

Sheet 2

– Au loin le paquebot. –
Parmi les voyageurs débarqués l'un deux hèle une voiture. Il donne une

Sheet 1

HUNGER
From the novel by Knut Hamsen

It is morning and the town is covered with mist. People are waiting in the port, turned towards the sea, a boat approaches, moors. – People disembark. —

On the quayside people say their last farewells. – They embark. – The voyagers who have disembarked, suitcases in their hands, busy, bump into the friends and family on the quayside who take one last look at the boat which is already far away.

Sheet 2

– The boat in the distance. –
Amongst the voyagers that have disembarked one of them hails a

adresse qu'il lit sur un papier. Les sabots du cheval martèlent quelques rues encore désertes. La voiture s'arrête devant un hôtel genre hôtel d'étudiants et commis voyageurs.

Sur le palier un garçon balaie, à moitié endormi. L'étranger le questionne lui montrant son papier. Le garçon lit un nom, cherche dans ses souvenirs; il a trouvé, de la main il décrit: 'un grand, qui a les joues creuses'. L'étranger approuve. Le garçon du geste fait vaguement qu'il est parti.

L'étranger inquiet questionne: où est-il parti ? – Le garçon a un geste d'ignorance. L'étranger anxieux hésite, puis fait prendre sa valise et s'installe à l'hôtel. –

Sheet 3

On longe quelques rues, des façades de maisons, qui deviennent de plus en plus pauvres. On arrive au quartier misérable.

Dans sa mansarde Johan dort. Il est couché tout habillé, entortillé dans une couverture trouée d'où ses pieds, ses chaussettes dépassent, recroquevillé contre le froid.

Dans la rue un boulanger relève brutalement le rideau de fer de sa boutique.

cab. He gives an address that he reads from a scrap of paper. The horse's hooves clip-clop on empty streets. The cab stops in front of a hotel for students and travelling salesmen.

On the threshold a boy is sweeping, half-asleep. The stranger asks him a question, showing his scrap of paper. The boy reads a name, looks for it in his memory; he has found it, he gestures with his hands: 'a tall man, with sunken cheeks'. The stranger nods. The boy gestures that he has left.

The stranger, worried, asks: where has he gone? – The boy shrugs. The stranger pauses anxiously, then picks up his suitcase and settles in the hotel. –

Sheet 3

The camera sweeps along some streets, the front of some houses, which become increasingly poor. We are coming to the poor quarter.

Johan is asleep in his garret. He is wearing all his clothes, wrapped up in a blanket full of holes, his feet, his socks protruding, huddled up against the cold.

In the street a baker abruptly lifts the iron curtain of his shop.

C'est le réveil-matin de Johan qui ouvre les yeux, a tout d'abord le geste mécanique de chercher à tâtons ses lunettes, puis s'assoit sur son lit et réfléchit. Dans la rue on vide avec fracas les poubelles. Johan se lève, s'approche de la fenêtre, s'assoit à son rebord.

It is Johan's wake-up call. He opens his eyes, fumbles mechanically for his glasses, then sits up and thinks. In the street, the bins are being noisily emptied. Johan gets up, goes to the window and sits on the edge.

Sheet 4

Le boulanger avant de recommencer son travail prend l'air à sa porte, suit des yeux le manège d'une vieille femme qui court devant le tombereau de la voirie pour lui disputer le contenu des boites à ordures qu'elle fouille d'un crochet. Johan a pris ses chaussures sans quitter sa place et tout en les enfilant se souvient de s'être présenté la veille au corps des sapeurs pompiers, où on l'évinça une première fois pour les lunettes. Il revint sans, fronçant les sourcils pour aiguiser son regard. L'inspecteur passa devant lui sans un mot, réprimant un sourire. On l'avait reconnu.

Sheet 4

The baker takes some fresh air at the door before starting work, his eyes following an old woman as she rummages in the dustcart with a hook. Johan has picked up his shoes without leaving his seat and as he puts them on he remembers applying to the fire service the day before, but was rejected because of his glasses. He went back without them, frowning to make himself look sharp. The inspector walked right past him, suppressing a smile. He had been recognised.

Johan a lacé ses chaussures.

Johan has tied his laces.

Le boulanger a commencé à aligner le pain frais sur les grils. – Johan quitte la fenêtre, s'approche d'une chaise sur laquelle

The baker has started to arrange the fresh bread on the grills. – Johan leaves the window, and goes to a chair on which

Sheet 5

il y a une cuvette et un papier gras, ouvre le papier qui a dû contenir sa

Sheet 5

there is a bowl and some greasy paper; he opens the paper which

nourriture et où il ne reste que quelques miettes sans formes. Il jette au loin le papier, verse l'eau d'un broc dans la cuvette, cherche du savon. Le récipient qui le contenait est vide. Alors dégoûté il se contente d'humecter les genoux de son pantalon. Un pâle rayon de soleil a pénétré dans la mansarde. Johan va sortir. À la porte il se ravise. Son terme n'est pas payé, il préfère enfouir le papier gras sous le lit, retaper lui-même les couvertures. Avant de sortir il s'assure qu'il ne risque pas de rencontrer le propriétaire dans l'escalier, et file en descendant les marches sur la pointe des pieds mais le plus rapidement possible, ce qui lui fait perdre l'équilibre qu'il rattrape bien heureusement à temps.

must have contained his food, but now there only a few crumbs. He throws the paper away, pours water from a jug into the bowl, gets some soap. The soap box is empty. Disgusted, all he does is sprinkle the knees of his trousers with water. A pale ray of sunshine has penetrated the garret. Johan is going to leave. But at the door he thinks better of it. He hasn't paid his rent, he prefers to thrust the greasy paper under the bed, patting down the blankets. Before leaving he makes sure he won't bump into the landlord on the stairs, and slips down the stairs on tiptoe as quickly as he can, which makes him lose his balance but he manages to keep it just in time.

Sheet 6

Dans la rue le soleil a transpercé la brume et se joue dans le cœur matinal des vies qui s'éveillent. Johan respire à pleins poumons l'air frais du matin.

Ce rayon qui le réchauffe lui fait redresser le torse et en marchant il se met à siffloter.

Les employés se hâtent vers leur travail. Johan arrivant à une petite place qui semble propice sort un crayon et un papier de ses poches, avise un banc, s'installe et s'apprête à écrire. Devant lui une fontaine offre son eau limpide aux jeux des

Sheet 6

In the street the sun has pierced through the mist and frolics in the hearts of those who are awakening. Johan breathes deeply the fresh morning air.

The ray of sunshine warms him and he stretches up, whistling as he walks along.

People hasten along to their place of work. Johan arrives at a small square that looks right and takes a piece of paper and a pencil from his pocket, finds a bench, sits down and gets ready to write. In front of him sparrows play in the clear water of a

moineaux. Auparavant Johan boit dans le creux de ses mains, se rafraîchit la tête; quand il revient à son banc il s'aperçoit qu'un vieillard s'y est installé, dévorant à belles dents pour déjeuner

Sheet 7

une saucisse. Il n'a pas mangé, à la vue de cette saucisse il a un sursaut, une grimace. Sa bonne humeur fait place à un malaise. Écœuré il décide d'aller écrire ailleurs. Prêt à partir il voit approcher une connaissance, un petit vieillard boiteux. Johan le salue. Mais le petit boiteux pour toute réponse esquisse à peine un signe de tête. La susceptibilité de Johan se réveille. Il fronce les sourcils, regarde son costume en effet peu présentable. Il y a même autour de lui des personnes qui auraient pu s'apercevoir de l'affront qu'on lui a infligé.

Justement un couple xxxxx[1] de jeunes femmes passait. Furieux il remonte la rue principale, quand il entend derrière

Sheet 8

lui le clopinement du boiteux.

Il s'arrête, décide à lui donner une leçon, et quand le boiteux passe il le dévisage avec mépris, sans un mot. Mais, à son grand étonnement, celui-ci fait le plus gracieux sourire avec un bonjour des plus amicals [sic].

fountain. Before he starts, Johan drinks from his cupped hands, freshens his head; when he gets back to his bench, he sees that an old man has sat down, hungrily munching a sausage for his lunch.

Sheet 7

He hasn't eaten, and seeing the sausage makes him start and pull a face. His good humour gives way to dizziness. Feeling sick he decides to go and write somewhere else. He is just about to go when he sees someone he knows approaching, an old man with a limp. Johan says hello to him. But the little man with the limp hardly nods in response. Johan feels offended. He frowns, looks at his suit which is in effect not presentable. Close by there are even people who might have seen the affront he has had to endure.

Indeed, just at that moment a xxxxx couple of women were passing by. Furious, he goes back up the high street, when he hears behind

Sheet 8

him the man hobbling along.

He stops, decides he is going to teach the man a lesson, and when the man with the limp passes he stares at him, without a word. But to his great astonishment, the man smiles at him gracefully as he gives

Dans son dos Johan ricane, mais au fond de lui-même n'est pas plus sûr que ça de n'avoir pas été un peu loin.

Aussi décide-t-il de faire preuve d'indulgence et dépassant le vieillard lui fait un signe de tête protecteur. Cette fois-ci on n'a même pas un regard pour lui, il le dépasse en fixant le bout de ses chaussures. Johan croise les bras et s'arrête – se moque-t-on de lui – Il sent la colère lui monter à la tête et s'élance à la suite du vieillard

Sheet 9

le rattrape, le retient par l'épaule.

Le petit boiteux se retourne, si étonné, si naïf, que Johan désemparé comprend qu'il est nerveux, qu'il est le dupe de sa faim. – Ils échangent une poignée de main, la conversation s'engage.

Quelle aubaine pour le petit boiteux, qui ne tarde pas à larmoyer, pleurer misère, et finir par demander de l'argent à Johan. De l'argent! Johan éclate d'un rire nerveux, de l'argent à lui, il trouve ça si drôle qu'il a une idée. Eh bien il lui donnera de l'argent, qu'il attende là un peu. En courant il enfile une ruelle, s'arrête sous une porte cochère, vivement enlève son gilet et monte le porter à l'échoppe d'un prêteur. Contre son gilet on lui remet une petite somme

him the friendliest greeting. Johan sniggers behind his back, but deep down isn't sure that he hasn't gone a bit too far.

So he decides to show indulgence and overtaking the old man nods at him protectively. This time the old man doesn't even look at him, he walks past staring at his shoes. Johan stops and folds his arms – is the old man making fun of him – he feels anger rising and runs after the old man

Sheet 9

catches up with him, and grabs him by the shoulder.

The little man with the limp turns around, so surprised, so innocent, that Johan finally understands that he is full of nerves, and that hunger has twisted his judgement. They shake hands and begin talking.

What a stroke of luck for the little old man with a limp, who soon starts snivelling, lamenting his fate, and ends up asking Johan for money. Money! Johan gives a burst of nervous laughter, asking money of him, he finds it so funny that he has an idea. Well he will give him some money, let him just wait a moment. He runs into a side-street, stops beneath an archway, quickly strips off his waistcoat and takes it up to a pawnshop. In exchange he gets a

d'argent, dont il fait deux parts

few pennies which he divides into two

Sheet 10

l'une qu'il remet au boiteux. L'autre dans la main, il va au plus pressé, entre dans une boutique de comestibles, dépose l'argent sur le comptoir, demande 'du pain et du fromage'. La marchande a un regard au comptoir et ironique elle jette 'du pain et du fromage pour toute la somme?' Oui pour toute la somme.

Sans sourciller Johan prend son paquet, s'incline et sort. Il va manger ses provisions sur un banc du square où aboutit la Rue Principale.

Les morceaux de pain et de fromage sont vite engloutis. Apres avoir ramassé précieusement les miettes sur ses genoux et les avoir mangées il s'apprête à se mettre au travail, sort son papier d'une poche, en fouille une autre

Sheet 11

une troisième, machinalement, porte la main à une poche du gilet, et quand il s'aperçoit qu'il n'a plus de gilet, se frappe le front. Il a laissé son crayon à l'échoppe du prêteur. Et comme il n'a pas un liard en poche il ne lui reste plus qu'à aller le chercher. Sans entrain il descend la Rue Principale et aperçoit de nouveau le couple de jeunes femmes

Sheet 10

one of which he gives to the man with the limp. With the other in his hand, he rushes off to the grocer's, puts the money on the counter, and asks for bread and cheese. The owner looks at the counter ironically and says: 'bread and cheese for that amount?' Yes, for that amount.

Without batting an eye Johan takes his packet, bows and leaves. He goes to eat his provisions on the bench in the square at the end of the High Street.

The bread and cheese are soon gone. After carefully picking the crumbs from his lap and eating them he gets ready for work, takes out his sheet of paper from his pocket, rummages in another pocket

Sheet 11

then a third one, mechanically, takes his hand to his waistcoat pocket, and when he realises that he no longer has a waistcoat, slaps his forehead. He has left his pencil at the pawn shop. And as he doesn't have a penny to his name all he can do is to go back and get it. Without hurrying he goes back down the High Street and sees once more the pair of

devant qui le vieillard lui avait
infligé l'affront. Quand il les croise,
il essaye, en tenant le haut de son
veston fermé, de cacher la chemise
sale et la cravate en lambeaux que
laisse à découvert la disparition du
gilet —[2]

young women in front of whom the
old man had insulted him. When he
goes past them, he tugs the top of
his jacket closed, to hide the dirty
shirt and the tattered tie that are
now in full view without his waist
coat —

Notes

1. Indecipherable.
2. The manuscript stops here in mid-sentence.

Filmography

Batcheff made twenty-five films (two being in alternate language versions), and prepared a filmscript which he was to direct. They are presented here in order of first public viewing, which is often the trade presentation, the general release occurring sometimes several weeks afterwards. Dates and cinema locations are those given in the film press of the time. These tend to give the details of trade presentations, and do not always announce the date of general release. Where we have not been able to find the date of general release, we have given the month in which a significant number of reviews have appeared in the film press, on the assumption that these will have occurred at the time of the film's general release. We have given the availability of films in the principal archives and/or details of commercially available copies. Where we have said 'none', this means that we are not aware of any extant copies. Synopses of those films we have not been able to consult are based on those given in the film press of the period.

1. *Claudine et le poussin ou Le Temps d'aimer*

Trade presentation	15 January 1924, Le Select
General release	14 March 1924
Director	Marcel Manchez
Production	Films Marcel Manchez
Script	Marcel Manchez
Camera	Maurice Forster
Distribution	Établissements Giraud
Length	1,700 metres
Main actors	Dolly Davis (Claudine); Pierre Batcheff (Claude de Puygiron); Jeanne Méa (Comtesse de Puygiron); Marthe Lepers (Madame de Portehaut); Maria Gandi (la paysanne); Gilbert Dalleu (l'abbé)
Availability	Cinémathèque française
Synopsis	Claude de Puygiron lives with his mother and his tutor, a priest, in a rural château. There is a car accident on the

road outside, in which Claudine, a Parisian actress, and her aunt are travelling. Claude's mother takes them in reluctantly, and Claude and Claudine soon fall in love, finding ways to get round the priest's chaperoning and ensuring that Claudine's aunt stays unwell. Claudine eventually leaves and Claude becomes suicidal. When his mother finds him holding a shotgun, she gives in and lets Claude leave for Paris.

2. PRINCESSE LULU

Premiere	25 February 1925, Palace Cinema, Montreux; 14 March 1925, Paris
General release	14 August 1925
Director	E. B. [Émile-Bernard] Donatien
Asst directors	André Gargour, M.-C. Bellaigue, Samuel Schnegg
Producers	Louis Aubert, Georges Hipleh Jr
Production	Établissements Louis Aubert, Paris; Agence Suisse du Cinéma, Montreux (G. Hipleh) Production
Script	E. B. Donatien, Camille de Morlhon
Camera	Emile Replin
Set design	E. B. Donatien
Editing	E. B. Donatien
Distribution	Star-Films Paris; Modernes-Films SA, Genève
Length	2,380 metres
Main actors	Lucienne Legrand (Lulu Juillard); Camille Bert (le père Juillard); Pierre Batcheff (Raoul Brounet); E. B. Donatien (Gingolph); Gil Clary (la mère Juillard)
Availability	None
Synopsis	Lulu's father is a drunken barge-owner. His employee, Gingolph, encourages him to drink so he can keep control of the business. Gingolph tries to rape Lulu, but she is saved by Raoul, who was passing by. She subsequently idolises her Prince Charming. Meanwhile things go from bad to worse; Lulu's mother, who has had to work in a chocolate factory to support her family, has been blinded in an accident. Gingolph lends money to them and asks for Lulu's hand in marriage in return, but Raoul pays off the debt and asks for Lulu himself. Gingolph, in a fury, tries to burn the barge where the engagement party is taking place, but the family manages

to escape, thanks to Lulu's mother who has recovered her sight and seen the smoke, and Gingolph dies.

3. *AUTOUR D'UN BERCEAU*

Trade presentation	7 March 1925, Gaumont-Palace
General release	15 May 1925
Directors	Georges Monca, Maurice Kéroul
Production	Grandes Productions Cinématographiques
Script	Maurice Kéroul
Camera	Paul Portier, Enzo Riccioni
Distribution	Grandes Productions Cinématographiques
Length	2,100 metres
Main actors	Geneviève Félix (Geneviève Marcy); Fernand Herrmann (René Fréville); Pierre Batcheff (Pierre de Sombierre); Charley Sov (le banquier Orlasse); Berthe Jalabert (Madame Fréville); Alice Tissot (Madame Ronfledur); Armand Numès (Martin)
Availability	None
Synopsis	René Fréville, secretary to the banker Orlasse, lives with his mother and is in love with his neighbour Geneviève. René's elegant friend, Pierre de Sombierre, steals 10,000 francs from money that Orlasse had entrusted to René, and flees the country. Orlasse holds René responsible and decides to have him arrested, but René in his turn flees the country, while his mother and Geneviève, who has moved in with her illegitimate child, work to reimburse Orlasse. Having scrimped and saved, Geneviève takes the money to Orlasse, only to see him being lynched by angry shareholders he has tricked. René returns, his innocence proved by a letter of confession from Pierre, who returns the money he stole. René adopts Geneviève's child as his own.

4. *LE DOUBLE AMOUR*

Trade presentation	25 June 1925, Salle Marivaux
General release	27 November 1925
Director	Jean Epstein
Production	Films Albatros
Script	Marie-Antonine Epstein

Camera	Maurice Desfassiaux, Nicolas Roudakoff
Set design	Pierre Kéfer
Distribution	Films Armor
Length	2,000 metres
Main actors	Nathalie Lissenko (Laure Maresco); Jean Angelo (Jacques Prémont-Solène); Pierre Batcheff (Jacques Maresco); Camille Bardou (Baron de Curgis)
Availability	Cinémathèque française
Synopsis	Laure Maresco, a singer, loves Jacques Prémont-Solène so much that she covers up for him when he gambles away money entrusted to her. He flees to the USA, while she is forced to earn a humble living to support the son Jacques gave her. Like his father, Jacques is a compulsive gambler and fritters away his mother's money despite her attempts to reform him. One evening, father and son (who are unaware of their relationship) play against each other at baccarat; the son loses and steals some chips. The father – now a respected industrialist – accompanies men from the casino to Laure's house, where the son confesses the theft. Laure reveals that he is Jacques's son. The father refuses to believe her. She forces a confrontation later at the police station by showing a letter written by the father twenty years before in which he confessed his theft. He repents, takes the blame for his son's theft, as she had done for him twenty years before, and compensates the casino handsomely. He tells them that they will henceforth live as a family in the USA.

5. *Feu Mathias Pascal*

Trade presentation	29 July 1925, Salle Marivaux
General release	February 1926
Director	Marcel L'Herbier
Asst director	Alberto Cavalcanti
Production	Cinégraphic-Albatros
Script	Marcel L'Herbier, from the novel by Luigi Pirandello
Camera	Jean Letort, Jimmy Berliet, Nicolas Roudakoff, Bourgassoff and Paul Guichard
Music	Joseph-Étienne Szyfer
Set design	Alberto Cavalcanti, Lazare Meerson

Distribution	Films Armor
Length	3,300 metres
Main actors	Ivan Mosjoukine (Mathias Pascal); Loïs Moran (Adrienne Paleari); Michel Simon (Jérôme Pomino); Marcelle Pradot (Romilde); Mme Barsac (veuve Piscatore); Jean Hervé (Térence Papiano); Pierre Batcheff (Scipion); Jaque Catelain (le client de l'hôtel)
Availability	Centre national de la cinématographie; Cinémathèque française
Synopsis	Mathias, a village librarian, has been ruined by an unscrupulous lawyer. He marries Romilde, with whom he has fallen in love, after courting her on behalf of his friend Pomino. His mother-in-law does everything she can to break up the marriage. Mathias's daughter dies the same day as his mother. Grief-stricken, Mathias flees by train, stopping off haphazardly in Monte Carlo, where in a few hours he wins 500,000 francs. On the train back home, he sees a newspaper report announcing his suicide. He decides not to reveal the error and leaves for Rome. In the second part of the film, under the name of Adrien, he lodges with the Paleari family, whose head, Anselmo, is keen on spiritualism. Mathias falls in love with the daughter, Adrienne, who is also being courted by the sinister Térence Papiano. At a séance, Papiano arranges that his brother, the epileptic Scipion, played by Batcheff, should steal 50,000 francs from Mathias, who cannot go to the police without revealing his true identity. He therefore decides to return home, only to discover that his wife has married Pomino. Mathias returns to Rome and Adrienne.

6. DESTINÉE

Private viewing	28 November 1925, Opéra de Monte Carlo
Trade presentation	9 December 1925, Théâtre des Champs-Élysées
Gala	Ministère des Affaires Étrangères, 12 December 1925
General release	March 1926 exclusively in Salle Marivaux
Director	Henry Roussell
Asst director	Pierre Delmonde
Production	Lutèce-Films
Script	Henry Roussell

Camera	Maurice Velle, Willy Faktorovitch
Music	André Gailhard
Distribution	Exclusivités Jean de Merly
Main actors	Isabélita Ruiz (Floria Alfina); Suzy Pierson (Mme de Tallien); Jean-Napoléon Michel (Bonaparte); Pierre Batcheff (Roland de Neuflize); Ady Cresso (Joséphine de Beauharnais); Christiane Favier (Pamela Egalité); Victoria Lenoir (Rosalia Strabini); Geymond Vital (Carlo Strabini); Raoul Villiers (Léonidas Gauthier); René Montis (Barras); James Devesa (Tallien); Louis Cari (David); Gaston Sylver (l'acteur Talma); Raphael Adam (Maréchal de Beaulieu); Pierre Delmonde (Salicetti); Georges-Augustin de la Noe (Masséna)
Availability	17.5mm print in a private collection
Synopsis	It is 1795. Floria Alfina, one of the Italian models of the painter David, is being courted by Roland, who pursues her into David's studio. The workshop is more like a salon for Parisian society. Her curses are translated by the relatively unknown Napoleon. Madame de Tallien, who is also there, arranges for Roland to give Floria French lessons at her home. The two fall in love, but Floria is promised to her foster-brother, Carlo Strabini. Napoleon is called upon to defend the Republic on 13th Vendémiaire, and Roland joins his army. Napoleon subsequently takes his army to Italy, ensuring that the Strabinis, his loyal supporters, go with him. At Lodi, near Milan, Carlo, blinded by jealousy of Roland, betrays the French to the Austrian army, imprisoning Floria to prevent her from warning the French. Napoleon leads his men to victory none the less, although Roland is wounded. Napoleon condemns Carlo and Floria (whom he believes to have been implicated) to a traitor's death. Carlo is shot, but Floria's innocence is proven, and she returns to tend Roland by his hospital bed.

7. *Le Secret d'une mère*

Trade presentation	7 July 1926
General release	July 1926
Director	Georges Pallu
Production	Nicae Film Production

Script	From the novel by Eugène Barbier, *Abandonné!*
Camera	Günzli Walter
Set design	Gaston David
Distribution	Exclusivité Agency
Length	2,000 metres
Main actors	Marise Maia (Denise Louvreuil); Pierre Batcheff (Marcel Vincent); Yanova (Juliette Louvreuil); Olga Noel (Marie Jeannin); Madame Desvergers (Catherine Baudot); Fabrice (Louvreuil)
Availability	None
Synopsis	Marcel Vincent, an aspiring artist, has fallen in love with a fellow student, Denise Louvreuil. He defends her against the unwanted advances of another student, and in the ensuing struggle is badly hurt. His stepmother comes to his bedside. She goes with him once he has recovered to Denise's parents' house where she recognises Denise's mother, Juliette, as the woman who gave her Marcel. Juliette had been raped when younger and had always refused to see Marcel, the result of that rape. Marcel, not understanding how she could abandon him, rejects her. One day Denise opens one of her mother's letters and discovers the secret. The years go by; Denise marries another and meets up with Marcel while on her honeymoon in Rome, where he is working, to beg him to return to his mother who is dying of sorrow. He marries and has a child, exhibiting a Maternity using his wife and child as models. He returns to Paris where he forgives his mother, and holds his two 'mothers' in his arms.

8. *LE JOUEUR D'ÉCHECS*

Trade presentation/ premiere	6 January 1927, Salle Marivaux
General release	January 1927
Director	Raymond Bernard
Asst directors	Jean Hémard
Production	Société des Films Historiques
Script	Raymond Bernard, Jean-José Frappa, Henri Dupuy-Mazuel

Camera	Marc Bujard, Joseph-Louis Mundviller, Willy Faktorovitch
Music	Henri Rabaud
Costumes	Eugène Lourié
Set design	Jean Perrier, Eugène Carré
Distribution	Jean de Merly
Length	139 mins
Main actors	Pierre Blanchar (Boleslas Vorowski); Charles Dullin (Baron de Kempelen); Édith Jehanne (Sophie Novinska); Camille Bert (Major Nicolaieff); Pierre Batcheff (Prince Serge Oblonoff); Marcelle Charles Dullin (Catherine II de Russie); Armand Bernard (Roudenko); Pierre Hot (le Roi Stanislas Poniatowski); James Devesa (Prince Orloff); Albert Préjean (le courrier du Tsar)
Availability	Centre national de la cinématographie. Copy restored by Kevin Brownlow and David Gill in the 'Thames Silents' series: DVD Image Entertainment, Region 1, released 29 July 2003 ASIN: B00009Q4W8; VHS Bfi Video Publishing, released 7 September 1998 ASIN: B00004CX1O
Synopsis	Boleslas Vorowski is Polish, and Serge Oblonoff Russian. They are friends, despite the tensions between their two countries, with Poland seeking independence. Sophie Vorowska is in love with Serge, but is also a fervent Polish patriot. When the tensions burst into conflict, she regretfully loosens her ties with Serge, and is drawn to the hot-headed Boleslas, who leads the independence movement against the Russians. When this is brutally crushed by the Russians, Baron de Kempelen, an inventor who is Sophie's guardian, hides Boleslas in one of his automata, a chess player. The Empress Catherine orders Kempelen to bring his automaton to St Petersburg, where she plays against him and loses. There is a masked ball, during which she and her officers come to suspect that the chess player is hiding Boleslas. The Empress orders the automaton to be shot, but Kempelen has switched places with Boleslas and dies. Serge helps Boleslas and Sophie to escape, sacrificing his love for Sophie.

9. *NAPOLÉON VU PAR ABEL GANCE*

Premiere	7 April 1927 (5,500 metres with two triptychs), Opéra
Trade presentation	9–10 May (directors); 11–12 May (critics), Apollo (full version spread over two days)
General release	14 November 1927
Director	Abel Gance
Asst directors	Henri Andréani, Pierre Danis, Henry Krauss, Anatole Litvak, Mario Nalpas, Viacheslav Tourjansky, Alexander Volkoff
Production	Société du Film Napoléon, Société Générale de Films
Script	Abel Gance
Camera	Jules Kruger; Louis Mundwiller (Brienne, Corsica)
Asst camera	Léonce-Henri Burel, Paul Briquet (for the triptychs), Marcel Eywinger, Roger Hubert, Georges Lucas, Émile Monniot, Émile Pierre
Music	Arthur Honneger
Art direction	Alexandre Benois, Georges Jacouty, Alexandre Lochakoff, Vladimir Meinhardt, Pierre Schildknecht, Pimenoff
Costume	Mme Augis, Georges Charmy, Mme Neminsky, Alphonse Sauvageau
Editing	Marguerite Beaugé
Asst editor	Henriette Pinson
Distribution	Gaumont–Metro-Goldwyn
Length	10,700 metres
Main actors	Albert Dieudonné (Napoléon Bonaparte); Edmond Van Daële (Robespierre); Alexandre Koubitzky (Danton); Antonin Artaud (Marat); Abel Gance (Saint-Just); Gina Manès (Joséphine de Beauharnais); Pierre Batcheff (Hoche); Yvette Dieudonné (Elisa Bonaparte); Eugénie Buffet (Laetitia Bonaparte); Nicolas Koline (Tristan Fleuri); Annabella (Violine Fleuri)
Availability	Centre national de la cinématographie
Synopsis	The film takes us from Napoleon's childhood through to the Italian campaign. We see him organising battles in the playground. As a young officer, he leaves Corsica, threatened by the nationalists, and arrives in Paris in the middle of the Terror. He shows himself to be a remarkable strategist by laying siege to the town of

Toulon. He is gradually attracted to Josephine, particularly during the Victims' Ball, where General Hoche was her gallant. He is the saviour of the day on Vendémiaire, and the Italian campaign, with the victory at Montenotte, turns him into the saviour of France.

10. *ÉDUCATION DE PRINCE*

Trade presentation	7 June 1927, Mogador
General release	11 November 1927
Director	Henri Diamant-Berger
Asst director	Maurice Daniel
Production	Natan
Script	André de Lorde and Henri Diamant-Berger, adapted from the play by Maurice Donnay
Camera	René Guissart
Music	Bétove
Set design	Martine, Milva
Costume	Paul Poiret
Distribution	Établissements Louis Aubert
Main actors	Edna Purviance (la reine Liska); Pierre Batcheff (Sacha); Jean Dax (Cercleux); Flora Le Breton (Raymonde); Albert Préjean (Hersch); Armand Bernard (Comte de Ronceval); Andrews Engelmann (Dimitri); Jean Joffre (le général Braoulitch); Bétove (le Premier Ministre); Pauline Carton (la concierge)
Availability	Cinémathèque française; Forum des Images. Copy reconstituted by Renée Lichtig in 1983.
Synopsis	René Cercleux, a wealthy but dissolute bon viveur, is asked by Queen Liska to show her son, Crown-Prince Sacha, how to socialise, so as to complete his rather severe education. She goes back to Silistria, and Sacha soon falls in love with Raymonde, a dancer. The Queen returns to Paris at Cercleux's suggestion, and almost gives in to his advances. There is trouble back in Silistria, as Dimitri the pretender has claimed the throne. Duty-bound, Sacha returns with his mother to be crowned. While this brings back calm politically, the two of them long for their lovers back in Paris. The Council advocates that Sacha should marry the daughter of the King of Illyria as a political expediency. Sacha demurs but asks

Cercleux to bring Raymonde to Silistria in secret so he can see her one last time. Meanwhile, Dimitri has launched an uprising; Sacha and his supporters are forced to flee the castle. They are caught and escorted back, only to discover that Raymonde and Hersch have managed to take Dimitri prisoner after a violent struggle. Sacha marries Raymonde, who has saved the country, and the Queen marries Cercleux.

11. *Le Bonheur du jour*

Trade presentation	4 July 1927, Moulin Rouge
General release	3 February 1928
Director	Gaston Ravel
Asst director	Tony Lekain
Production	Franco-Film
Producer	Jacques Haïk
Script	Adapted from the play by Edmond Guiraud
Camera	Henri Gondois, Robert Batton
Set design	Tony Lekain
Distribution	Franco-Film
Main actors	Elmire Vautier (Madame Plessiers); Francine Mussey (Germaine d'Aguzon); Pierre Batcheff (Jean Plessiers de Chavignac); Suzanne Munte (Madame d'Aguzon); Henry Krauss (le docteur Plessiers); Maurice Schutz (Monsieur d'Aguzon)
Availability	None
Synopsis	Geneviève de Chavignac loves Bertrand, but both families are poor so they decide not to marry. He flees to Africa, where he dies in a plane crash. Geneviève, realising that she is pregnant, marries the good doctor Plessiers. Twenty-five years later, her son Jean is in love with Germaine. He discovers letters in an old desk revealing his mother's secret and his illegitimacy. Unable to stay in his mother's house, he decides, like his father, to flee to Africa. The family and Germaine go after him; his mother shows him the marriage certificate for a marriage that she and Bertrand had never been able to regularise. He and Germaine marry a year later.

12. *La Sirène des tropiques*

Trade presentation	21 December 1927, Théâtre des Champs-Élysées
General release	30 December 1927
Directors	Henri Etiévant, Mario Nalpas
Asst director	Luis Buñuel
Production	La Centrale Cinématographique
Script	Maurice Dekobra
Artistic director	Jacques Natanson
Camera	Albert Duverger, Paul Cotteret, Maurice Hennebains
Set design	Pierre Schildknecht, Eugène Carré
Distribution	Établissements Louis Aubert
Length	2,060 metres
Main actors	Josephine Baker (Papitou); Pierre Batcheff (André Berval); Régina Dalthy (Marquise Sévéro); Régina Thomas (Denise); Georges Melchior (le Comte Sévéro); Kiranine (Alvarez); Adolphe Candé (le directeur)
Availability	Centre national de la cinématographie; DVD Kino, Region 1, released 21 June 2005 ASIN: B0009CTTX8
Synopsis	Marquis Sévéro wants to divorce his wife and marry his stepdaughter Denise, who loves an engineer in Sévéro's employ, André Berval. Sévéro sends Berval to prospect his territories in the Antilles, instructing his man there, Alvarez, to ensure that Berval does not return. Berval saves Papitou from being raped by Alvarez, who subsequently ambushes Berval and leaves him for dead. Papitou, who has fallen in love with Berval, saves him, and the two of them catch Alvarez stealing gold from Sévéro's mines. Meanwhile, the Marchioness and Denise have come to the Antilles, realising that Berval is in danger. The three of them return to Paris; Papitou, desperate to be with Berval, follows them as a stowaway on a liner. In Paris, she works as a governess, but is spotted dancing by the director of a music hall who persuades her to join him, promising that he will make sure she can meet Berval. The director tells his friend Sévéro about this, who realises that he can use it to his advantage. He engineers a meeting at his house, where Denise sees Papitou in Berval's arms, allowing Sévéro to break off the engagement. The men agree to fight a duel. Sévéro fires

first but misses; Berval fires into the air, but Papitou
shoots Sévéro from her hiding place at just that
moment. Realising how much Berval loves Denise,
however, she sacrifices herself, explaining to Denise the
misunderstandings and returning to the Antilles.

13. *L'ÎLE D'AMOUR*

General release	3 February 1928, exclusively at Aubert-Palace (no trade presentation)
Directors	Jean Durand, Berthe Jean Durand
Asst director	Marcel Marceau
Production	Franco-Film
Script	Jean Durand, from the novel *Bicchi* by Saint-Sorny
Camera	Maurice Velle, Jacques Montéran, Colas
Set design	Eugène Carré, Pierre Schildknecht
Distribution	Franco-Film
Length	2,247 metres; 78 mins
Main actors	Claude France (Xénia Smith); Pierre Batcheff (Bicchi); Jean Garat (Harry Smith); Thérèse Kolb (la mère); Berthe Dagmar (une femme); Mistinguett; Yvonne Armor (la fiancée); Alice Roberte (la nurse); Victor Vina (Jean de Serlys); Aldo Rossano (Bozzi)
Availability	Centre national de la cinématographie
Synopsis	Rich American Harry Smith and his daughter Xénia come to Ajaccio for philanthropic work. Bicchi offers his services as a guide, and Xénia, after buying him decent clothes, sees his natural elegance. Bicchi saves a child's life by removing him from the path of Harry Smith's car, and ends up in hospital, where Xénia visits him. Madly in love with her, he leaves the hospital to sing under her window, collapsing from the effort. When recovered, he helps her set up a poorhouse for children and older people; she declares her love to him. In a moment of joy, Bicchi traces a cross – sign of death – on the door of one of his enemies. There is an opening gala for the hospital built by Smith, where Mistinguett performs. Bicchi and Xénia spend the night together. That night, Bicchi's enemy, Bozzi, is assassinated, and Bicchi is the suspect. He confesses so as to protect Xénia's honour, but she reveals that they were together.

Bicchi and Xénia later leave Ajaccio on the Smiths'
yacht.

14. *Vivre*

Trade presentation	9 July 1928, Empire
General release	July 1928
Director	Robert Boudrioz
Production	Phénix-Films A.G.–Studios Réunis
Script	Emmanuel Alfieri, adapted from the play by Hans Müller
Camera	Paul Portier, Adolf Otto Weitzenberg
Set design	Hays
Distribution	Star Films
Length	3,055 metres
Main actors	Elmire Vautier (Jeanne); Bernhard Goetzke (professeur Granval); Pierre Batcheff (baron Derozier-Schell); Adolphe Candé (le domestique)
Availability	None
Synopsis	After many years of research Professor Granval has discovered a serum that cures tuberculosis, although his faculty colleagues are hostile. He has neglected his wife, Jeanne, who seeks affection. She eventually strikes up a close friendship, but not love, with Baron Derozier, a fact that even Granval, absorbed as he is in his work, eventually realises. Derozier contracts tuberculosis, and Granval, caught between jealousy and professional conscience, injects him with the serum, but Derozier dies the next day. Granval is arraigned before the medical council. Jeanne argues to him that he should protect his work by claiming that he killed Derozier in a crime of passion. Granval refuses to impugn his wife's honour in this way, and at the hearing refuses to answer their questions. Jeanne is about to spin the story she has concocted when the autopsy results announce that Derozier had committed suicide with opiates. Granval understands that he must devote more attention to his wife.

15. *Le Perroquet vert*

Trade presentation	13 October 1928
General release	19 October 1928
Director	Jean Milva
Production	Films A.R.C.
Script	Jacques de Casembroot, adapted from the novel by Princess Bibesco
Camera	Marc Bujard
Set design	Eugène Carré, Jean d'Eaubonne, Géa (Georges-Charles Augsburger)
Distribution	Compagnie Vitagraph de France
Length	1,654 metres
Main actors	Édith Jehanne (Natacha Dalgouroukine); Pierre Batcheff (Félix Soltikoff); Maxudian (le père); Jeanne Berangère (l'aïeule); Mme Alberti (Nianka); Jim Gérald (Gordon)
Availability	Cinémathèque Royale de Belgique
Synopsis	Natacha's childhood was blighted by two things: the death of her brother, and the refusal of her father to buy her a green parrot, symbol in his eyes of misfortune. Her grandmother reveals the family's curse: brother–sister incest. Many years later, her father is preparing a coup d'état with his right-hand man, Félix Soltikoff, who has a price on his head. A traitor tries to kill Félix, but Natacha's father takes the fatal blow. Grateful for the help that Félix's mother has given to her father in his last days, Natacha takes Félix to Paris, where the two fall in love. They are just about to be married when the grandmother arrives and recognises Félix as Natacha's brother, as his mother had once been her father's mistress. Natacha decides to enter a convent.

16. *Les Deux Timides*

Trade presentation	5 December 1928, Empire
General release	1 March 1929
Director	René Clair
Asst directors	Georges Lacombe, Georges Lampin
Production	Albatros-Sequana
Script	René Clair adapted from the play by Eugène Labiche and Marc Michel

Camera	Robert Batton, Nicolas Roudakoff
Set design	Lazare Meerson
Length	1,739 metres, 76 mins
Main actors	Pierre Batcheff (Jules Frémissin); Véra Flory (Cécile Thibaudier); Jim Gérald (Anatole Garadoux); Maurice de Féraudy (Thibaudier); Françoise Rosay (la tante de Jules Frémissin); Anna Lefeuvrier (la cousine Garadoux); Yvette Andreyor (Madame Garadoux); Madeleine Guitty (Annette, la bonne); Louis Pré Fils (le cousin Garadoux)
Availability	Cinémathèque française
Synopsis	Frémissin, a lawyer, is defending Garadoux for abusing his wife. While he is in full flow, the court is distracted by a mouse; already a shy man, Frémissin becomes confused, ending up by asking for the maximum penalty for his client. Garadoux spends two years in prison; now divorced and part of the community, he tries to obtain Cécile Thibaudier's hand in marriage by courting her father, as she does not care for him. She meets Frémissin at a soiree, but he is too shy to take it further, despite a reciprocal attraction. Pushed by his aunt, Frémissin goes to see Cécile, and the two of them declare their love on a walk through the fields; but Cécile reveals that she is now promised to Garadoux, and urges Frémissin to talk to her father. Frémissin goes to see Cécile's father, but he is too shy to ask for his daughter's hand, and the father too shy to enquire as to the reason for the visit; the two of them end up dropping off to sleep. Garadoux, who has seen his rival and recognised him as his old lawyer, tries to frighten Frémissin off by wearing a mask and threatening him with a gun. Despite some hesitation, Frémissin goes to the Thibaudiers' house where the Garadoux family will be witnesses for the engagement. Some village children let off crackers, and both Frémissin and the Garadoux clan believe that masked bandits have attacked. Frémissin none the less overcomes his shyness and manages to enter the house with the notary and a policeman, where he denounces Garadoux as a wife abuser. The two families fight, and the matter ends up in court. Thibaudier and Frémissin, each as shy as the other, pluck up courage by getting drunk before the hearing, which ends up in fisticuffs

once more after Frémissin's successful speech.
Thibaudier promises his daughter to Frémissin.

17. MONTE-CRISTO

Trade presentation	27 May 1929, Empire
General release	25 October 1929 (Part 1), 1 November 1929 (Part 2)
Director	Henri Fescourt
Asst director	Armand Salacrou
Producer	Louis Nalpas
Script	Henri Fescourt and Armand Salacrou adapted from the novel by Alexandre Dumas and Auguste Maquet
Artistic director	Frank Daniau-Johnson
Camera	Julien Ringel, Henri Barreyre, Goesta Kottula, Maurice Hennebain
Editing	Jean Louis Bouquet
Set design	Boris Bilinsky, Bertin et Moreau
Costumes	Boris Bilinsky
Distribution	Les Productions Réunies
Length	5,740 metres. Restored version 5,230 metres/218 mins
Main actors	Jean Angelo (Edmond Dantès, comte de Monte-Cristo); Lil Dagover (Mercédès); Gaston Modot (Fernand de Mortcerf); Marie Glory (Valentine de Villefort); Pierre Batcheff (Albert de Mortcerf); Jean Toulout (Monsieur de Villefort); Bernhard Goetzke (l'abbé Faria); Henri Debain (Caderousse); Tamara Stezensko (Haydée)
Availability	Centre national de la cinématographie, Cinémathèque française (reel missing). Restored version (by ZZ Productions) screened by the Franco-German TV channel Arte in their series 'Le Muet du mois', 23–4 September 2006.
Synopsis	Edmond Dantès, second in command of the ship *Le Pharaon*, belonging to Morrel, returns to Marseille to discover that he has been promoted to captain, thus ensuring his future for his impending marriage to Mercédès. He is thrown into jail, however, betrayed by three men: Caderousse, sailor on *Le Pharaon*, jealous of Edmond's promotion; Fernand Mondego, Edmond's rival for Mercédès; and de Villefort, the public prosecutor, whose father is compromised by a letter in Edmond's possession. In the notorious prison of the

Château d'If, Edmond meets Abbé Faria, who educates him and also reveals the location of an immense treasure on the island of Monte-Cristo. When the old man dies, Edmond escapes by substituting himself for Faria's corpse, and finds the treasure. He uses part of his fortune to save Morrel, who supported his father, from bankruptcy, and he then turns to his vengeance. He engineers the incarceration of Caderousse and his foster-son Benedetto for the murder of a jeweller. He lures Fernand and Mercédès's son, Albert, to his under ground palace on Monte-Cristo, and makes a friend of him. Albert introduces him to Parisian high society as the Count of Monte-Cristo. The Count organises a soiree where Fernand's betrayal of a former ally is revealed in a theatrical sketch. This becomes the talk of the town, and in a confrontation, the Count reveals who he is; Fernand commits suicide. The Count extracts Benedetto from prison and creates a new identity for him as a wealthy foreign prince. De Villefort breaks off his daughter's engagement with the son of Morrel, so that he can acquire a wealthy son-in-law. The contract is about to be signed when the police come to arrest Benedetto, who has just tried to murder his foster-father, Caderousse. De Villefort, as prosecutor general, tries Benedetto, but at the trial it is revealed that he himself is Benedetto's father, whom he had left for dead; de Villefort goes mad when the Count in turn reveals who he is.

18. *Un Chien andalou*

Premiere	6 June 1929, Studio des Ursulines
Director	Luis Buñuel
Asst director	Pierre Batcheff
Producers	Luis Buñuel, Pierre Braunberger
Production	Studio-Films (Paris)
Script	Luis Buñuel, Salvador Dalí
Editing	Luis Buñuel
Camera	Albert Duverger
Set design	Pierre Schildknecht
Distribution	Studio-Films (Paris)

Length	18 mins
Main actors	Pierre Batcheff (l'homme); Simonne Mareuil (la jeune femme); Salvador Dalí (un frère des écoles); Jaime Miratvilles (un frère des écoles); Luis Buñuel (l'homme au rasoir); Fano Messan (l'androgyne)
Availability	Centre national de la cinématographie; DVD Bfi Video Publishing, released 25 October 2004 ASIN: B000621P6A
Synopsis	In a 'prologue', a man (Buñuel) strops a razor and slits a woman's (Mareuil's) eye. Eight years later, a man (Batcheff) cycles in a street dressed in a suit overlaid with a mantelet and topples over. The woman cradles him as he lies in the street. She lays out his tie and mantelet on her bed. On the other side of the room he stares at hole in his hand out of which ants are crawling. This image dissolves into a female bather's underarm hair, then into a sea-urchin, and finally into the head of an androgynous woman standing in the street and poking a severed hand with a cane. She is surrounded by a horrified crowd, and observed by an increasingly excited Batcheff and Mareuil. The crowd is dispersed by a policeman, the androgyne puts the severed hand in a box, and is run over by a car. Batcheff pursues Mareuil, caressing her breasts and buttocks, his eyes upturned and his mouth drooling blood. Mareuil runs away. Batcheff grabs some ropes lying on the floor and pulls two pianos covered with dead donkeys and trailing two Marist brothers towards her. She escapes into the next room which is a replica of the first, Batcheff's hand with the ants being caught in the door. Mareuil sees him also lying on a bed in the room to which she has escaped. A stranger rings the door, turning out to be Batcheff as well. He orders Batcheff to remove the mantelet and frills, and throws them out of the window, ordering Batcheff to stand in the corner of the room with his hands up. The stranger gives Batcheff some books from a school desk; they change into revolvers, and Batcheff shoots his double who falls in a park. A group of strangers take him away. We return to the room where Mareuil stares intently at a death's–head moth; Batcheff suddenly appears and abruptly places his hand over his

mouth, effacing it. Mareuil defiantly puts lipstick on her lips, and hair appears on Batcheff's face where the mouth should be; Mareuil looks under her arm and sees that her underarm hair has disappeared. She pokes her tongue out at Batcheff and opens the door on to a windswept beach, where she meets a new man. They walk along the beach and come across the mantelet and frills worn by Batcheff, casting them away. A final tableau entitled 'in the spring' shows us the new man and Mareuil buried in sand and covered with insects.

19. *ILLUSIONS*

Trade presentation	14 January 1930, Empire
General release	March (?) 1930
Director	Lucien Mayrargue
Production	S.I.F.A. (Sociedad Independiente Filmadora Argentina)
Script	Lucien Mayrargue
Artistic director	Lyco Laghos
Camera	Willy, Alphonse Gibory
Set design	Lucien Carré
Distribution	Loca-Films
Length	2,200 metres (CNC version without intertitles 1,545 metres; 54 mins)
Main actors	Mary Serta (Valentine); Pierre Batcheff (Henry); Gaston Jacquet (Gérard); Esther Kiss (Odette); Pola Illéry (une soubrette); Ninon Bernard (une paysanne)
Availability	Centre national de la cinématographie; unrestored version without intertitles
Synopsis	Gérard finds a packet of letters in a taxi one night, with the photograph of a young couple. As he reads the letters, which were written by a woman, he relives the courtship of Henry and Valentine, the attempt by Odette, Valentine's best friend, to have Henry for herself, Valentine's threatened suicide and her eventual separation from Henry. He sees an advert in the paper a few days later announcing that the Countess de Moslay mislaid her love letters. He takes them to her, believing that he can step into Henry's place, only to discover that Valentine is now an old lady, and that she is happily married to Henry.

20. *LE ROI DE PARIS*

General release	7 August 1930
Director	Leo Mittler
Producer	Marcel Hellmann
Production	Exclusivités Jean de Merly, Greenbaum-Film
Script	Curt J. Braun, Michael Linsky, adapted from the novel by Georges Ohnet
Camera	Curt Courant, Max Brink
Music	Walter Goehr
Main actors	Suzanne Bianchetti (la duchesse de Marsignac); Marie Glory (Lucienne); Ivan Petrovitch (Pedro Gil); Gabriel Gabrio (Rascol); Pierre Batcheff (Henri); Pierre Juvenet (Amorreti)
Availability	None
Synopsis	Rascol persuades the young Argentinian dancer Pedro to take him as his manager, and he turns him into the 'king of Paris', with a view to using him as a lure for rich women. The Duchess de Marsignac is much taken with him, although her son, Henri, disapproves to such an extent that he leaves his mother's house to live with his friend Amorreti and his daughter Lucienne. Lucienne, with whom Pedro has fallen in love, deceives Pedro into confessing that he does not really love the Duchess while the Duchess is listening. The Duchess, still too much in love with Pedro, helps him to escape from the police. Pedro, rejecting the life of the con artist, argues with Rascol, and in the ensuing struggle, Rascol dies. Amorreti helps him leave the country.

21A. *LES AMOURS DE MINUIT*

Premiere	7 January 1931, Palais Rochechouart
General release	20 January 1931
Directors	Augusto Genina, Marc Allégret
Asst director	Yves Allégret
Production	Établissements Braunberger-Richebé, Carl Froelich Film
Script	Georg C. Klaren, Maurice Kroll, Carl Behr
Camera	Roger Hubert, Theodore Sparkuhl
Editing	Denise Batcheff, Jean Mamy
Music	Jean Delannay, Philippe Parès, Georges Van Parys

Length	97 mins
Main actors	Pierre Batcheff (Marcel); Danièle Parola (Georgette); Jacques Varennes (Gaston Bouchard); Josseline Gaël (Fanny)
Availability	Cinémathèque française (last reel missing)
Synopsis	Marcel has stolen money from the bank where he works, and is leaving the country by train. The man in the compartment with him, Gaston, an escaped murderer, sees that Marcel's wallet is stuffed full of notes. When they arrive at the station, Marcel waits for Gaston in the café, and starts a conversation with Georgette, who turns out to be Gaston's girlfriend, although he calls her his sister when he returns to join them. He asks Georgette to take Marcel to the cabaret where she is a dancer, and he will join them later. Georgette is taken with Marcel and decides not to steal his money, as Gaston had wanted her to. Gaston beats her just before she is called on stage, where she sings a sad song, 'Amours de minuit'. After the show Marcel joins Georgette in her room, where she and Gaston are arguing. Gaston attacks Marcel, takes his money and escapes. Marcel confesses to Georgette that he has stolen the money from his bank, but that he wants to put it back before anyone realises it has been taken. The police arrive, and Marcel is arrested because he has no papers. Georgette seduces the captain of the boat on which Gaston is escaping, and he and the captain come to blows. Georgette retrieves Marcel's wallet and papers in the confusion, and he is freed from the police station. Gaston arrives and shoots Georgette before being arrested by the police. Marcel visits Georgette in hospital after he has returned the money.

21b. *Mitternachtsliebe* (German version of preceding film)

General release	4 September 1931
Directors	Augusto Genina, Carl Froelich
Production	Établissements Braunberger-Richebé, Carl Froelich Film, Friedrich Pflughaupt
Script	Georg C. Klaren, Maurice Kroll, Carl Behr
Camera	Roger Hubert, Theodore Sparkuhl

Editing	Denise Batcheff, Jean Mamy
Music	Philippe Parès, Georges Van Parys
Sound	Carlo Paganini
Length	109 mins
Main actors	Danièle Parola (Georgette); Josseline Gaël (Fanny); Pierre Batcheff (Walter Thalberg); Hans Adalbert Schlettow (Bagdanoff)
Availability	None

22. LE REBELLE

General release	10 August 1931
Director	Adelqui Millar
Production	Films Paramount
Script	Martin Brown, Louise Long, Benno Vigny adapted from the play by Lajos Zilahy
Camera	Philip Tannura
Main actors	Pierre Batcheff (Boris Sabline); Suzy Vernon (Maria Ivanovna); Paule Andral (Mme Alexandra); Jeanne Brazine (la chanteuse); Thomy Bourdelle (le général Platoff); André Réhan (Spoliansky); Georges La Cressonnière (le lieutenant Glinka)
Availability	None
Synopsis	Maria has agreed to marry Boris, a young medical student researching a serum, even though she does not really love him. War breaks out and Boris is sent to the front. Maria tries to persuade General Platoff to transfer Boris back into a laboratory where he will be of more use, but the General refuses. Boris reacts badly to criticism of his poor military skills, and after striking the General, is condemned to death. Maria tries to obtain his pardon from the General, and the two fall in love with each other. The General decides to pardon Boris, but when he reveals to Boris that his release is thanks to his wife, Boris tries to kill him. The enemy attacks at that moment and Boris goes out to seek death, but the General takes a bullet intended for Boris. Faced with the General's courage and selflessness, Boris realises why his wife loves him, and gives Maria her freedom.

23A. *BAROUD* (ENGLISH VERSION)

Trade presentation	28 September 1932, Prince Edward Theatre, London
General release	27 February 1933
Director	Rex Ingram, Benno Vigny
Co-director	Alice Terry
Assistant	Tomás Cola
Producer	Rex Ingram
Production	Gaumont British Picture Corporation
Script	Rex Ingram, Peter Spencer
Camera	Léonce-Henri Burel, P[aul] Portier, A. [Sepp] Allgeier, Marcel Lucien, T. Tomatis
Set design	Jean Lafitte, Georges Wakhévitch (uncredited)
Music	Louis Lévy
Editor	Lothar Wolff
Distribution	Ideal
Length	91 mins
Main actors	Rex Ingram (André Duval); Pierre Batcheff (Si Hamed); Felipe Montes (Si Allal, caïd de Ilued); Rosita Garcia (Zinah, his daughter); Arabella Fields (Mabrouka, a slave); Andrews Engelmann (Si Amarok); Dennis Hoey (Captain Labry); Laura Salerni (Arlette)
Availability	British Film Institute
Synopsis	Close friends Si Hamed and André Duval are both sergeants in a squadron of spahis patrolling Morocco. The squadron stops off in Illouet, ruled by Si Hamed's father Si Allal, where Si Hamed's sister Zinah spots André from afar and falls for him. The squadron goes on to Marrakech, and the two men go to a cabaret where the singer Arlette falls for Si Hamed. André leaves them, and stops a group of soldiers from molesting Zinah and her chaperone. He arranges a secret meeting with her in the local cemetery, unaware that the lovers have been seen by an informer, who tells Si Hamed. Si Hamed is torn between his friendship and Islamic law, which rules that the seducer should be killed. When the two men meet, André is so effusive about the woman he has met (and whose identity he is unaware of) that Si Hamed cannot bring himself to kill his friend. One of Si Allal's caravans has been destroyed by a neighbouring tribe, led by Si Amarok, who has asked Si Allal for his daughter's

hand in marriage. When Si Allal is told by a survivor of the caravan's fate and that Si Amarok is the culprit, Si Amarok declares war ('baroud') in the meeting. Not long after, Si Amarok's fighters attack Si Allal's fortress. The fortress is saved by a squadron of spahis, but Zinah has been wounded by Si Amarok. André and Si Hamed leave; Si Allal promises André that he will have everything his heart desires.

23B. *BAROUD* (FRENCH VERSION)

General release	18 November 1932, exclusively at Gaumont-Palace
Directors	Rex Ingram, Alice Terry
Assistant	Thomas Cola
Producer	André Weill
Production	Gaumont British Production
Script	Rex Ingram, André Jaegerschmidt, Benno Vigny
Camera	L[éonce-Henri] Burel, [Paul] Portier, M[arcel] Lucien
Set design	Jean Lafitte, Georges Wakhévitch (uncredited)
Music	Louis Lévy
Editor	Lothar Wolff
Distribution	Gaumont
Length	91 mins
Main actors	Philippe Moretti (Si Allal, caïd d'Illouet); Rosita Garcia (Zinah, sa fille); Pierre Batcheff (Si Hamed); Roland Caillaux (André Duval); Arabella Fields (Mabrouka); Andrews Engelmann (Si Amarock); Roger Gaillard (le capitaine Labry); Colette Darfeuil (Arlette)
Availability	Centre national de la cinématographie

24. *AMOUR . . . AMOUR . . .*

General release	26 September 1932
Director	Robert Bibal
Producer	Léon Poirier
Production	Gaumont, Franco-Film, Aubert
Script	Pierre Batcheff, from a story by Paul Maret
Camera	Georges Million, G. Goudard
Set design	Robert-Jules Garnier
Music	André Demurger
Sound	Marcel Royné, R. Paris

Length	76 mins, 2,045 metres
Main actors	Adrien Le Gallo (Monsieur Vander), Henri Marchand (Paul Berton), Colette Broïdo (Jacqueline), Sylvio de Pedrelli (Max Stern), Marcel Delaître (Labrousse)
Availability	Cinémathèque Royale de Belgique
Synopsis	Paul, the shy but model employee of Vander, a Parisian jeweller, loves bank typist Jacqueline, but she falls for jewel thief Max, whom the police are trying to catch. Jacqueline is stood up by Max, who realises he is being tailed, and she spends the evening with Paul. The next day, Paul is mistakenly arrested as he tries to cash a cheque for Vander. Although Paul is cleared, Vander sacks him for his increasingly erratic behaviour. He meets Jacqueline, also sacked, and tries to impress her by claiming that Vander's car is his own; they drive off. Meanwhile, Max and his gang lure Vander to a hotel in Fontainebleau so as to steal a valuable pearl necklace, the same hotel where Paul and Jacqueline have stopped. The police arrive, hot on the gang's tail, and Max is foiled. Paul pretends that someone else has stolen Vander's car. Vander, delighted to recover his car, reinstates Paul, and takes the lovers back to Paris.

Bibliography

Where we have not been able to source items directly in their original format, we have given the location of press clippings. These are either in the private Collection Roche-Batcheff (abbreviated CRB), or in the Collection Rondel of the Bibliothèque Nationale de France (abbreviated CR); in the latter case we have given the name and catalogue number of the relevant file.

Abel, Richard (1984), *French Cinema: The First Wave, 1915–1929*, Princeton, NJ: Princeton University Press.

Abel, Richard (1988) (ed.), *French Film Theory and Criticism: A History/Anthology, 1907–1939*, vol. 1: 1907–1929, Princeton, NJ: Princeton University Press.

Abel, Richard (1994), *The Ciné Goes to Town: French Cinema, 1896–1914*, Berkeley, CA: California University Press.

Abel, Richard (2005), 'Memory Work: French Historical Epics, 1926–1927', *Film History*, 17, pp. 352–62.

Albera, François (1995), *Albatros: des Russes à Paris, 1919–1929*, Milan/Paris: Mazzotta/ Cinémathèque Française.

Alby, Marianne (1928), 'Idéal masculin', *Cinémagazine*, 24 (15 June), pp. 421–3.

Ami du peuple (1931), '*Les Amours de minuit*', *L'Ami du peuple* (23 January) [CRB].

Anri, Luc (1930), '*Illusions*', *Écho* (17 January) [CR *Illusions* 8°Rk5265].

Aragon, Louis and André Breton (1928), 'Le Cinquantenaire de l'hystérie (1878–1928)', *La Révolution surréaliste*, 11 (15 March), pp. 20–2.

Aranda, J. Francisco (1975), *Luis Buñuel: A Critical Biography*, translated and edited by David Robinson, New York: Da Capo.

Arnoux, Alexandre (1929), '*Un Chien andalou*', *Les Nouvelles littéraires* (11 October) [CRB].

Aron, Robert (1929), 'Films de révolte', *La Revue du cinéma*, 5 (15 November), pp. 41–5.

Aron, Robert (1988), 'Films of Revolt', in Richard Abel, *French Film Theory and Criticism: A History/Anthology, 1907–1939*, vol. 1: 1907–1929, Princeton, NJ: Princeton University Press, pp. 432–6.

Artaud, Antonin (1925), 'Lettre aux médecins-chefs des asiles de fous', *La Révolution surréaliste*, 3 (15 April), p. 29.

Artaud, Antonin (1961), *Œuvres complètes*, vol. 3, Paris: Gallimard.

Artaud, Antonin (1964), *Œuvres complètes*, vol. 4, Paris: Gallimard.

Artaud, Antonin (1972), *Collected Works*, vol. 3, translated by Alastair Hamilton, London: Calder & Boyars.

Auriol, Jean-George (1929), '*Un Chien andalou*', *L'Ami du peuple* (21 June) [CR *Un Chien andalou* 8°Rk9399].

Austin, Guy (2003), *Stars in Modern French Film*, London: Arnold.

Barancy, A.-F. (1928), '*Les Deux Timides* d'après Labiche', *L'Avenir* (6 December) [CRB].

Barbier, Eugène (1924), *Abandonné!*, Paris: R. Chiberre.

Batcheff, Pierre (1926), 'Article inédit de M. Pierre Batcheff', *Argus de la presse* [Avignon], 14 August [CRB].

Batcheff, Pierre (1930), 'M. Pierre Batcheff tournera son propre film', *La Cinématographie française* (25 October) [CRB].

Becker, Jean-Jacques and Serge Berstein (1990), *Victoire et frustrations 1914–1929* (Nouvelle Histoire de la France contemporaine, vol. 12), Paris: Seuil.

Bensard, Patrick (1995), 'Joséphine Baker: *La Sirène des tropiques*', text dated August 1994 in the programme for La Cinémathèque de la Danse à la Cinémathèque Française (15 January), 'Rythmes et continents noirs', p. 6.

Bernard-Derosne, Sabine (1929), 'Les Grandes Vedettes de l'écran: Pierre Batcheff', *Minerva*, 205 (14 July), p. 16.

Berner, Raymond (1928), '*L'Île d'amour*', *Le Matin* (2 March) [CR *L'Île d'amour* 8°Rk5232].

Berner, Raymond (1929), 'Jean Milva quitte la France', *Mon ciné*, 410 (26 December), p. 4.

Berressem, Hanjo (1996), 'Dali and Lacan: Painting the Imaginary Landscapes', in *Lacan, Politics, Aesthetics*, edited by W. Apollon and R. Feldstein, Albany, NY: State University of New York Press, pp. 263–93.

Bibesco, Marthe Lucie Lahovary (1924), *Le Perroquet vert*, Paris: B. Grasset; repr. Paris: A. Fayard, 1928. Translated into English by Martin Cowley as *The Green Parrot*, London: Selwyn & Blount, 1928; repr. New York: Turtle Point, 1994.

Billard, Pierre (1995), *L'Âge classique du cinéma français: du cinéma parlant à la Nouvelle Vague*, Paris: Flammarion.

Bonneau, Albert (1926), '*Destinée!* Le Film – l'interprétation', *Cinémagazine*, 9 (26 February), pp. 414–18.

Bonneau, Albert (1927), '*Éducation de prince*', *Cinémagazine*, 24 (17 June), p. 585.

Breton, André (1922), 'Entrée des médiums', *Littérature*, 6 (1 November), pp. 1–16. Repr. in André Breton, *Œuvres complètes*, vol. I, Paris: Gallimard, 1988, pp. 273–9.

Breton, André (1928), *Nadja*, Paris: Gallimard. Repr. in André Breton, *Œuvres complètes*, vol. 1, Paris: Gallimard, 1988, pp. 643–753.

Breton, André (1929), 'Second Manifeste', *La Révolution surréaliste*, 12 (15 December), pp. 1–17. Translated as *Manifestoes of Surrealism*, Ann Arbor, MI: University of Michigan Press, 1969.

Breton, André (1972), *Manifestoes of Surrealism*, translated from the French by Richard Seaver and Helen R. Lane, Ann Arbor, MI: University of Michigan Press.

Breton, André (1988), *Œuvres complètes*, vol. 1, Paris: Gallimard.

Breton, André (1992), *Œuvres complètes*, vol. 2, Paris: Gallimard.

Breton, André (1999), *Œuvres complètes*, vol. 3, Paris: Gallimard.

Breton, André and Paul Éluard (1930), *L'Immaculée Conception*, Paris: Éditions surréalistes. Reprinted in André Breton, *Œuvres complètes*, vol. 1, Paris: Gallimard, 1988, pp. 839–84.

Bronfen, Elizabeth (1998), *The Knotted Subject: Hysteria and its Discontents*, Princeton, NJ: Princeton University Press.

Brownlow, Kevin (1983), *Napoleon: Abel Gance's Classic Film*, New York: A. A. Knopf.

Brownlow, Kevin (1984), 'Another Napoleon?', *Home Movie*, 1:1, pp. 5–7.

Brownlow, Kevin (1990), 'Thames Silents: Raymond Bernard's *The Chess Player*', *Sight and Sound*, 60:1, p. 2.

Brunius, Jacques Bernard (1929a), '*Un Chien andalou*', *La Revue du cinéma*, 4 (15 October), pp. 67–8.

Brunius, Jacques Bernard (1929b), 'La Revue des revues: croyant bien faire', *La Revue du cinéma*, 5 (15 November), pp. 78–9.

Brunius, Jacques-Bernard (1987), *En Marge du cinéma français*, Lausanne: L'Âge d'Homme. Originally published Paris: Arcanes, 1954.

Buñuel, Luis (1927), 'College', *Cahiers d'art,* 10. Translated in Francisco Aranda, *Luis Buñuel: A Critical Biography*, translated and edited by David Robinson, New York: Da Capo, 1975, pp. 272–3 and Paul Hammond (ed.), *The Shadow and its Shadow: Surrealist Writings on the Cinema*, London: British Film Institute, 1978, pp. 34–5.

Buñuel, Luis (1929a), '*Un Chien andalou*', *La Révolution surréaliste*, 12 (15 December), pp. 34–7.

Buñuel, Luis (1929b), '*Un Chien andalou*', in *The Collected Writings of Salvador Dalí*, edited and translated by Haim Finkelstein, Cambridge: Cambridge University Press, 1998, pp. 128–34.

Buñuel, Luis (1978), 'Notes on the Making of *Un Chien andalou*', in *The World of Luis Buñuel: Essays in Criticism*, edited by Joan Mellen, New York: Oxford University Press. Originally appeared in *Art in Cinema*, edited by Frank Stauffacher, San Francisco Museum of Art, 1947. Translated by G. L. McCann Morley.

Buñuel, Luis (1982), *Mon Dernier Soupir*, Paris: Robert Laffont.

Buñuel, Luis (1984), *My Last Breath*, translated by Abigail Isreal, London: Jonathan Cape.

Burch, Noël (1973), *Marcel L'Herbier*, Paris: Seghers ('Cinéma d'aujourd'hui', 78).

Cadars, Pierre (1982), *Les Séducteurs du cinéma français (1928–1958)*, Paris: Henri Veyrier.

Caillois, Roger (1935), 'Mimétisme et psychasthénie légendaire', *Minotaure*, 7, pp. 5–10.

Carné, Marcel (1931), '*Les Amours de minuit*', *Hebdo-Film*, 2 (10 January), p. 14.

Casembroot, Jacques de (1925), 'Ce que le Public en pense: de J. de Casembroot à Neuilly-sur-Seine', *Cinéa-Ciné pour tous*, 46 (1 October), p. 35.

Chataignier, Jean (1930), '*Illusions*', *Le Journal* (14 March) [CR *Illusions* 8°Rk5265].

Cinéa (1925a), 'On tourne!', *Cinéa-Ciné pour tous*, 36 (1 May), pp. 16–17.

Cinéa (1925b), '*Destinée*', *Cinéa-Ciné pour tous*, 46 (1 October), pp. 32–3.

Cinéa (1929), '*Monte-Cristo*', *Cinéa-Ciné pour tous*, 135 (15 June), p. 27.

Cinémagazine (1923), 'On monte', *Cinémagazine*, 37 (14 September), p. 374.

Cinémagazine (1928a), 'Courrier des lecteurs', *Cinémagazine*, 17 (27 April), pp. 154–7.

Cinémagazine (1928b), 'Courrier des lecteurs', *Cinémagazine*, 28 (13 July), pp. 80–1.

Cinémagazine (1928c), '*Destinée*: reprise', *Cinémagazine*, 35 (31 August), p. 323.

Cinématographie française (1924a), '*Claudine et le poussin ou Le Temps d'aimer*', *La Cinématographie française*, 246 (16 February).

Cinématographie française (1924b), 'Association', *La Cinématographie française*, 311 (18 October), p. 29.

Cinématographie française (1924c), '*Feu Mathias Pascal*', *La Cinématographie française*, 321 (27 December), pp. 9, 11.

Cinématographie française (1925a), 'Chez "Albatros"', *La Cinématographie française*, 329 (21 February), p. 21.

Cinématographie française (1925b), 'Deux grands films français: *Autour d'un berceau* et *La Douleur*', *La Cinématographie française*, 332 (14 March), p. 7.

Cinématographie française (1925c), '*Autour d'un berceau*', *La Cinématographie française*, 332 (14 March), p. 17.

Cinématographie française (1925d), '*Feu Mathias Pascal*', *La Cinématographie française*, 352 (1 August), pp. 12–13.

Cinématographie française (1925e), '*Destinée*', *La Cinématographie française*, 360 (26 September), p. 26.

Cinématographie française (1926a), '*Napoléon*', *La Cinématographie française*, 403 (24 July), p. 23.

Cinématographie française (1926b), 'Avant-première: ce que sera *Le Joueur d'échecs*', *La Cinématographie française*, 412 (25 September), p. 93.

Ciné-Miroir (1926), 'Nos Jeunes Premiers: André Roanne', *Ciné-Miroir*, 100 (15 June), p. 178.

Ciné-Miroir (1928), 'Du Studio à la ville: Pierre Batcheff nous écrit', *Ciné-Miroir*, 162 (11 May), p. 315.

Ciné-Miroir (1929), 'En Marge de l'écran: l'affaire du *Collier de la reine*', *Ciné-Miroir*, 206 (15 March), p. 167.

Ciné-Miroir (1931), 'Avec les Artistes du *Général*', *Ciné-Miroir*, 318 (8 May), p. 307.

Cinémonde (1932), '*Baroud*', *Cinémonde*, 212 (10 November), p. 919.

Collet, Jean, Michel Marie, Daniel Percheron and Jean-Paul Simon (1976), *Lectures du film*, Paris: Albatros.

Cosnier, Jacqueline (1985), 'Masochisme féminin et destructivité', *Revue française de psychanalyse*, 49, pp. 551–68.

Courrier cinématographique (1931), '*Les Amours de minuit*', *Le Courrier cinématographique*, 22:2 (10 January), p. 25.

Courrière, Yves (2000), *Jacques Prévert: en vérité*, Paris: Gallimard.

Croze, Jean-Louis (1925a) 'Nous avons nos vedettes . . . mais nous ne savons pas les imposer', *Ciné-Miroir*, 69 (1 March), p. 77.

Croze, Jean-Louis (1925b), '*Feu Mathias Pascal*', *Comœdia*, 4607 (1 August), p. 1.

d'Agraives, Jean (1924), *Le Temps d'aimer*, Paris: Mon ciné.

d'Ahetze, J.-C. (1930), 'Costume et cinéma: ce qu'ils devraient porter à l'écran', *Pour vous*, 99 (9 October), p. 7.

d'Ast, R. (1932), '*Baroud*', *Liberté* (5 October) [CR *Baroud* 8°Rk2096].

d'Herbeumont, Louis (1924), '*Claudine et le poussin*', *Cinéopse*, 54 (1 February), pp. 193–4.

Dalí, Salvador (1929), '*Un Chien andalou*', in *Mirador*, 39 (24 October), p. 6, in *The Collected Writings of Salvador Dalí*, edited and translated by Haim Finkelstein, Cambridge: Cambridge University Press, 1998, pp. 134–6.

Dalí, Salvador (1930), 'L'Âne pourri', *Le Surréalisme au service de la révolution*, 1 (July), pp. 9–12, in *The Collected Writings of Salvador Dalí*, edited and translated by Haim Finkelstein, Cambridge: Cambridge University Press, 1998, pp. 223–6.

Dalí, Salvador (1976), *The Unspeakable Confessions of Salvador Dalí*, as told to Andre Parinaud, translated from the French by Harold J. Salemsom, New York: Morrow. Originally published in French as *Comment on devient Dalí: les aveux inavouables de Salvador Dalí*, Paris: Robert Laffont, 1973.

Dassonville, Robert (1931), '*Les Amours de minuit*', *L'Écran du Nord* (23 January) [CRB].

de Mirbel, Jean (1924), '*Claudine et le poussin*', *Cinémagazine*, 11 (14 March), pp. 461–2.

Derain, Lucie (1925a), '*Le Double Amour*', *La Cinématographie française*, 348 (4 July), pp. 13–15.

Derain, Lucie (1925b), '*Feu Mathias Pascal*', *La Cinématographie française*, 353 (8 August), p. 27.

Derain, Lucie (1925c), '*Destinée*', *La Cinématographie française*, 371 (12 December), pp. 16–18, 40.

Derain, Lucie (1927a), '*Le Joueur d'échecs*', *La Cinématographie française*, 428 (15 January), p. 24.

Derain, Lucie (1927b), '*Napoléon*', *La Cinématographie française*, 441 (16 April), p. 25.

Derain, Lucie (1927c), '*Éducation de prince*', *La Cinématographie française*, 450 (18 June), p. 30.

Derain, Lucie (1927d), '*Le Bonheur du jour*', *La Cinématographie française*, 453 (9 July), p. 38.

Derain, Lucie (1928), '*Les Deux Timides*', *La Cinématographie française*, 528 (15 December), p. 37.

Desclaux, Pierre (1927), 'Une Enquête de *Mon ciné*: nos lecteurs nous disent', *Mon ciné*, 255 (6 January), p. 19.

Desclaux, Pierre (1928), 'Le Public aime les héros sportifs', *Mon ciné*, 355 (6 December), pp. 12–13.

Desclaux, Pierre (1930), 'Les Versions étrangères', *Mon ciné*, 456 (13 November), p. 7.

Desnos, Robert (1966), 'Cinéma d'avant-garde', in Robert Desnos, *Cinéma*, Paris: Gallimard, 1966, pp. 189–92. Originally published in *Documents*, 7 (December 1929).

Desnos, Robert (1978), 'Avant-Garde Cinema', in Paul Hammond (ed.), *The Shadow and its Shadow: Surrealist Writings on the Cinema*, London: British Film Institute, pp. 36–8.

Donnay, Maurice (1895), *Éducation de prince*, Paris: P. Ollendorff, repr. 1907. New editions Paris: Société d'Éditions Littéraires et Artistique, 1907; Paris: A. Fayard, 1911; Paris: Fayard, 1912; Paris: Jules Tallendier, 1927, illustrated with stills from the film.

Doré, Claude (1929a), 'Nos Enquêtes: l'influence du partenaire', *Ciné-Miroir*, 207 (22 March), p. 183.

Doré, Claude (1929b), 'Dans nos studios: on tourne *Illusions*', *Ciné-Miroir*, 233 (20 September), p. 606.

Doré, Claude (1930), 'Pierre Batcheff devient metteur en scène', *Ciné-Miroir*, 288 (10 October), p. 647.

Downing, Lisa and Sue Harris (eds) (2007), *From Perversion to Purity: The Stardom of Catherine Deneuve*, Manchester: Manchester University Press.

Drummond, Phillip (1977), 'Textual Space in *Un Chien andalou*', *Screen*, 18:3, pp. 55–119.

Drummond, Phillip (2004), 'Domains of Cinematic Discourse in Buñuel's and Dalí's *Un Chien andalou*', in Isabel Santaollalla, Patricia d'Allemand, Jorge Díaz Cintas *et al.* (eds), *Buñuel, siglo XXI*, Zaragoza: Prensas Universitarias de Zaragoza, pp. 101–10.

Duhamel, Marcel (1972), *Raconte pas ta vie*, Paris: Mercure de France.

Dumas, Alexandre (1981), *Le Comte de Monte-Cristo*, Paris: Gallimard.

Dupont, Georges (1928), 'Claude France', *Cinémagazine*, 2 (13 January), pp. 59–62.

Durgnat, Raymond (1968), *Luis Buñuel*, Berkeley, CA: University of California Press.

Dyer, Richard (1992), 'Don't Look Now: The Instabilities of the Male Pin-Up', in Richard Dyer, *Only Entertainment*, London: Routledge, pp. 103–19.

Dyer, Richard (1993a), 'Seen to Be Believed: Some Problems in the Representation of Gay People as Typical', in Richard Dyer, *The Matter of Images: Essays on Representation*, London: Routledge, pp. 19–51.

Dyer, Richard (1993b), 'Coming Out as Going In: The Image of the Homosexual as a Sad Young Man', in Richard Dyer, *The Matter of Images: Essays on Representation*, London: Routledge, pp. 73–92.

Eager, Gerald (1961), 'The Missing and Mutilated Eye in Contemporary Art', *The Journal of Aesthetics and Art Criticism*, 20:1, pp. 49–59.

Écho (1928), '*Vivre*', *L'Écho* (20 July) [CR *Vivre* 8°Rk10000].

Edwards, Gwynne (1982), *The Discreet Art of Luis Buñuel: A Reading of his Films*, London: Boyars.

Ellenberger, Allan R. (1999), *Ramon Novarro: A Biography of the Silent Film Idol, 1899–1968; with a Filmography*, Jefferson, NC: McFarland.

Épardaud, Edmond (1924), '*Claudine et le poussin ou Le Temps d'aimer*', *Cinéa-Ciné pour tous*, 6 (1 February), p. 16.

Épardaud, Edmond (1925), 'La Collaboration Marcel L'Herbier – Luigi Pirandello dans *Feu Mathias Pascal*', *Cinéa-Ciné pour tous*, 43 (15 August), pp. 9–11.

Épardaud, Edmond (1927), '*Le Joueur d'échecs*', *Cinéa-Ciné pour tous*, 77 (15 January), pp. 14–16.

Épardaud, Edmond (1928), '*Les Deux Timides*', *Cinéa-Ciné pour tous*, 123 (15 December), pp. 24–5.

Européen (1932), '*Baroud*', *Européen* (2 December) [CR *Baroud* 8°Rk2096].

Ezra, Elizabeth (2000), 'A Colonial Process: Josephine Baker's French Films', in Elizabeth Ezra, *The Colonial Unconscious: Race and Culture in Interwar France*, Ithaca, NY: Cornell University Press, pp. 97–128.

Farnay, Lucien (1927), '*La Sirène des tropiques*', *Cinémagazine*, 52 (30 December), pp. 587–8.

Farnay, Lucien (1928), 'Les Présentations de la Franco-Film: *L'Île d'amour*', *Cinémagazine* (9 March), 10, pp. 424–6.

Fescourt, Henri (1959), *La Foi et les montagnes, ou le septième art au passé*, Paris: Paul Montel.

Finkelstein, Haim (1998), *The Collected Writings of Salvador Dalí*, edited and translated by Haim Finkelstein, Cambridge: Cambridge University Press.

Flügel, John Carl (1930), *The Psychology of Clothes*, London: Hogarth and Institute of Psycho-Analysis.

Foster, Hal (1993), *Compulsive Beauty*, Cambridge, MA: MIT Press.

Foster, Richard and Pamela Tudor-Craig (1986), *The Secret Life of Paintings*, Woodbridge: Boydell, pp. 75–95.

Fotiade, Ramona (2004), '*Un Chien andalou*', in Phil Powrie, *The Cinema of France*, London: Wallflower, pp. 20–9.

Fotiade, Ramon (2007), 'From Ready-Made to Moving Image: The Visual Poetics of Surrealist Cinema', in *The Unsilvered Screen: Surrealism on Film*, edited by Graeme Harper and Rob Stone, London: Wallflower, pp. 9–22.

Francis, Terri (2005), 'Embodied Fictions, Melancholy Migrations: Josephine Baker's Cinematic Celebrity', *Modern Fiction Studies*, 51:4, pp. 824–45.

Frank, Nino (1928), 'Un Russe naturalisé français par sa carrière: Pierre Batcheff', *Pour vous*, 6 (27 December), pp. 8–9.

Frank, Nino (1932), '*Baroud*', *Pour vous*, 210 (24 November), p. 8.

Frantel, Max (1929), '*Vivre*', *Le Matin* (11 January) [CR *Vivre* 8°Rk10000].

Frantel, Max (1932), 'Les Derniers Moments de Pierre Batcheff', *Comœdia* (16 April 1932) [CR Pierre Batcheff 8°Rk17740].

Freud, Sigmund (1955), 'The Uncanny', in *The Standard Edition of the Complete Psychological Works of Sigmund Freud*, vol. 17, London: Hogarth, pp. 217–56.

Gaillard, Henri (1923), 'Nos Réalisateurs: Robert Boudrioz', *Cinémagazine*, 45 (9 November), pp. 207–11.

Gauteur, Claude and Ginette Vincendeau (1993), *Jean Gabin: anatomie d'un mythe*, Paris: Nathan.

Gauthier, Christophe (2002), 'Le Cinéma passé en revues (1926–1927): informer ou promou-voir?', exhibition catalogue (11 October 2002–31 January 2003). Available electronically at http://www2.bifi.fr/cineregards/article.asp@sp_ref=221&ref_sp_type=6&revue_ref=23 (accessed 25 December 2007).

Gilles, Christian (2000), *Le Cinéma des années trente par ceux qui l'ont fait. Tome I. Les Débuts du parlant: 1929–1934*, Paris: L'Harmattan, pp. 187–93.

Gordeaux, Paul (1932), '*Baroud*', *L'Écho* (18 November) [CR *Baroud* 8°Rk2096].

Gorel, Michel (1929), 'Films d'essai', *Cinémonde*, 49 (26 September), p. 855.

Goudal, Jean (1976), 'Surréalisme et cinéma', in Alain and Odette Virmaux (eds), *Les Surréalistes et le cinéma*, Paris: Seghers, pp. 303–17. First published in *La Revue hebdomadaire* (February 1925), pp. 343–57.

Goudal, Jean (1978), 'Surrealism and Cinema', in Paul Hammond (ed.), *The Shadow and its Shadow: Surrealist Writings on the Cinema*, London: British Film Institute, 1978, pp. 49–56. Also in Richard Abel (ed.), *French Film Theory and Criticism: A History/Anthology, 1907–1939*, vol. 1: 1907–1929, Princeton, NJ: Princeton University Press, 1988, pp. 353–62.

Guérin, Raymond (1932), 'La Mort de Pierre Batcheff', *Ciné-Miroir*, 369 (29 April), p. 291.

Guido, Laurent (2002), 'Le Dr Ramain, théoricien du "musicalisme"', *1895*, 38, pp. 67–100.

Hammond, Bryan and Patrick O'Connor (1988), *Josephine Baker*, London: Cape.

Hansen, Miriam (1986), 'Pleasure, Ambivalence, Identification: Valentino and Female Spectatorship', *Cinema Journal*, 25:4, pp. 6–32. Revised version in *Babel and*

 Babylon: Spectatorship in American Silent Film, Cambridge, MA: Harvard University Press, 1991.

Hansen, Miriam (1991), *Babel and Babylon: Spectatorship in American Silent Film*, Cambridge, MA: Harvard University Press.

Harvey, John (1995), *Men in Black*, London: Reaktion.

Hayes, Graeme (2004), 'Framing the Wolf: Alain Delon, Spectacular Masculinity, and the French Crime Film', in Phil Powrie, Ann Davies and Bruce Babington (eds), *The Trouble with Men: Masculinities in European and Hollywood Cinema*, London: Wallflower, pp. 42–53.

Hayward, Susan (2001), 'Setting the Agenders: Simone Signoret – The Pre-Feminist Star Body', in Alex Hughes and James Williams (eds), *Gender and French Cinema*, Oxford: Berg, pp. 107–24.

Hayward, Susan (2002), 'Simone Signoret (1921–1985) – The Body Political', *Women's Studies International Forum*, 23:6, pp. 739–47.

Hayward, Susan (2003) *Simone Signoret: The Star as Cultural Sign*, London: Continuum.

Hayward, Susan and Sarah Leahy (2000), 'The Tainted Woman – Pathology and its Displacement: Simone Signoret's Body as Site of Retribution', in Ulrike Sieglohr (ed.), *Heroines without Heroes: Female Identities in Post-War European Cinema 1945–51*, London: Cassell, pp. 76–88.

Heard, Gerald (1924), *Narcissus: An Anatomy of Clothes*, London: Kegan Paul, Trench, Trubner.

Hebdo-Film (1925), '*Feu Mathias Pascal*', *Hebdo-Film* (1 August).

Hebdo-Film (1931), '*Le Rebelle*', *Hebdo-Film*, 811 (12 September), pp. 14–15.

Hennard, Jean (1924), 'Ceux qui tournent en Suisse: Donatien et sa troupe', *Revue suisse du cinéma*, 12 (7 June), pp. 3–4.

Henry, Pierre (1925), 'En marge de l'écran', *Cinéa-Ciné pour tous*, 39 (15 June), pp. 5–6.

Henry, Pierre (1926), 'Les Étoiles d'aujourd'hui: Simonne Mareuil', *Cinéa-Ciné pour tous*, 56 (1 March), pp. 21–2.

Higginbotham, Virginia (1979), *Luis Buñuel*, Boston: Twayne.

Icart, Roger (1983), *Abel Gance ou le Prométhée foudroyé*, Lausanne: L'Âge d'homme.

Jay, Martin (1994), *Downcast Eyes: The Denigration of Vision in Twentieth-Century French Thought*, Berkeley, CA: University of California Press.

Jeanne, René (1928), '*L'Île d'amour*', *Rumeur* (10 February) [CR *L'Île d'amour* 8°Rk5232].

Kaplan, Nelly (1994), *Napoléon*, London: British Film Institute.

King, Barry (1985), 'Articulating Stardom', *Screen*, 26:5, pp. 27–50.

King, Norman (1984), *Abel Gance: A Politics of Spectacle*, London: British Film Institute.

King, Norman (1990), 'History and Actuality: Abel Gance's *Napoléon vu par Abel Gance* (1927)', in Susan Hayward and Ginette Vincendeau (eds), *French Film: Texts and Contexts*, London: Routledge, pp. 25–36.

Klein, Jean-Claude (1990), 'La Revue nègre', in Olivier Barrot and Pascal Ory (eds), *Entre deux guerres: la création française entre 1919 et 1939*, Paris: François Bourin, pp. 363–77.

Kolb, Jean (1928), '*Le Perroquet vert*', *Mon ciné*, 320 (5 April), p. 17.

Kolb, Jean (1929), 'Parlez-nous du public: Pierre Batcheff nous dit', *Mon ciné*, 383 (20 June), p. 12.

Kovács, Stephen (1980), *From Enchantment to Rage: The Story of Surrealist Cinema*, Rutherford, NJ/London: Fairleigh Dickinson University Press/Associated University Presses.

Kramer, Steven Philip and James Michael Welsh (1978), *Abel Gance*, Boston: Twayne.

L'Herbier, Marcel (1979), *La Tête qui tourne*, Paris: Belfond.

Labiche, Eugène (1882), 'Les Deux Timides', in *Théâtre complet*, vol. 4, Paris: Calmann-Lévy, pp. 155–208.

Lacan, Jacques (1973), *Le Séminaire. Livre XI. Les quatre concepts fondamentaux de la psychanalyse*, Paris: Seuil.

Lacan, Jacques (1986), *Le Séminaire. Livre VII. L'éthique de la psychanalyse*, Paris: Seuil.

Lacan, Jacques (1992), *The Ethics of Psychoanalysis 1959–1960: The Seminar of Jacques Lacan. Book VII*, edited by Jacques-Alain Miller, translated by Dennis Porter, London: Tavistock/Routledge.

Lacan, Jacques (1994), *The Four Fundamental Concepts of Psychoanalysis*, edited by Jacques-Alain Miller, translated by Alan Sheridan, Harmondsworth: Penguin.

Lagrange, M. (1932), '*Baroud*', *L'Ami du film* (21 October) [CR *Baroud* 8°Rk2096].

Laumann, E. M. (1926), *Le Secret d'une mère*, Paris: Jules Tallendier.

Laumann, E. M. (1927), *Le Dernier des Capendu*, Paris: Jules Tallendier.

Laury, Jean (1932), '*Baroud*', *Le Figaro* (20 November) [CR *Baroud* 8°Rk2096].

Le Chanois, Jean-Paul (1979), 'Préface', *La Revue du cinéma*, vol. 1 (fiftieth anniversary facsimile edition), Paris: Pierre L'Herminier, pp. ix–xxii.

Le Chanois, Jean-Paul (1996), *Le Temps des cerises: entretiens avec Philippe Esnault*, Arles: Actes Sud/Lyon: Institut Lumière.

Le Sonn, Loig (2004), 'Thérapeutes de la "timidité" et rééducateurs de "l'initiative": la filiale française de l'Institut Pelman (1924–1941), paravent thérapeutique des nouvelles professions salariées', Laboratoire Printemps-CNRS (Université de Versailles Saint-Quentin-en-Yvelines). Available electronically at http://www.printemps.uvsq.fr/Com_leso.htm#_ftnref f8 (accessed 8 December 2007).

Leahy, Sarah (2002), 'Bardot and Dance: Representing the Real?', *French Cultural Studies*, 13, pp. 49–64.

Leahy, Sarah (2003), 'The Matter of Myth: Bardot, Stardom and Sex', *Studies in French Cinema*, 3:2, pp. 71–81.

Leahy, Sarah (2004), ' "Neither Charm nor Sex Appeal": Just What is the Appeal of Simone Signoret?', *Studies in French Cinema*, 4:1, pp. 29–40.

Lebreton, René (1928a), '*Le Perroquet vert*', *Comœdia* (14 October) [CR *Le Perroquet vert* 4°Rk7316].

Lebreton, René (1928b), '*Vivre*', *Comœdia* (11 July) [CR *Vivre* 8°Rk10000].

Lenauer, Jean (1929), 'Deux nouveaux films: *Le Mystère du Château de Dé*, et *Un Chien andalou*', *Pour vous*, 30 (13 June), p. 4.

Lenoir, Jacqueline (1928a), 'Les Grandes Enquêtes de *Ciné-Miroir*: brune ou blonde?', *Ciné-Miroir*, 169 (29 June), p. 419.

Lenoir, Jacqueline (1928b), 'Leur Violon d'Ingres: Pierre Batcheff', *Ciné-Miroir*, 176 (17 August), p. 534.

Lenoir, Jacqueline (1928c), 'Nous avons aussi . . . Pierre Batcheff', *Cinématographie française*, 526 (30 November), p. 17.

Lequin, Yves (1992), ' "Métissages imprudents"?', in Yves Lequin (ed.), *Histoire des étrangers et de l'immigration en France*, Paris: Larousse, pp. 379–99.

Liebman, Stuart (1986), '*Un Chien andalou*: The Talking Cure', *Dada/Surrealism*, 15, sp. no. 'Dada and Surrealist Film', pp. 143–58.

Lomas, David (2000), *The Haunted Self: Surrealism, Psychoanalysis, Subjectivity*, New Haven, CT: Yale University Press.

McGerr, Celia (1980), *René Clair*, Boston: Twayne.

Mairgance, Maurice (1930), '*Illusions*', *L'Ami du peuple du soir* (27 January) [CR *Illusions* 8°Rk5265].

Marguet, Jean (1928), '*Le Perroquet vert*', *Cinémagazine*, 43 (26 October), pp. 162–3.

Matthews, John H. (1971), *Surrealism and Film*, Ann Arbor, MI: University of Michigan Press.

Méré, Charles (1932), 'Baroud', *Comœdia* (25 October) [CR *Baroud* 4°Rk2096].

Millet, J.-K. Raymond (1928), 'Nos Jeunes Premiers: Pierre Batcheff', *Ciné-Miroir*, 156 (30 March), p. 215.

Mital, Bernard (1931), 'Une Heure chez Pierre Batcheff', *Mon ciné*, 503 (8 October), p. 6.

Mitry, Jean (1960), *René Clair*, Paris: Éditions universitaires.

Mohy, Simone (1943), 'Visages derrière l'écran: les jeunes premiers', *Ciné-Mondial*, 83 (2 April), pp. 6–7.

Mon ciné (1925a) [short note], *Mon ciné*, 155 (5 February), p. 14.

Mon ciné (1925b), 'Nous apprenons que . . .', *Mon ciné*, 161 (19 March), p. 5.

Mon ciné (1926), 'Vous avez la parole', *Mon ciné*, 229 (8 July), pp. 2, 21.

Mon ciné (1928), 'Sports et cinéma', *Mon ciné*, 327 (24 May), pp. 8–9.

Mon ciné (1930a), 'Deux Époques', *Mon ciné*, 414 (23 January), p. 7.

Mon ciné (1930b), 'Vous avez la parole', *Mon ciné*, 417 (13 February), pp. 2 and 14.

Mon ciné (1930c), 'Vous avez la parole', *Mon ciné*, 424 (3 April), pp. 2 and 14.

Mon ciné (1930d), 'Vous avez la parole', *Mon ciné*, 433 (5 June), pp. 2 and 14.

Mon ciné (1930e), 'Vous avez la parole', *Mon ciné*, 434 (12 June), pp. 2 and 14.

Mon ciné (1931a), 'Vous avez la parole', *Mon ciné*, 465 (15 January), pp. 2 and 14.

Mon ciné (1931b), 'Vous avez la parole', *Mon ciné*, 467 (29 January), pp. 2 and 14.

Mon ciné (1931c), 'Vous avez la parole', *Mon ciné*, 468 (5 February), pp. 2 and 14.

Mon ciné (1931d), 'Vous avez la parole', *Mon ciné*, 489 (2 July), pp. 2 and 14.

Mondragon (1949), 'Comment j'ai compris *Un Chien andalou*', *Revue du Ciné-Club*, 8–9. Reprinted in Pierre Renaud, 'Symbolisme au second degré: *Un Chien andalou*', *Études cinématographiques*, 22–23, 1963, pp. 147–57 (pp. 149–50).

Moniteur du Puy-de-Dôme (1932), '*Le Rebelle*', *Moniteur du Puy-de-Dôme* (17 January) [CRB].

Morris, Cyril Brian (1972), *Surrealism and Spain*, Cambridge: Cambridge University Press.

New York Times (1933), '*Love in Morocco* (1931): On the Sands of Morocco', *New York Times* (20 March). Available electronically at http://movies.nytimes.com/movie/review?res=9401E4D61F3BEF3ABC4851DFB5668388629EDE (accessed 5 January 2008).

Nîmes Journal (1932), '*Le Rebelle*', *Nîmes Journal* (28 January) [CRB].

Normand, Suzanne (1929), '*Un Chien andalou*', *Vient de paraître* (1 December) [CRB].

Nowell-Smith, Geoffrey (1977), 'Minnelli and Melodrama', *Screen*, 18:2, pp. 115–18.

O'Leary, Liam (1993), *Rex Ingram: Master of the Silent Cinema*, Le Giornate del cinema muto/London: British Film Institute. Originally published Dublin: Academy, 1980.

O'Shaughnessy, Martin (1994), 'Jean-Paul Belmondo: masculinité et violence', *Projets féministes*, 3, pp. 112–30.

Olivet, René (1929a), '*Les Deux Timides*', *Cinémonde*, 25 (11 April), p. 440.

Olivet, René (1929b), '*Le Chien andalou*' [sic], *Cinémonde*, 52 (17 October), p. 900.

Olivet, René (1929c), '*Monte-Cristo*', *Cinémonde*, 53 (24 October), p. 920.

Orta, Madeleine (1928), 'Joséphine Baker dans *La Sirène des tropiques*', *Cinéa-ciné pour tous*, 100 (1 January), pp. 31–3.

Paris-midi (1926), '*La Comédie du bonheur*', *Paris-midi* (10 November) [CR Rt3745 vol. 6].

Pérez, Gilberto (2004), 'The Sliced Eye and the Primal Scene Identification and Interpretation in *Un Chien andalou*', in Isabel Santaolalla, Patricia d'Allemand, Jorge Díaz Cintas *et al.* (eds), *Buñuel, siglo XXI*, Zaragoza: Prensas Universitarias de Zaragoza, pp. 397–404.

Petit Niçois (1931), '*Le Rebelle*', *Petit Niçois* (26 October) [CRB].

Petitbeau, Abel (1924), '*Le Temps d'aimer ou Claudine et le poussin*', *Mon ciné*, 121 (12 June), p. 22.

Piazza, François (1949), 'Considérations psychanalytiques sur le *Chien andalou* de Luis Buñuel et Salvador Dalí', *Psyché*, 27–8, pp. 147–56.

Pierret-Marthe (1929), '*Monte-Cristo*', *Cinémonde*, 33 (6 June), pp. 570–1.

Pigasse, A. (1925), '*Feu Mathias Pascal*', *Gazette de France* (8 August). Extract cited in *La Cinématographie française*, 360 (26 September 1925) [CR *Feu Mathias Pascal* 8° Rk 4353].

Pirandello, Luigi (1904), *Il fu Mattia Pascal*, Rome: Nuova Antologia.

Pirandello, Luigi (1910), *Feu Mathias Pascal*, translated by Henry Bigot, Paris: Calmann-Lévy.

Ploquin, Raoul (1925), '*Le Double Amour* est terminé', *Cinématographie française*, 337 (18 April), p. 12.

Ponty, Janine (1988), *Polonais méconnus: histoire des travailleurs immigrés en France dans l'entre-deux-guerres*, Paris: Publications de la Sorbonne.

Pour vous (1928a), '*Les Deux Timides* de Labiche par René Clair', *Pour vous*, 3 (6 December), p. 8.

Pour vous (1928b), 'Jeu de la veillée de Noël', *Pour vous*, 5 (20 December), pp. 12–13.

Pour vous (1931), 'Cinéma parlant: la question des langues (histoire, théorie, . . .)', *Pour vous*, 121 (12 March), p. 2.

Powrie, Phil (1992), 'Reflections on/from the Ruined Eye', *SuperReal: The British Journal of Surrealism*, 1, pp. 6–13.

Powrie, Phil (1998), 'Masculinity in the Shadow of the Slashed Eye: Surrealist Film Criticism at the Crossroads', *Screen*, 39:2, pp. 153–63.

Powrie, Phil (2000), '*Bleu, blanc, rouge*: Masochism and the Distinction between Verbal and Visual Automatism', *Australian Journal of French Studies*, 37:1, pp. 40–51.

Powrie, Phil, with Éric Rebillard (2004), 'Sauvage et mignon: a star study of Pierre Batcheff', in Isabel Santaolalla, *et al.* (eds), *Buñuel, siglo XXI*, Zaragoza: Institucíon Fernando el Católico/Prensas Universitarias de Zaragoza, pp. 413–18.

Powrie, Phil, Bruce Babington, Ann Davies, Chris Perriam (2007), *Carmen on Film: A Cultural History*, Bloomington, IN: Indiana University Press.

Presse (1926), '*La Comédie du bonheur*', *La Presse* (10 November) [CR Rt3745 vol. 6].

Prévert, Pierre (1965), 'Témoignages: Pierre Prévert', *Études cinématographiques*, 38–9, pp. 49–55.

Prévert, Pierre and Jacques Prévert (1965), 'La Parole est à Pierre et à Jacques Prévert', *Image et son*, 189, pp. 6–17.

Progrès du Nord (1931), '*Le Rebelle*', *Progrès du Nord* (11 September) [CRB].

Querlin, Marise (1925), 'À propos de *Chouchou poids-plume*', *Cinéa-Ciné pour tous*, 44 (1 September), pp. 20–1.

Ramain, Paul (1925), 'L'Influence du rêve sur le cinéma', *Cinéa-Ciné pour tous*, 40 (1 July), p. 8. In Richard Abel (ed.), *French Film Theory and Criticism: A History/Anthology, 1907–1939*, vol. 1: 1907–1929, Princeton, NJ: Princeton University Press, pp. 362–3.

Ramain, Paul (1928), 'Les Films de "recherches"', *Cinémagazine*, 28 (13 July), pp. 60–2.

Ramain, Paul (1930), 'Réflexions sur un film mal compris: *Un Chien andalou*', *Cinéa-Ciné pour tous*, 2 (April), pp. 6–7.

Régent, Roger (1929a), '*Les Deux Timides*', *Pour vous*, 36 (25 July), p. 5.

Régent, Roger (1929b), 'Simonne Mareuil', *Pour vous*, 47 (10 October), p. 4.

Régent, Roger (1930a), '*Illusions*', *Pour vous*, 62 (23 January), p. 6.

Régent, Roger (1930b), '*Le Roi de Paris*', *Pour vous*, 90 (7 August), p. 5.

Régent, Roger (1930c), 'Premiers tours de manivelle', *Pour vous*, 101 (23 October), p. 14.

Renaud, Pierre (1963), 'Symbolisme au second degré: *Un Chien andalou*', *Études Cinématographiques*, 22–3, pp. 147–57.

Richardson, Michael (2006), *Surrealism and Cinema*, Oxford: Berg.

Robin, Jean (1928), 'Les Présentations de la "Star Film": *Vivre*', *Cinémagazine*, 29 (20 July), pp. 102–3.

Roque, Jules (1928), 'Chronique du cinéma', *Vie Marseillaise et de Provence* (4 February) [CRB].

Rose, Phyllis (1989), *Jazz Cleopatra: Josephine Baker in Her Time*, New York: Doubleday.

Sadoul, Georges (1975), *Histoire générale du cinéma. 5, L'Art muet: 1919–1929. Premier volume, L'Après-guerre en Europe*, Paris: Denoël.

Saint-Sorny (1922), *Bicchi*, Paris: Émile-Paul frères.

Samuels, Charles Thomas (1972), *Encountering Directors*, New York: Putnam.

Sandro, Paul (1987), *Diversions of Pleasure: Luis Buñuel and the Crises of Desire*. Columbus, OH: Ohio State University Press. The chapter on *Un Chien andalou* was first published as 'The Space of Desire in *An Andalusian Dog*', *1978 Film Studies Annual*, pp. 57–63.

Sannier, Mireille (1930), 'De l'Autre Côté des sunlights: Pierre Batcheff va faire de la mise en scène', *Cinémonde*, 104 (16 October), p. 665.

Saubes, Pierre (1929), 'Fakirs . . . fumistes et *Chien andalou*', *Cinégraph* (December) [CR *Un Chien andalou* 8° Rk 9399].

Sauvage, Marcel (1931), '*Le Rebelle*', *Pour vous*, 144 (20 August), p. 12.

Schor, Ralph (1996), *Histoire de l'immigration en France*, Paris: Armand Colin.

Short, Robert (2002), *The Age of Gold: Surrealist Cinema*, Washington, DC: Creation (Persistence of Vision, vol. 3).

Siegel, Jeanne (1961a), 'The Image of the Eye in Surrealist Art and its Psychoanalytic Sources. Part One: The Mythic Eye', *Arts Magazine*, 56:6, pp. 102–6.

Siegel, Jeanne (1961b), 'The Image of the Eye in Surrealist Art and its Psychoanalytic Sources. Part Two: Magritte', *Arts Magazine*, 56:7, pp. 116–19.

Silverman, Kaja (1992), *Male Subjectivity at the Margins*, New York: Routledge.

Sirinelli, Jean-François (1993), 'La France de l'entre-deux-guerres: culture et société', in Jean-François Sirinelli, Robert Vandenbussche and Jean Vavasseur-Desperriers, *La France de 1914 à nos jours*, Paris: Presses universitaires de France, pp. 87–106.

Solomon-Godeau, Abigail (1997), *Male Trouble: A Crisis in Representation*, London: Thames & Hudson.

Soupault, Philippe (1979), '*Les Amours de minuit*', in Philippe Soupault, *Écrits de cinéma*, Paris: Plon, pp. 215–16. First published in *L'Europe nouvelle*, 686 (4 April 1931), pp. 471–2.

Spa, Robert (1927), '*La Sirène des tropiques*', *Le Figaro* (24 December) [CRB].

Spectateur (1931), 'Pierre Batcheff', *Le Spectateur* (12 April) [CR *Pierre Batcheff* 8°Rk17740].

Starobinski, Jean (1968), 'Freud, Breton, Myers', *L'Arc*, 34, pp. 87–96.

Studlar, Gaylyn (1996), *This Mad Masquerade: Stardom and Masculinity in the Jazz Age*, New York: Columbia University Press.

Sweeney, Carole (2004), *From Fetish to Subject: Race, Modernism, and Primitivism, 1919–1935*, Westport, CT: Praeger.

Tedesco, Jean (1925), 'L'Art de Marcel L'Herbier a-t-il évolué?', *Cinéa-Ciné pour tous*, 44 (1 September), pp. 7–8.

Tedesco, Jean (1927), '*Napoléon vu par Abel Gance*', *Cinéa-Ciné pour tous*, 83 (15 April), pp. 9–10.

Thiher, Allen (1979), 'Surrealism's Enduring Bite: *Un Chien andalou*', in Allen Thiher, *The Cinematic Muse: Critical Studies in the History of the French Cinema*. Columbia, MO: University of Missouri Press, pp. 24–37. Previously published in *Literature/Film Quarterly*, 5:1 (1977), 38–49.

Toulouse, Édouard (1931), 'L'Hôpital psychiatrique', *Prophylaxie mentale*, 30 [pagination unknown].

Trévise, Robert (1925a), '*Le Double Amour*', *Cinéa-Ciné pour tous*, 41 (15 July), p. 27.

Trévise, Robert (1925b), '*La Princesse Lulu*', *Cinéa-Ciné pour tous*, 44 (1 September), p. 27.

Trévise, Robert (1925c), '*Destinée*', *Cinéa-Ciné pour tous*, 51 (15 December), pp. 26–7.

Trévise, Robert (1928), '*L'Île d'amour*', *Cinéa-Ciné pour tous*, 105 (15 March), p. 28.

Tribourg, Alain (1930), 'Du Cinéma français', *Cinémonde*, 63 (2 January), p. 9.

Tual, Denise (1980), *Le Temps dévoré*, Paris: Fayard.

Tual, Denise (1987), *Au Cœur du temps*, Paris: Carrère.

Turim, Maureen (2004), '*Napoléon vu par Abel Gance*', in Phil Powrie (ed.), *The Cinema of France*, London: Wallflower, pp. 11–18.

Vaché, Jacques (1919), *Lettres de guerre*, Paris: Au Sans Pareil.

Vailland, Roger (1929), 'Les Films d'avant-garde', *Paris-Midi*, 14 October. Reprinted in *Le Grand Jeu et le cinéma*, edited by Alain and Odette Virmaux, Paris: Paris Expérimental, 1996, pp. 43–4.

van Etten, Henry (1929), *Publications des études criminologiques: organe de l'association des élèves et anciens élèves de l'Institut de Criminologie de l'Université de Paris*, 4, 'La Musique dans les prisons', pp. 1–11 [CRB].

Vavasseur-Desperriers, Jean (1993), 'L'Impossible Retour à l'avant-guerre (1919–1931)', in Jean-François Sirinelli, Robert Vandenbussche and Jean Vavasseur-Desperriers, *La France de 1914 à nos jours*, Paris: Presses universitaires de France, pp. 43–86.

Véray, Laurent (2000) (ed.), *Abel Gance, nouveaux regards*, sp. no. *1895*, 31.

Véray, Laurent (2005), '1927: The Apotheosis of the French Historical Film?', *Film History*, 17, pp. 334–51.

Vernes, Stéphane (1924), '*Claudine et le poussin*: ce que le public en pense', *Cinéa-Ciné pour tous*, 17 (15 July), p. 32.

Vezyroglou, Dimitri (2000), 'Chemins croisés: René Clair et la société Albatros (1926–1928)', in Noël Herpe and Emmanuelle Toulet (eds), *René Clair ou le cinéma à la lettre*, Paris: Association Française de Recherches sur l'Histoire du Cinéma, pp. 121–37.

Vignaud, Jean (1929), 'Notre Opinion: réclamations', *Ciné-Miroir*, 198 (18 January), p. 35.

Villette, Raymond (1927), '*Éducation de prince*', *Mon ciné*, 300 (17 November), p. 10.

Villette, Raymond (1930), '*Le Roi de Paris*', *Mon ciné*, 448 (18 September), p. 5.

Villette, Raymond (1931a), '*Les Amours de minuit*', *Mon ciné*, 474 (19 March), p. 5.

Villette, Raymond (1931b), '*Le Rebelle*', *Mon ciné*, 506 (29 October), p. 5.

Vincendeau, Ginette (2000), *Stars and Stardom in French Cinema*, London: Continuum.

Vincent-Bréchignac, Jean (1930), '*Illusions*', *Pour vous*, 69 (13 March), p. 5.

Virmaux, Alain and Odette Virmaux (1976), *Les Surréalistes et le cinéma*, Paris: Seghers.

Vuillermoz, Émile (1924), '*Claudine et le poussin*', *Le Temps* (29 March) [CR *Claudine et le poussin* 8°Rk2945].

Vuillermoz, Émile (1925a), '*Feu Mathias Pascal*', *Le Temps* (8 August). Extract cited in *La Cinématographie française*, 360 (26 September 1925) [CR *Feu Mathias Pascal* 8° Rk 4353].

Vuillermoz, Émile (1925b), '*Feu Mathias Pascal*', *L'Impartial français* (16 August).

Wahl, Lucien (1929a), '*Vivre*', *Pour vous*, 7 (3 January), p. 5.

Wahl, Lucien (1929b), 'De Labiche à René Clair: *Les Deux Timides*', *Pour vous*, 15 (28 February), p. 7.

Wahl, Lucien (1929c), '*L'Île d'amour*', *Pour vous*, 18 (21 March), p. 5.

Wahl, Lucien (1929d), 'La Dernière Incarnation de Monte-Cristo', *Pour vous*, 28 (30 May), p. 7.

Wahl, Lucien (1929e), '*Le Joueur d'échecs*', *Pour vous*, 41 (29 August), p. 5.

Wahl, Lucien (1931), '*Les Amours de minuit*', *Pour vous*, 113 (15 January), p. 5.

Williams, Linda (1976), 'The Prologue to *Un Chien andalou*', *Screen*, 17:4 (1976–7), pp. 24–33.

Williams, Linda (1981), *Figures of Desire: A Theory and Analysis of Surrealist Film*. Urbana, IL: University of Illinois Press.

Williams, Michael (2003), *Ivor Novello: Screen Idol*, London: British Film Institute.

Index